A Guide To Rational Living

A Guide
To
Rational Living

by
Albert Ellis Ph.D. 1913-
and
Robert A. Harper Ph.D.

PRENTICE - HALL, INC.

ENGLEWOOD CLIFFS, N.J.

Acknowledgments

GRATEFUL ACKNOWLEDGMENT is made to Dr. Raymond J. Corsini, Dr. Frances R. Harper, Rhoda Winter Russell, and Brooking Tatum, who read the original draft of the manuscript of this book and who made valuable critical comments and suggestions. Full responsibility for the contents of the book, however, remains with the authors.

Table of Contents

A Guide To Rational Living

1 \ How Far
Can You Go
With Self-Analysis?

PEOPLE OFTEN SAY to us, "Look, let's suppose that your principles of rational therapy actually work. Let's suppose that you really can, as you claim, teach any intelligent human being not to be desperately unhappy about practically anything. If all this is true, why don't you just put your theories in a book and let us read them. That way, we'd save a whale of a lot of time, trouble, and treasure going for psychotherapy."

We usually demur.

Self-analysis, we point out, has distinct limitations. No matter how clearly the principles of self-help are stated, people often misunderstand or distort them. They read into these principles what they *want* to read—and ignore some of their most salient aspects. They oversimplify, edit out most of the author's carefully stated *ifs, ands,* and *buts,* and use the most cautiously stated rules as if they were breezy slogans which can be cavalierly applied to any afflicted person in any situation.

Worse yet, the amount of lip-service which thousands of readers give to psychological, moral, social, and other principles in which they stoutly *say* they believe is amazingly vast. "I just don't know how to thank you," they keep saying and writing, "for having written that wonderful book! I keep re-reading it all the time and it's been the *greatest* help to me." But when you correspond or speak with them further, you are startled to find that they often are doing nothing along the lines you painstakingly described in your "wonderful book"—or that their actual behavior is diametrically opposed to your advocacies.

1

This is the unique advantage of intensive psychotherapy over almost any other form of reconstructive teaching: it provides for systematic and periodic check on whether the therapist's message is *really* getting home to the patient or client. Somewhere in the early part of treatment, the active-directive, rational psychotherapist (quite unlike the passive orthodox psychoanalyst or the non-directive therapist, with whom we respectfully but wholeheartedly disagree) clearly indicates to the emotionally disturbed individual that not only is he off beam, but that if he wants to get on a saner course he is going to have to see that he is thinking and acting in one or more irrational ways and is going to have to forcefully challenge his illogical assumptions and begin to think and act in more rational and less self-defeating ways.

"Very well," says the average cooperative patient after a fairly short period of this kind of therapy, "I think I pretty much see what you mean. I'm going to try to do as you say and challenge my own nonsense that is creating my emotional disturbance." And he does try, and soon (perhaps even the very next session) comes back to report significant progress. He reports, for example (as one of our patients stated a few months ago), "Say, this is really great! I did exactly what you told me to do. Instead of groveling before my wife, as usual, when she laid me out for having come to see you, supposedly telling tales about her, and spending money for treatment, I remembered what you said. 'What is *her* motive,' I asked myself, 'for being angry? I'll bet that, just as the Doctor said, she's really sick herself, underneath, and is just trying to cover up for her own weakness by laying me out. But this time I'm not going to take her so seriously and let myself get upset by her weakness.' And I didn't. I didn't let it bother me at all."

"Fine!" said the therapist, feeling that perhaps this patient really was learning how to question his own assumptions regarding himself and his wife and to act more rationally in record time. "And then, when you didn't let it bother you, what did you do, how did you behave toward your wife?"

"Oh, that was easy!" said the patient. "I just said to myself again—just like you told me to, Doctor—'Look, I'm not going to let this sick female get away with this kind of stuff any longer. I've taken enough of it for much too long now. Enough is enough!' And I really let her have it. I wasn't afraid, as I usually would be, and I told her exactly what I thought of her, how goddam stupid she was, how you agreed with me that she was giving me too hard a time, and how if she kept up that kind of stuff any longer I'd push her goddam teeth in and make her swallow them. Oh, I really let her have it! Just like you told me."

"I did? I told you *that?*" asked the appalled therapist. And for the next few sessions, by careful repetition and the use of the simplest examples tailored to order this particular patient and his level of understanding, he was able—finally!—to show him that what he really meant. Yes, the patient should first learn to question his wife's motives, and not take her disapproval too seriously; but that he should *also* learn not to condemn her (or anyone else) for being the way she was, but should try to accept and forgive her shrewishness and sympathetically help her, if possible, to overcome it. Eventually (actually, after three and a half months of rational psychotherapy on a once-a-week basis), this patient did learn a great part of the message that the therapist did his best to convey to him, but only after persistent repetition by the therapist, backsliding by the patient, more explanation by the therapist, renewed experimental attempts by the patient to apply what he thought were the therapist's instructions, still more corrective repetitions by the therapist, and so on, until reasonably final victory now, at the present writing, seems in sight.

This, then, is one of the main advantages of intensive psychotherapy: its repetitive, experimenting, revising, practicing nature. And this is what no book, sermon, article, or series of lectures, no matter how excellently expositive and explicative, can fully give. This is why the authors of this book intend to continue doing individual and group psychotherapy and training other psychotherapists. Whether we like it or not, the great majority of seriously disturbed people can not be expected to really get at the root of their problems and rid themselves of their needless anxiety and hostility without some amount of intensive, direct contact with a competent therapist. It would be perfectly lovely, from the standpoint of the patient, the therapist, and society, if this were not so; but let us face it: it is.

Now for a look at the other side of the fence. While *most* emotionally disturbed individuals only benefit to a limited extent by reading and hearing material designed to help them understand and combat their disturbances, *some* do derive considerable, albeit rarely complete, help thereby. A case in point is that of the fifty-year-old engineer who visited one of the authors after reading his book, *How to Live with a Neurotic* (1957). This man had a wife who was obviously psychotic and with whom he had had a most difficult time getting along for the twenty-eight years of their marriage. He reported that, until he read the book, he had been continually angry at her because of her behavior; but after reading it twice, almost all his anger vanished and he was able to live quite peaceably, though not entirely happily, with her and to devote himself much more effectively to protecting their three children from some of the effects of her erratic behavior.

"One passage in the book particularly helped me," this gentleman reported, "After I read and re-read that passage several times, almost all my anger against my wife seemed to melt away, as if by magic. It really impressed me very much."

"And what was that passage?" the therapist asked.

"In your chapter on how to live with a person who remains emotionally disturbed, you say, 'all right, Jones gets drunk every night and he is noisy— what do you expect a drunk to be—sober?' That really hit me. And I asked myself: 'What do you expect your crazy wife to be—sane?' That did it. Of course, I couldn't expect *her* to be sane. But I could expect *me* to be. Ever since then, would you believe it? I've been acting a heck of a lot differently—more sanely."

And as far as the therapist could see, he had been acting in a manner much more rational and less self-defeating since he took this particularly pertinent passage in this book to heart.

Another instance is even more spectacular. An ex-patient, whom we shall call Bob Smith spent a year and a half in a state hospital (several years ago) with a diagnosis of paranoid schizophrenia. He has been working in the community for the past five years and doing remarkably well. Not only has he been able to work steadily and to take care of his family, but he has also been of considerable aid to many other emotionally disturbed individuals.

But Bob Smith has had his problems. For a couple of years he has not been able to talk to his parents (who, as might be expected, have their own personality difficulties). He has been on the verge of divorcing his wife. He has been afraid to do many things he would have liked to do, particularly in relation to approaching various people and discussing intimate or "embarrassing" situations with them. In many ways—even as you and I—he has been terribly bottled up, defensive, and hostile.

Came the dawn—to be precise, May 26, 1960. After running across the article, "An Impolite Interview With Albert Ellis," in the March and May 1960 issues of the iconoclastic magazine, *The Realist*, and tracking down some of the main papers on rational psychotherapy published in professional journals, Bob Smith went through mental mood changes "the likes of which I never felt before." He suddenly learned a simple fact: "People and things are not in themselves upsetting. Rather, it is our telling ourselves that they are upsetting which upsets us."

This main tenet of what Bob Smith refers to as the "anti-unhappiness formula," which is his own simplified restatement of twelve principles of rational psychotherapy first presented in a paper at the American Psychological Association annual meeting in Chicago in August, 1956, and later published in the *Journal of General Psychology* (1958), remarkably changed his life. Almost immediately, he began talking to his parents, getting along much better with his wife, and discussing with people exactly the things he had fearfully refrained from discussing for years.

Not only did he effect some almost incredible unblockings in his own thinking and doing, but Bob Smith also began talking to others, sending out leaflets, writing letters, and doing a host of other things that he hopes will lead to a "chain reaction" of interest in rational living. He believes that by continuing this chain, and inducing important people and statesmen to think sanely and stop upsetting themselves with the belief that *other* people and events are upsetting them, unusual strides toward world peace may eventually be taken. Whether he is right or wrong about this, he has certainly helped himself to think straight and is now leading a more productive and peaceful existence.

So it *can* be done. With or without prior psychological sophistication, an individual can read or hear about a new idea, can forcefully set about applying it to his own thought and action, and can carve amazingly constructive changes in his own psyche. Not everyone, of course, can or will do this. And few of those who, theoretically, are able to do so, actually ever will. But some can; and some will.

History gives us several outstanding instances of individuals who significantly changed themselves and helped change others by hard-headed thinking. Zeno of Citium, for example, who flourished in the third century B.C., and founded the Greek stoic school of philosophy. The Greek philosopher, Epicurus; the Phrygian, Epictetus; the Roman emperor, Marcus Aurelius; the Dutch Jew, Baruch Spinoza. These were just a few of the outstanding rational thinkers who, after reading about the teachings of still earlier thinkers (Heraclitus and Democritus, among others), and doing some tall thinking of their own, not only enthusiastically adopted philosophies of life radically different from their original beliefs but—what is more to the point for purposes of our present discussion—actually began to *live* these philosophies, to *act* in accordance with them.

All this, mind you, without benefit of what we today would call formal psychotherapy. Granted, of course, that these were outstanding individuals; and that, in the entire history of mankind, their number seems to have been relatively few. But the important thing is that they did it—did see the light of another's reasoning and did use this enlightenment for their own saner living.

Can basic personality change then, really be effected except by intensive psychotherapy? Most modern authorities strongly say "No!" Thus, Freud, Rank, Reich, Rogers, and Sullivan all stoutly contend that certain therapeutic conditions must exist and continue over a period of time if basic personality change is to be effected in disturbed individuals. But all possible weight of authoritative quoting hardly proves anything other than that the quoted authorities agree.

Our own position is this: Granted that basic personality disturbance *usually* is so deep-seated and longstanding that it *almost always* requires persistent psychotherapeutic help to overcome, this is by no means *always* true. Although basic constructive personality change—as opposed to temporary symptom removal—seems to require fundamental modifications in the ideologies and value systems of disturbed individuals, there is probably *no* single condition which is absolutely necessary for the induce-ment of such changed attitudes and behavior patterns. Many conditions, such as those listed by the therapists mentioned in our last paragraph, or such as we list in several of our previously published papers on rational psychotherapy, are highly desirable. But all that seems to be necessary is that the individual *somehow* come up against significant life experiences *or* learn about others' experiences *or* sit down and think for himself *or* enter a relationship with a therapist who will help him reconstruct his basic attitudes toward himself and others.

Let us, then, not denigrate self-analysis, however limited, for the most part, it tends to be. Rare, almost to the point of being non-existent, are those who fully perform it. But it does exist; it can be effectively done.

In one sense, indeed, self-analysis is a requisite for *all* basic personality change. For even when a disturbed individual does receive competent, ade-quate, persistent therapeutic help, and even when this help is truly salu-tary, unless it is highly *accompanied* by persistent and forceful self-analysis, it will tend to produce superficial and non-lasting results. As we often ex-plain to our psychotherapy patients and marriage counseling clients, par-ticularly during the early treatments, it is not what the therapist tells the individual that helps this individual overcome his emotional disturbances, but what the patient or client *does* with what the therapist tells him.

More concretely: although the effective therapist must somehow teach his patients to think straight, he cannot at any time really think *for* them. Even though he may temporarily advise them exactly what to do in a given life situation, and although they may benefit immensely from following his ad-vice, he must eventually get them to think for themselves—otherwise, they will never be cured, and will always be dependent upon him or on others.

This means that therapy, in essence, largely consists of teaching the pa-tient effective self-analysis: How, specifically, to observe his own feelings and actions, how to evaluate them objectively instead of moralistically or grandiosely, and how to change them, by consistent effort and practice, so that he may achieve the things that he most wants to do in this brief span of human existence while, simultaneously, not interfering seriously with the preferences of others. Self-analysis, in this sense of the term, is not merely an important but actually a requisite aspect of successful psycho-therapy.

Which brings us to one of the main purposes of writing this book. Not only do we hope that it will reach many individuals who have never had (though many of them well could use some) psychotherapeutic help of any sort, and that it will help some of the more earnest and work-oriented of these individuals to think more clearly and act more effectively in regard to their personality problems. We also hope that it will serve as useful supplementary reading for the millions of Americans who have had or are now having some amount of psychotherapeutic assistance.

Continually, in our separate but similar practices of psychotherapy and marriage counseling, patients and clients ask us: "What can we read that will help us while we are undergoing therapy? Have you any kind of a reading list to supplement our work with you?" In answer to these questions, we try to suggest some suitable reading for these patients and have included some references for this purpose in the bibliography at the end of this volume.

Since, however, we do a particular kind of treatment that we call rational psychotherapy which is, as yet, practiced by only a minority of therapists, and since most of the published material in the area of self-analysis and of personality evaluation and treatment only partially includes some of our most utilized principles (and includes many other views we consider to be of highly dubious validity), we find great difficulty in referring our inquirers to even a single book that we would consider to be adequate supplementary reading. The present volume incorporates our attempt to provide the kind of book that goes distinctly beyond our two earlier and less comprehensive books in this area—*How to Live with a Neurotic* and *Creative Marriage*.

A few words of caution, before we go on to the meat of our material. First of all, we should like to note that this book is *not* to be considered a technical and full exposition of our theories and techniques of rational psychotherapy. These have been briefly expounded in several articles in professional literature and will be comprehensively discussed in a weighty tome that will, we hope, soon be forthcoming. In this book, on which we have been working for the past several years, we shall present details of the experimental and clinical evidence for our point of view and shall give concrete descriptions of clinical applications of this viewpoint.

To those who want to get specific help from this book, we must again warn—no book, including this one, can meet in every detail your particular desire for help. There is always something unique about your individual situation, therefore a book cannot be a fully adequate substitute for personalized psychotherapy or counseling. It can, however, nicely supplement or reinforce any individual help you are getting; and, as noted above, in some instances, it can encourage a degree of self-analysis on your part that *may* result in your much more adequately handling some of your major problems.

Still another *caveat*. Remember that the English language, including those variations of it in this book, is limited. Because we, like other writers in the field of mental health, use words such as "creativity," "happiness," "love," "maturity," and "problem-solving," do not jump to the conclusion that we are handing out the same old, hackneyed, pollyanish, "spiritual" message that you may have long ago considered and rejected as being of no practical value in your life. Superficially, some of the things we say may sound like "positive thinking," let-us-pray-for-the-best-ism, orthodox stoicism, or other utopian credo. Actually, they are not. Try reading the anti-unhappiness principles we present in this book; then try thinking and acting on them. We confidently expect that you, like many of our individual and group psychotherapy patients, will find that we've "got something there."

Here, then, is our plan for straight thinking and rational living. Read it carefully and with all due allowances for our limitations as communicators and yours as a receiver of intelligence. No matter how good the rules of living that we set before you, remember that what reads easily and simply may be quite difficult and complicated to believe and to act upon. Do not assume that because you have read and understood some of our practical suggestions for improving your life functioning that—*that is that.* That is *not* that: you still have again and again to go through the usual (or unusual) time-consuming and energy-exacting task of seeing, challenging, and blocking out old self-defeating behavior patterns and learning new, self-fulfilling ways of thinking, perceiving, feeling, and doing.

Well, happy thinking!

You Feel
As You Think

2

"WHAT YOU SAY, Dr. Harper, seems on the surface to be plausible and sensible. And it would be all very nice if human beings actually worked as simply as you indicate that they do! But, frankly, what you and Dr. Ellis call your theory of rational psychotherapy sounds to me, when you probe a little into it, very superficial, antipsychoanalytic, and like a few pages out of the how-to-lift-yourself-by-your-bootstraps school of slick magazine psychology."

The speaker, Dr. B——, was a member of a group of educators to whom I had been asked (as both authors of this book frequently are) to describe the tenets of rational therapy. And he was partly right. Some of our ideas on RT *do* sound superficial. And they *are* contrary to the point of view of orthodox psychoanalysis—though not too far from some of the views of those who follow the teachings of Alfred Adler, Karen Horney, Harry Stack Sullivan, Erich Fromm, and the psychoanalysts who stress the newer "ego psychology."

Still, I couldn't help taking my heckler somewhat to task—not because I thought I could change his mind, for who can unfreeze the prejudices of a trained psychotherapist?—and not because I itched to put him in his place (for the luxury of venting one's spleen on others is, as we shall show later in this book, no reward for the truly rational person), but because I thought that his objections might be turned to good account to demonstrate one of the main principles of RT for the rest of my audience.

"You are presumably objecting," I said, "to our view that human feelings

9

and emotions are much different from, and more than, thoughts and ideas, and that they cannot be changed, as I have just said they could, simply by changing the person's thinking. Is that your main point?"

"It is. We have fifty or a hundred years' history of experimental and clinical findings that prove entirely otherwise."

"Perhaps so. But suppose we forget this hundred years of history for a moment and concentrate on the history of the last few moments. Just a short while ago, as I was giving my talk on rational therapy, you were having some real intense emotional feelings, were you not?"

"I certainly was! I was feeling that you were an idiot and should not be allowed to go on spouting such nonsense."

"Fine," I said, as the rest of my audience gleefully howled. "But you also," I persisted, "had another emotion, just before you stood up to speak against me did you not?"

"I did? What kind of an emotion do you mean?"

"Well, unless I miss being worth my salt as a clinician, I would say that, judging from the high and uneven pitch of your voice as you just spoke, you had at least a little bit of anxiety about getting up among your peers here and voicing your anti-Harperian opinion. Am I totally incorrect about this?"

"—Uh—" My antagonist hesitated for several long seconds (while the knowing smiles of the members of the audience were now in my favor). "No—. I guess you're not totally incorrect. I did have some anxiety just before speaking and during the first part of my words; though it's all gone now."

"All right. Just as I imagined, then. You had two emotions while I was speaking: anger and anxiety. And now, at this present moment, you seem to have neither. Is that correct too?"

"Definitely. I am no longer anxious or angry—though perhaps I feel a little pity for you for still holding to what I think is an untenable position." Touché! Again the smiles were behind him.

"Good. Maybe we'll go into the feeling of pity for me a little later. But let's, for a moment, get back to the anxiety and anger. Would I be quite wrong in assuming that behind your anger was some chain of sentences such as: "That idiot, Harper—along with that other nincompoop colleague of his, Ellis—is mouthing the veriest of hogwash. There ought to be a law against his boring us to tears with this kind of stuff at what might otherwise be a highly scientific meeting'?"

"Precisely! How did you guess?" Again the chorus of snickers was pretty solidly behind him. I continued:

"It must, again, be my clinical intuition. Anyway, you did have such a thought, and you were angry. And our thesis in rational therapy is just that: that your thought—'Dr. Harper is not only mouthing hogwash but he *shouldn't* be allowed to do so'—is the real and virtually sole source of your anger. Indeed, in one sense of the term, this thought *is* your anger. Moreover, our thesis is that the reason you are not, at this present moment, still angry, is because you have replaced the original thought with quite a different one, namely: 'Oh, well, even if he's wrong, Dr. Harper really believes this nonsense; and if the poor fellow wants to keep believing it, that's *his* problem.' And this new thought, I and Dr. Ellis would contend, is at the heart of your present state of feeling, which you quite accurately describe, I think, as 'pity.'"

Before my opponent could say anything further, another member of the audience interjected: "Suppose you are right about Dr. B——'s feelings of anger and now pity. What about his anxiety?"

"I was just going to get around to that," I replied. "According, again, to the theories of rational therapy, what happened in connection with his anxiety was as follows. As I was talking, and as he was inciting himself to anger by telling himself what an impossible person I was, Dr. B—— was also saying to himself something along these lines: 'Just wait till Harper stops talking! Boy, have I something to say that will show everyone what an idiot he is (and what a bright boy I really am for being able to see what an idiot he is and show him up before everyone!). Let me see, now, how shall I squelch him, when I get the chance?'

"And then, I further suggest, Dr. B—— tested several opening sentences in his mind, rejected some of them quickly, thought others might do, and kept looking for still better ones with which to annihilate my thesis. Not only, however, did he objectively try to discover the best set of phrases and sentences he could use against me, but he also kept saying to himself: 'What will the other members of the group think? Will they think I'm just as foolish as Harper? Will they be swayed by his charm? Will they think that I'm just jealous of his and Ellis's success with patients and with their writings? Will it *really* do me any good to open my big mouth against him?'

"These self-created and self-perpetuated sentences of Dr. B——'s, I hypothesize, caused him to be anxious—and, as I noted before in regard to his anger, in a certain sense *were* his anxiety. Is that, Dr. B——, not so? Am I so wide from the mark again?"

"You're probably not entirely wrong," my opponent acquiesced, with more than a shade of embarrassed redness on his face and nearly-bald pate, "but doesn't everyone, do not all of us, say things to ourselves like this before we get up to talk about almost anything in public?"

"We most certainly do," I heartily agreed. "And, believe me, I am using your internalized sentences as an example here only because they are an illustration of what virtually all of us do. But that's just the point I am trying to make—that precisely because all of us keep telling ourselves these kinds of sentences, we are more or less anxious before speaking in public. Because we tell ourselves (a) 'I might make a mistake and fall on my face before this group of my peers' and, much more important, tell ourselves (b) 'And wouldn't that be *awful* if I did make a mistake and fall on my face in public?'—precisely because we tell ourselves these catastrophizing sentences, we almost immediately began to *feel* anxious. Otherwise, if we told ourselves only sentence (a) but instead of (b), said to ourselves quite a different sentence, which we might call (b'), namely, "So what? If I make a mistake and fall on my face, it won't be great, but it still won't be *awful*—if *this* is what we told ourselves at (b'), we would practically never be anxious."

"But suppose," the same educator who had first asked about Dr. B——'s anxiety interrupted again, "suppose you are right, Dr. Harper, in regard to how B—— was creating his anxiety. How do you explain its later disappearance, in terms of your theory of RT?"

"Very simply again. Having screwed up sufficient courage to speak in spite of his self-created anxiety, Dr. B—— found that, even though he did perhaps partly fall on his face, at least to the extent of not fully annihilating me, the world did *not* come to an end, and no actual catastrophe occurred. At worst, he found that I kept standing up to his assault and that some of the members of the audience still seemed to be on my side, although perhaps some also sided with him. So he changed his internalized sentences to something like:

" 'Oh, well. Harper still doesn't really get my point and see what falsehoods he's propounding here, and some of these other people are still on his side, but that's just too damned bad. You can always fool some of the people some of the time, and I just can't expect it to be any different. I'll just bide my time, continue to present my view, and even if I don't win everyone over to it, I can still effectively hold it myself.'

"With this *new*, anticatastrophizing chain of sentences, Dr. B—— has dispelled the anxiety he previously caused himself and is now, as he again has probably accurately reported, more pitying than angry or upset. Is that not correct?"

My opponent again hesitated a moment; then replied "I can only repeat that you may be partially correct, and that there may be *something* in what you say; but I'm still not entirely convinced."

"Nor did I expect that you would be. I just wanted to use your own example to induce you to give this matter some additional thought, and try to encourage the rest of the members of this audience to do likewise. Maybe rational psychotherapy is, as you say, superficial and overly slick. All I am asking is that you professional people give it an honest try and see for yourself whether it really is."

As far as I know, I have never, to this day, convinced my heckler of the soundness of our RT position. But at least three other members of my audience that day are now RT enthusiasts—who, with their students, as well as in relation to every potential crisis in their own lives, are beginning more incisively to see that human emotions and feelings are *not* magically existent in their own right, and do *not* mysteriously flow from totally unconscious or repressed somatic needs and psychic desires. Rather, they almost always, in the case of adolescents and adults, and even in that of fairly young children, directly stem from ideas, thought, attitudes, or beliefs, and can usually be radically changed by modifying the thinking processes that keep creating them.

All of which brings us to the paramount thesis of this book: namely, that *man can live the most self-fulfilling, creative, and emotionally satisfying life by intelligently organizing and disciplining his thinking.* All the pages that follow will, in one way or another, bear testimony to this central, rational psychotherapeutic view.

Feeling Well
by Thinking Straight

3

"WHAT DO YOU mean by a person's intelligently organizing and disciplining his thinking?" we are often asked by our patients, friends, and professional associates.

Answer: "Exactly that. Just what we say."

"But when you say that by rationally and realistically organizing and disciplining his thinking a human being can live the most self-fulfilling, creative, and emotionally satisfying life, you make that 'life' sound like a cold, intellectual, mechanical, and, to be candid, rather unpleasant affair."

"Maybe so. But isn't it possible that it *sounds* that way because most of us have been propagandized to believe, by our parents, teachers, and other purveyors of information, that highly 'emotional' experiences are the only 'real' way of 'living it up' and 'getting the most out of life'? Isn't it likely that fiction writers and dramatists, in particular, by sentimentally rationalizing some of their own 'emotional' excesses, have often been responsible for spreading the dubious notion that unless one keeps roller-coasting from deep depression to brief manic joy and then down to the bogs of despair again one is 'not really living'?"

"Oh, come now! Aren't you exaggerating?"

"Yes, probably. But aren't *you?*"

"I'm not sure. Surely you don't, in your own personal lives, always behave like cold-blooded, big-brained, emotion-squelching individuals who never *feel* any sorrow, pain, joy, elation—or *anything?*"

"We hope we don't. And we can get affidavits from sundry past and

14

present wives, sweethearts, friends, and co-workers to prove that we don't. But whoever said that well-organized, rational thinking was incompatible with intense emotion?"

"We did, if you'll recall, right at the beginning of this chapter. And as yet you rational therapy boys haven't done a thing to disprove our statement. Where's your evidence?"

"Oh, yes; to be sure. You *did* say that rational thinking appears to lead to 'a cold, intellectual, mechanical, and, to be candid, rather unpleasant' kind of life."

"Well?"

"Well what? It's *your* hypothesis. And, according to the first principles of science, the onus of proof is invariably on the individual who hypothesizes, and surely not on him who doubts the original assumption. You seem to be assuming that just because reason *may* interfere with the sensing and expression of intense emotion (and we definitely grant that it *may*) that it therefore *must* so interfere. When and how are you going to prove *that?*"

"A good point," our questioners often admit. "Reasoning *need* not interfere seriously with intense emotion but isn't it nonetheless true that it normally *tends* to do so?"

"Not that we've ever found—nor that anyone else ever seems to have incontrovertibly proved. It may well be true that reasoning normally blocks highly exaggerated, disorganizing, or pathologically excessive emotion. Indeed, that is one of our main tenets of rational therapy—that since a human individual finds it virtually impossible to think of two major things at exactly the same moment, and since emotion is normally created by thinking, the more an excessively or pathologically emoting (or what is generally called an emotionally disturbed) individual thinks, the less he can at one and the same time continue to sustain his pathological state of feeling."

"Then you've practically admitted our charge," our questioners often interject at this point. "You've just said that rational thinking and intense emotion cannot co-exist and that the former drives away the latter."

"Nothing of the sort! You've illegitimately substituted the word 'intense' —which we did *not* use—for the words 'exaggerated,' 'disorganizing,' and 'excessive.'"

"What a silly quibble! Aren't they the same?"

"Not necessarily. Intense emotion may be—often, in fact, clearly is— quite appropriate, realistic, and salutary. Intense feelings of love may be experienced in connection with a most suitable object (such as a truly fine member of the other sex). It may be expressed quite appropriately by treating the beloved affectionately and inducing him or her to be your steady companion or mate. And it may lead to highly fortunate results, for example, inducing the lover to work harder at his art or profession or encouraging him to feel more kindly to others. Exaggerated, disorganizing, or excessive love, on the other hand, would rarely if ever lead to these actions or results."

"Your main point seems to be, then," interject our skeptics, "that although disorganizing emotion is largely incompatible with rational thinking, intensely *pleasant* emotions are not. Is that correct?"

"Most correct. We would contend, in fact, that truly rational thinking almost inevitably leads to pleasant emotions of varying degrees of intensity. And, perhaps even more importantly, we particularly hold that once human reason is properly maximized and utilized to rid people of their disorganizing and disruptive feelings—that is, of their severe emotional blockings caused by many dreadful kinds of anxiety and anger—only *then* can highly pleasurable and productive feelings consistently exist. We say, in other words, the more reason, the more emotion—of a fortunate and joy-evoking kind."

"Very interesting. But this is *your* hypothesis. And, as you so cleverly noted before, the onus is now on *you* to prove the validity of this view."

"Right. And prove it we shall, in the remaining pages of this book, by presenting a mass of clinical, experimental, personal, and other data. But the most important and most unique proof of all, in some ways, is one that you will have to try for yourself."

"Who—*us?*"

"Yes—you. If you really want to see whether the theories we are about to present and back up are of more than passing worth to you—and that, after all, is what you are really interested in,—then we would strongly advise you to keep, for the most part, your present appropriately skeptical frame of mind, but also experimentally to put it in abeyance from time to time and give yourself a chance *to try out* our rational viewpoint in some aspects of your own life. Take some area in which you think you are needlessly unhappy—some grief, guilt, or grandiosity that keeps repetitively ravaging you—and try, really try, some of our thinking formulas on yourself in connection with these personal miseries. Don't accept what we say on faith, no matter how persuasive we may seem. Try our notions for yourself, *see* to what results they lead."

"Seems fair enough. Maybe we shall try."

"O.K., then. Let's see if we can get on with some of the evidence to back our basic theories of rational living and *pleasant* emoting."

At this point, we generally swing into some of the basic theories behind the principles of rational living which we shall now briefly delineate for our readers.

As noted, human feeling is really a product of, and in some ways a form of, human thinking. Does this mean that *all* emotions and creativity can or should be controlled by reason and intellect? Not exactly.

The human individual has four basic processes, all of which are indispensable to his behaving adequately and all of which are interconnected: (1) He perceives or senses—that is, sees, tastes, smells, feels, hears. (2) He moves or acts—walks, eats, swims, throws, climbs, and so forth. (3) He feels or emotes—loves, hates, fears, becomes guilty, feels depressed. (4) He reasons or thinks—remembers, imagines, hypothesizes, concludes, solves problems.

Ordinarily, none of these four basic processes is experienced in isolation by the human adult. Take, first of all, perceiving. If a man perceives or senses something (for example, sees an apple), he also tends, at the very same time, to think about it (figure out whether it is suitable food); to have some feelings about it (to desire or not to desire it); and to do something about it (to pick it up or throw it away).

By the same token, if an individual moves or acts (say, he picks up a stick), he also tends to perceive what he is doing (for example, to see and touch the stick); to think about his act (imagine what he might do with this particular kind of stick); and to have some emotion about it (to like it or dislike it).

Again: if anyone thinks about something (for example, about a crossword puzzle), he will simultaneously tend to perceive (see) it; to have feelings about it (react favorably or unfavorably to it); and to move in connection with it (use a pencil to write on it or put aside the page on which it is printed).

Finally: if one emotes about something or some person (say, hates another individual), he will also tend to perceive (see, hear, touch) this person; think about him (remember him, figure out how to avoid him); and take some kind of action in regard to him (run from him or punch him in the jaw).

We function, then, as a single organism—perceiving, moving, thinking, and emoting simultaneously and interrelatedly. These four basic life processes are *not* distinctly different ones, each of which begins where the others leave off. Instead, they all significantly overlap and are in some respects aspects of the *same thing*.

Thus, thinking, aside from consisting of bioelectric changes (which are, of course, motor processes) in the brain, and in addition to consisting of remembering, learning, comparing, and problem-solving, also is—and to some extent has to be—sensory, motor, and emotional behavior.

Instead, therefore, of saying, as we usually vaguely say, "Jones thinks about this puzzle," we could more accurately note that "Jones perceives-moves-feels-*and*-THINKS about this puzzle. Because, however, Jones's motives in regard to the puzzle may be *largely* focussed upon solving it, and only *incidentally* on seeing, manipulating, and emoting about it, we may justifiably state that he thinks about the puzzle without our specifically mentioning that he *also* perceives, moves, and feels in relation to it. But we should never forget that Jones (like everyone else) is not really able, except for a split-second or two, *just* to think about the puzzle.

Question: Since thinking is only one of the four basic human processes, and really never can be totally separated from perceiving, moving, and feeling, why is it given top billing in the system of rational psychotherapy?

Answer: For reasons which will shortly, we hope, be made clear. But let us first point out that it is emoting—or, rather, the controlling of our emotions—rather than thinking or problem-solving that seems to be the main problem of human living today. This was not always so. Man, in competition with other animals, once had the problem of seeing, moving, and thinking better than they did, in order to ensure his own survival. Today, after inventing eyeglasses, radar, aircraft, electronic calculators, and other perceiving-moving-thinking aids, he rules supreme on this earth and is literally seeking other worlds to conquer.

Only in the emotional area has man as yet made remarkably few advances. In spite of amazing progress in other areas, he still is not appreciably more emotionally mature, stable, and happy than he was in past centuries. Indeed, he is in some ways more childish, emotionally uncontrolled, and mentally ill than ever.

Some progress has of course been made in the emotional area. In the field of psychological diagnosis and psychotherapy, sparked largely by the brilliant insights of Sigmund Freud and his followers, considerable understanding of emotional disturbance and its treatment has already been achieved. In the biochemical realm, the use of drugs, shock treatment, brain surgery, and other twentieth century techniques are every day adding to our knowledge of why human beings become psychologically distraught and what can be done to help them regain their emotional equilibrium.

Nonetheless, perhaps the outstanding problem of our day is that of controlling or changing human emotion and thereby alleviating almost universal neurosis and psychosis. Which leads us to ask: What *is* the emotional process, and *how* can we go about making it better serve human ends?

4

What
Your Feelings
Really Are

WHAT THE DEVIL *is* emotion?

Hundreds of profound books and articles have tried to answer this question—none of them, as yet, with absolute certainty. Let us now, with something short of a perfect answer as our goal, see if we can shed a little light on this difficult subject.

Emotion, we have already indicated, is a complicated life process that is inseparably connected with perceiving, moving, and thinking. It is not *one* thing but a combination of several seemingly diverse, yet actually closely related, phenomena. The famous neurologist, Stanley Cobb, has given this somewhat technical description of this elusive state of feeling:

"My suggestion is that we use the term 'emotion' to mean the same thing as (1) an introspectively given affective state, usually mediated by acts of interpretation; (2) the whole set of internal physiological changes, which help (ideally) the return to normal equilibrium between the organism and its environment, and (3) the various patterns of overt behavior, stimulated by the environment and implying constant interaction with it, which are expressive of the stirred-up physiological state (2) and also the more or less agitated psychological state (1). An emotion is not a private mental state, nor a set of static qualities abstracted from such a state, nor a hypothalamic response with intense autonomic discharge, nor a pattern of behavior viewed in purely objective terms, nor a particular stimulus-situation, even though it has some emotogenic meaning for distinguishable things, nor is it the entire set of them viewed as constituting a merely addi-

19

tive whole. An emotion is rather *an acute disturbance, involving marked somatic changes, which is experienced as a more or less agitated feeling.* There are associated inferences, of varying degrees of explicitness, as to the meaning of what is happening. Both the feeling and the behavior which expresses it, as well as the internal physiological responses to the stimulus-situation, constitute a dynamically interrelated whole, which *is* the emotion. Thus, *an emotion is at once physiological, psychological, and social* since other persons are usually the most highly emotogenic stimuli in our civilized environment."

Question: Is Dr. Cobb's definition of emotion final and fully acceptable to all modern psychologists and neuropsychiatrists?

Answer: No, it is not. As English and English point out in their recent *Comprehensive Dictionary of Psychological and Psychoanalytic Terms,* it is virtually impossible as yet to define emotion without referring to several conflicting theories.

There is, however, considerable agreement today that there is no *single* cause or result of what we call emotion. At minimum, emotions arise through a three-way process: First, through some kind of physical stimulation of the special emotional center of the brain (called the hypothalamus) and the nerve network of the body (called the autonomic nervous system). Second, through the perceiving and the moving (technically called the sensori-motor) processes. And third, through desiring and thinking (technically, conation and cognition).

Normally, the emotional centers of the human organism (the hypothalamus and the autonomic nervous system) as well as the perceiving, moving and thinking centers of the organism, especially the cerebral centers of the brain and the millions of fibers of the central nervous system which go to the arms, legs, skin, and other end-organs of the body, are in a certain moderate state of excitability and receptivity at any given time. Then a stimulus of a certain intensity impinges upon the emotional centers and excites or damps them. This stimulus can be (in rather unusual cases) directly applied to the emotional centers—for example, by electrically stimulating parts of the brain or by giving the individual exciting or depressing drugs which quickly act on parts of his brain or autonomic nervous system. Or the stimulus (more usually) can be indirectly applied, through the individual's perceiving, moving, and thinking, and through his thereby affecting central-nervous-system and brain pathways which, in turn, are connected with and influence the emotional (hypothalamic and autonomic) centers.

If you wish to control your feelings, then, you may do so in three major ways. Suppose, for example, you are highly excitable and wish to calm down. You can directly influence your emotions by electrical or biochemical means—such as by getting shock treatment or by taking barbiturates or tranquilizing drugs. Or, secondly, you can work through your perceiving-moving (sensori-motor) system—for example, by doing relaxation exercises, by dancing, or by Yoga breathing techniques. Or, thirdly, you can counteract your excitability by using your willing-thinking processes—that is, by reflecting, thinking, or telling yourself to calm down.

Which combination of these three means of controlling your emotional state will be most effective in any given instance will depend largely on how intense your emotion is to begin with and in what direction and how extensively you wish to change or control it.

Question: If three effective methods of controlling one's emotions are available, why is only one of these methods emphasized in rational psychotherapy and in your present discussion?

Answer: For several important reasons. For one thing, we are not specialists in medicine or biophysics and therefore do not feel that advocating pharmacological or bioelectrical methods of emotional control is our cup of tea. Nor are we adequately versed in physiology, relaxation or movement techniques, Yoga methods, or other pathways to sensori-motor control over one's emotional responses. We therefore are more than willing to leave investigations and remedial work in these areas to others more versed in these fields.

We believe that it is highly probable, moreover, that biophysical and sensori-motor techniques for affecting human emotions are, unless combined with thinking-desiring methods, of limited usefulness and effectiveness. Thus, a person may be brought out of a depression by the use of drugs or relaxation techniques. But unless this individual begins to think more clearly and acquire more self-confidence, he will usually tend to become depressed again when the drugs are withdrawn or the movement exercises are halted. For *permanent* and *deep-seated* emotional changes to be effected, thinking changes, or drastic modifications of the individual's philosophy of life, appear to us to be necessary in most instances.

Finally, we are particularly interested in what the emotionally disturbed individual can do to help himself, rather than what others (such as biochemists, physicians, or physiotherapists) can do to help him. In many instances, it is most important that he seek outside physical help to control his emotional outbursts or severe inhibitions. But the less dependent he is on drugs or physical apparatuses, the better. And our rational methods of inducing him to think for and help himself are ideally suited, we believe, for his own independent application. Once he learns these techniques and persistently practices them for awhile he should have little or no further need of our, or anyone else's, outside assistance.

We are not, then, opposed to controlling self-defeating emotions by drugs, relaxation techniques (such as those of Jacobsen, or Schultz and

Luthe), dance therapy, Yoga exercises, or other physical approaches. We believe that under some circumstances these techniques may be effective in controlling or modifying runaway or over-inhibited feelings. Although we are not enthusiasts for more drastic physical treatment, such as electro-shock treatment and brain surgery, we can admit the legitimacy of its cautious and occasional usage.

The main theme of this volume and of the principles of rational therapy, however, is that for the most thoroughgoing and permanent changes (rather than mere suppression, diversion, or repression) of disturbed feeling to occur, the use of reason and logic is a virtual necessity. This is because a huge element (though not the whole) of emoting essentially *is*, or is at least directly influenced by, thought.

Question: Granted that bioelectrical, pharmacological, and sensori-motor approaches to emotional change may be limited; but is not the rational approach to conscious thought equally superficial? Have not the psychoanalysts and other investigators long ago established the fact that much of human behavior, and especially of *emotional* behavior, is *un*con-sciously motivated and controlled? How can an individual, if this is true, learn to control and change the thoughts that create his feelings when he is not necessarily aware of these thoughts because they lie buried deeply in his unconscious mind?

Answer: A very good point! And one that cannot be answered in a word. As we shall keep showing throughout this volume, what the orthodox Freudians and many other psychoanalysts keep cavalierly referring to as "deeply unconscious thoughts" are, in the vast majority of instances, what Freud originally called "preconscious" ideas. That is to say, they are thoughts and feelings (or what we personally like to call internalized phrases and sentences) that are not *immediately* accessible to the individual's awareness, but that he can fairly easily learn to infer and observe, by working back from the behavior which they induce him to perform.

We firmly believe that the average intelligent individual, even though he is seriously emotionally disturbed, can learn to perceive the cerebral self-signalings that invariably lie behind and motivate his emotions and can succeed in deciphering the "unconscious" messages which he is continually transmitting to himself. Once he clearly sees, understands, and begins to challenge and question the declarative and exclamatory sentences which create his feelings, his "unconscious" thoughts will become quite accessible to consciousness, and his power of emotional self-control will be enormously enhanced.

Enough of our own vague promises! Let us more specifically note that a large part of what we call emotion is nothing more nor less than a certain kind—a biased, prejudiced, or strongly evaluated kind—of thinking. What we usually label as thinking is a relatively calm and dispassionate appraisal of a given situation, an objective comparison of many of the elements in this situation, and a coming to some conclusion as a result of this comparing or discriminating process.

Thus, a thinking person may observe a piece of bread, see that one part of it is mouldy, remember that eating this part previously made him ill, and therefore cut off the mouldy part and eat the non-mouldy section of the bread. An emoting individual, on the other hand, will tend to observe the same piece of bread and remember so violently or prejudicially his previous experience with the mouldy part that he may quickly throw away the whole piece of bread and go hungry.

The emotional person, in this instance, is doing as much thinking as is the non-emotional individual but he is doing a different *kind* of thinking—thinking which is so prejudiced or circumscribed by an unpleasant prior experience that it is now limited, biased, overgeneralized, and ineffective. Because the thinking person is relatively calm, he uses the maximum information available to him—that is, the information that mouldy bread is unpleasant to eat but that non-mouldy bread is good. Because the emotional person is relatively excited, he uses only part of the information available—that is, that the mouldy bread is unpleasant.

What we call the thinking individual is a person who is less strongly biased by his previous experience than he whom we label "emotional." In consequence, he is in a better position to *employ* all the information he may gather about a current life situation and its possible connections with his past. Although he seriously *considers* his prior experiences, he is less overwhelmed by them. Consequently, he is much more flexible and liable about making his current discriminations and decisions.

Question: Hadn't you better watch your step? After first making a four-way division of human behavior into the acts of perceiving, moving, thinking, and feeling, you are now talking about a "thinking" and an "emotional" individual as if you had never made your previous distinctions.

Answer: Right you are! There are, of course, no exclusively thinking or exclusively emotional persons, since we still insist that everyone, almost simultaneously, perceives, moves, thinks, *and* feels. However, to use our previous terminology, some people perceive, move, THINK, and feel; while others perceive, move, think, and FEEL. The latter, as we just noted above, do a kind of thinking different from the former, and hence *predominantly* feel; while the other with their calmer and less prejudiced type of cogitation, may be said to be those who *predominantly* think. All people, however, are thinkers *and* emoters—even if, when making use of conventional language, (though we are often sorely tempted to coin our own) we arbitrarily, to some extent, have to divide the two.

Perhaps it will make things a bit clearer (and this is admittedly murky territory in which we are treading) if we note that much of what we call emotion would really seem to be a certain kind of thinking or discriminating —a kind that is strongly slanted or biased by previous perceptions or experiences; that is often accompanied by sharp bodily responses, such as feelings of pleasure or nausea; and that is likely to encourage the emoting person to take some kind of positive or negative action—to go comfortably toward or run wildly away from the stimulus that seems to be (but by no means always is) causing the thinking and its emotional concomitants.

In other words: emotion in some major respects seems to be a kind of semi-logical, fixated, prejudiced, or bigoted thought; while thinking seems to be a relatively calm, unbiased, reflective kind of discrimination. Thus, if we calmly compare one apple with another, we may *thoughtfully* conclude that it is fuller, less blemished, and redder, and that therefore it is more likely to be a good apple. But if we have had very pleasant prior experiences with blemished apples (if we, for instance, successfully bobbed for one at a Halloween party and were enabled, as a prize, to kiss the prettiest girl present) or if we have had most unpleasant prior experiences with unblemished apples (if we ate too many one day and became ill), we may excitedly, rashly, and prejudicially—that is, *emotionally*—conclude that the blemished apple is the better one and may start eating it.

It would appear, then, that thinking and emoting are closely interrelated and at times differ mainly in that thinking is a more tranquil, less activity-directed mode of discrimination; while emoting is a less tranquil, more somatically involved, and more activity-directed mode of behavior. It would also appear that among adult humans reared in a social culture which includes a well-formulated language, thinking and emoting usually accompany each other, act in a circular cause-and-effect relationship, and in certain (though hardly all) respects are essentially the *same thing* so that one's thinking *becomes* one's emotion and emoting *becomes* one's thought.

By the same token—in accordance with the interrelationship between all four major human behavior processes, as we outlined—one's thinking and emoting also become one's (sensori-motor) action and one's action becomes one's thinking and emoting. For example, by thinking about and enjoying the thought of swimming, one pushes oneself into the water and eventually learns to swim; and the more one swims, the more one often (though not always) comes to think about and enjoy the thought and practice of it.

Question: Are you really saying that *all* emotion is a kind of thought? Do you seriously believe that emotion can under *no* circumstance exist without thinking?

Answer: No, we do not believe or say that. It is possible (although in the case of the adult human being not absolutely certain) that emotion can *briefly* exist without thought. An individual, for instance, steps on your toe and you spontaneously, immediately become angry. Or you hear a piece of music and you instantly begin to feel warm and excited. Or you learn that a close friend has died and you begin to feel sad. Under these circumstances, you may feel emotional without doing any associated thinking.

Perhaps, however, even in these cases, in which emotion appears to rise instantaneously and unpremeditatedly, you do, with split-second rapidity, start thinking to yourself: "This person who stepped on my toe is a black-guard!" or "This music is wonderful!" or "Oh, how awful it is that my friend died!" Perhaps only *after* you have had these rapid-fire and "unconscious" thoughts you *then* begin to become emotional.

In any event, assuming that you don't, at the very beginning, have any conscious or unconscious thought accompanying your emotion, it appears to be virtually impossible to sustain an emotional outburst without bolstering it by repeated ideas. For unless you keep telling yourself something on the order of "This person who stepped on my toe is a blackguard!" or "How could he do a horrible thing like that to me!" the pain of having your toe stepped on will soon die and your immediate reaction will die with the pain.

Of course, you may keep getting your toe stepped on and the continuing pain may sustain your anger. But assuming that your physical sensation stops, your emotional response, in order to last, has to be bolstered by some kind of thinking. Otherwise, by what magical process could it endure?

Similarly with pleasant feelings. By continuing to listen to certain musical compositions and having the sensations (aural and kinesthetic) obtained thereby, your emotion of warmth and excitement may be sustained. But even under these circumstances you will have difficulty in *perpetuating* your feelings of pleasure unless you keep telling yourself something like: "This music is fine!"; "Oh, how I love those harmonies!"; "What a wonderful composer the writer of this piece was!"; and so on.

In the case of the death of one of your close friends or relatives, you normally will find it easy to become depressed, since you have lost a relationship with someone who is truly dear to you. But even in this instance you will find it difficult to sustain your emotion of depression for any period of time unless you keep reminding yourself: "Oh, how terrible it is that he has died!" or "How could he have died so young?" or something of that sort.

Even then, when thinking does not immediately precede or accompany feeling (which would apparently be rarely if ever), it would seem that sustained emotion normally is associated with thinking and that it is positively or negatively evaluative thinking, and in fact, serves as the sustaining force behind the feeling. We say "normally" because it is theoretically possible for emotional circuits, once they have been made to reverberate by some physical or psychological stimulus, to keep reverberating under their own power.

It is also possible for drugs or electrical impulses to keep acting directly on emotion-carrying nervous circuits (such as the cells of the hypothalamus and autonomic nervous system) and thereby to keep one emotionally aroused once arousal has started. Usually, however, these types of continued direct stimulation of the emotion-producing centers do not occur. They seem to be limited largely to pathological conditions.

Question: Granting that thinking processes usually precede, follow, and sustain human feeling, need it still be true that these thinking processes literally consist of words, phrases, and sentences that people "say to themselves?" Does *all* thinking consist of self-verbalizations?

Answer: Perhaps not and we certainly do not want to take an absolutist position. We much prefer to state that by the time a person who is not suffering from some severe psychotic disturbance (such as deep-seated schizophrenia) reaches adulthood, he has normally been conditioned to do almost all, if not absolutely all, his thinking, and consequently his emoting, in terms of self-talk or internalized phrases and sentences.

Man is a uniquely language-creating animal and he begins to learn from very early childhood to formulate his thoughts, perceptions, and feelings in words, phrases, and sentences. Unless, as we have noted, some very serious disease process intervenes, the human tendency to think in words, rather than in pictures, sounds, touch units, or other possible methods of internal representations, is nearly complete by adolescence or adulthood. If this is so (and we know of no evidence to the contrary), then for all practical purposes the phrases and sentences that we keep telling ourselves usually *are* or *become* our thoughts and emotions.

To illustrate this human propensity, let us take the example of a man who has been interviewed for a job. Before the interview, he will often start talking to himself along the following lines:

"I wonder if I'll get this job . . . I wish I didn't have to face the interview I'm about to take, because it's not very enjoyable and I may be refused . . . But if I don't face the interview, I certainly won't get the job. . . . Besides, what difference does it make if I am refused? I really have nothing to lose thereby . . . While if I don't get the job, I may have a lot to lose . . . The only thing to do, then, is to take the interview, get it over with and see whether or not I get the job."

By telling himself these kinds of sentences, this man is thinking. For all practical purposes, his sentences *are* his thinking.

If, however, this same individual becomes highly emotional, he may say certain different sentences:

"Suppose I go for this interview, make a fool of myself, and don't get the job ... *That would be awful!* ... Or suppose I go for the interview, get the job, and then prove to be incompetent ... *That would be frightful!*"

Or this same individual may say still different sentences to himself:

"Suppose I go for the interview, make a favorable impression, and get the job ... *That would be wonderful!* ... My wife and friends would look up to me and think I had done very well ... *And that would be fine!*"

By telling himself these kinds of sentences, and including the negative evaluation *"That would be awful!"* or the positive evaluation, *"That would be wonderful!"*, this individual changes his calm thinking into excited emoting. And, for all practical purposes, his evaluative internalized sentences *are* his emotion.

It would appear, then, that positive human emotions, such as feelings of love or elation, are often associated with or result from internalized sentences stated in some form or variation of the phrase "This is good!" and that negative human emotions, such as feelings of anger or depression, are frequently associated with or result from sentences which are stated in some form or variation of the phrase "This is bad." Without an adult human being's employing—on some conscious or unconscious level—such sentences as these, much of his emoting would simply not exist.

Question: If what you say is true, how is it that so few men and women, including few members of your own psychological profession, clearly see that thinking and emoting are basically the same kind of thing and that they stem from internalized words, phrases, and sentences? Is this because of their ignorance?

Answer: In part, yes. Many people, including psychologists and psychiatrists, just don't bother to look very closely at so-called emotions and therefore remain ignorant of their ideological basis. Others look closely enough, but only in the light of some preconceived dogma, such as classical psychoanalytic dogma. We have found that some persons trained to think of human behavior in rigid Freudian terms will no more consider the possibility that emotion may be understood and radically changed by observing and changing the sentences that create it than will some religious fundamentalists consider anything other than their interpretation of certain Biblical passages.

But that is exactly what we, non-Freudians and non-fundamentalists, insist: that if human emotions are usually, as we contend they are, in large part the result of thinking, one may appreciably control or revamp one's emotions by controlling or revamping one's thoughts. Or, more concretely stated: if one wishes to control one's emotions, one may appreciably do so by changing the internalized sentences, or self-talk, with which one created them in the first place.

This, again, is the main message of this book: that human thinking and the emotions usually associated with this thinking can be controlled or changed by parsing the thoughts and emotions into the essential sentences of which they consist and then changing these sentences. We hold, more specifically, that sustained negative emotions—such as depression, anxiety, anger, and guilt—are almost always unnecessary and that they can be largely eradicated if people will learn to think consistently straight and to follow up their straight thinking with effective action.

Question: Can *all* negative emotions be extirpated by controlling one's thinking?

Answer: Hardly. Many emotional outbursts, such as fits of anger or fear, seem to be spontaneous and almost instantaneous results of perceiving and moving (sensori-motor) processes which are either of innate origin or result from early acquired visceral conditioning. Thus, if you make a loud noise behind someone's back or aim a swiftly moving vehicle at him, he will normally tend to experience fear, while if you keep cooking fine meals for someone or satisfying him sexually, he will normally tend to experience liking or love.

These kinds of emotions, based on distinct threats to an individual's security or on the satisfaction of his sensory pleasures, tend to be biologically rooted and probably have their source in primitive pleasure-pain processes. It is difficult to see how people could survive for long without *some* emotional leanings of this nature.

Many emotions, moreover, even though they are hardly necessary for human survival, appear to add appreciably to human well-being and in this sense are almost indispensable to a happy existence. One's joy or elation at hearing a beautiful piece of music, watching a lovely sunset, or successfully finishing a difficult task is not exactly life-preserving. But an existence bereft of feelings like these would indeed be drab and non-rewarding.

Anyone, therefore, who would attempt to control human emotions out of existence would be tackling a goal of dubious value. To succeed at such a task would be to dehumanize men and women and make their lives meaningless.

The ancient and medieval philosophers who apotheosized man's achieving a state of pure "soul" or pure intellect, devoid of all the "crass" emotions, were actually asking for a super-robot or automaton which, like some of our modern electronic computers, would be quite effective in solving certain problems but which would not be capable of any pleasure or satisfaction. What would the *point* of such a super-"human" being be?

Question: Then ridding the world of emotion, or substituting intellect for feeling, is definitely not your main goal—is that correct?

Answer: Quite correct. If anything, one of our main goals is to help many inhibited and apathetic individuals to achieve *more* honest-to-goodness feeling, *higher* pitches of emotion. We are all in favor of human emotional experience. All that we oppose is negative, self-defeating, highly exaggerated emotionalizing. And in the remainder of this book we shall try to present some specific techniques for dealing with and controlling this self-sabotaging brand of over or under-emotionalizing.

Thinking Yourself
Out of
5   *Emotional Disturbances*

MOST PSYCHOTHERAPY PATIENTS are difficult customers, but this one was abusing the privilege. No matter how often I (A.E.) would try to show her that she had control over her own destiny, if only she *believed* that she had, she kept parrying my arguments with all kinds of excuses and evasions.

"I know you're right," she said, "about those other patients of yours who are able to control their feelings but I just can't seem to do it. Maybe I'm different. Maybe they've got something that I'm missing."

"Yes, maybe they have got something that you haven't," I agreed. "Recently acquired corks to plug the holes in their head. And I've shown them where to get the corks. Now how come I'm having so much trouble showing you?"

"Yes, how come you haven't shown me? God knows, I've tried to see what you keep telling me."

"You mean God knows you keep *thinking* you're trying to see. But maybe that's just the trouble—you've convinced yourself that you're really trying to see how you're bothering yourself with the nonsense you keep drumming into yourself all the time; and having convinced yourself that you're trying, you actually find no need for trying any longer. So you quickly give up and don't actually try to see anything. Now, if I could only get you to *work* at observing and changing your own self-defeating internal sentences, you'd be surprised how quickly and drastically your enormous feelings of anger against your mother and your brother would go away."

"But how can I *work* at a thing like that?—it's so indefinite."

30

"It only *seems* indefinite—because you make little actual effort to grasp it: to see what your own sentences are and to examine the philosophic premises behind them. Actually, it's no different from working at playing the piano or playing tennis—which you once told me you do very well."

"Oh, but that's different. Playing tennis is something physical. It's not at all like thinking or getting angry or anything like that."

"Ah, now I think I've got you!" I exclaimed.

"What do you mean?" she asked. And it was almost laughable (had it not been so tragic) how fearfully startled she was at the thought that I *might* now have her, and that she consequently might have to surrender her neurosis.

"You say that playing tennis is something physical. And on the surface, of course, it is. You make muscle movements with your eyes and your arms and your hands, and somehow the ball keeps going over the net. And, looking at your muscles moving and the ball flying, you think of the whole process as physical, almost mechanical."

"But isn't it?"

"No, it definitely isn't. Suppose your opponent hits the ball to you. Your object is to hit it back over the net, preferably in a place where he or she will not be able easily to reach and return it. So you run after the ball (using your legs), reach out for it (using your arms), swing at it (using your arms and wrist), and so on. But what *makes* you run this way or that way, stretch out or pull back your arms, turn your wrist to the left or right?"

"What makes me—? Well, I guess my eyes do. I *see* that the ball is over here or over there, and I *see* where I want to place it, and I move accordingly."

"Fine. But do you see *by magic*? And do you somehow mysteriously, magically get your sight to direct your legs this way, your arms that way, your wrist still another way?"

"No, it's not any magic. It's—. It's—." My patient was frankly troubled.

"Could it," I asked, "could it possibly be *thinking*? Could it be that you see, as you say, your opponent's ball going over here or over there, and you *think* it would be wise to return it over on this or that corner of the court, and you *think*, again, that you can reach the ball by stretching out your arm a little more in this direction, and your wrist in this other direction, and so on and so forth?"

"You mean, I really am not as mechanical and physical, all along, in my actions as I think I am, but I am really directing these actions by my thinking? You mean I am continually telling myself, while playing the game, to do this and that, and to stretch my arm out here or turn my wrist over this way, and so forth? Is that what you mean?"

"Well, *isn't* that what you are really doing while you are playing this so called *physical* game of tennis? Aren't you, during every single minute of the play, continually *directing* your arm to do this and your wrist to do that? And aren't you doing this directing by real, hard, concerted thinking?"

"Come to think of it—and I must admit I never have thought of it that way before—I guess I really am. I'll be darned! The whole thing—why, the whole thing's really mental, isn't it?"

"Yes, isn't it? Even this highly 'physical' game is really largely mental. And you keep working, working at this game—and not only working by running, stretching, turning your wrist, and so on, but working at *thinking* about what to do during the game. And it's this latter work, the work at thinking, that really makes you a better tennis player, eventually, than you originally were. The main practice, in fact, that you do at playing tennis, is *thinking* practice. Isn't it?"

"When you put it that way, I guess it is. Funny! And I thought it was physical and little else. I guess I'm beginning to see now what you mean by *working* at changing my sentences and changing my emotions. Just as in tennis, I work at changing my stance and my stroke and other things. And, as you say, it's really working at thinking, and not just at mechanical changes."

"Exactly. Now if I can get you to accept the same concept that you use at tennis (even though you've been unaware for years just *what* you've been doing to improve your game) and to apply this to changing your sentences, and particularly those behind your disordered emotions, your game of life will begin to improve almost as quickly and as well as your game of tennis has in the past."

With this kind of an ideological breakthrough effected, it was not so difficult, thereafter, to induce this previously defensive and stubborn patient to work at her emotional disturbances. Nor is it too difficult to get almost any patient to work in a similar manner—once the basic *idea* of working at changing one's own sentences is got over to him or her.

Back, now, to our main theme. Granted that human emotions are both necessary and desirable (as we have willingly admitted at the end of the last chapter), the important question remains: Are sustained *negative* emotions, such as enduring fear or hostility, necessary?

The answer to this question is: In large part, no. Sustained negative feelings, other than those caused by continuous physical pain or discomfort, are usually the result of ignorance or disturbance and for the most part may be eliminated by knowledge and straight-thinking.

How do we reach this conclusion? Simply by extending some of the concepts of thinking and emoting which we have been presenting in the first chapters of this book. For if sustained feelings usually are the result of an individual's conscious or unconscious thinking, (that is, his internalized sentences), then it would appear that it is rarely the things that occur to us from the outside that make us sad or glad. It is, rather, our perceptions, attitudes, or self-verbalizations about these outside events.

This principle, which we have recently rediscovered from the materials of many psychotherapeutic sessions with scores of clients, was originally realized by several ancient Greek and Roman philosophers, and perhaps best stated by the famous stoic, Epictetus, who in the first century A.D. wrote in *The Enchiridion:* "Men are disturbed not by things, but by the views which they take of them." William Shakespeare, many centuries later, rephrases this thought in *Hamlet:* "There's nothing either good or bad but thinking makes it so."

As a case in point, let us turn for a moment to Geraldine, one of my highly intelligent and efficient thirty-three-year-old female patient who had come to see me (R.A.H.) about six months after she had obtained a divorce. Although she had been decidedly unhappy in her marriage to an irresponsible and dependent husband, she had been no happier since her divorce. Her husband had drunk to excess, run around with other women, and had been unable to hold a job. But when she came to see me, she was beginning to think she had made a mistake in divorcing him. I said:

"Why do you think it was a mistake to divorce your husband?"

"Because I think divorce is wrong," she replied. "I think when people get married, they should stay married."

"Yet you do not belong to a religious group that takes that position. You do not believe that marriages are somehow made and sealed in heaven, do you?"

"No, I don't even believe in a heaven. I just *feel* it is wrong to get divorced and I blame myself for having gotten one. I have been even more miserable since I got it than I was when living with my husband."

"But look," I asked, "Where do you think your feelings about divorce being wrong originated? Do you think you were born with them? Do you think that human beings have built-in feelings, like built-in taste buds, that tell them how to distinguish right from wrong? Your taste buds tell you what is salty, sweet, or bitter. And are your feelings supposed to tell you what is right, wrong, or indifferent?"

The young divorcée laughed. "You make it sound pretty silly. No, I don't suppose I was born with feelings about what is right or wrong. I had to learn to feel as I do." ANTI-SCRIPTURE

Seeing a good opening, I rushed in where less directive and less rational therapists often fear to tread. "Exactly," I said. "You had to learn to feel as you do. And what is learned can be unlearned or modified. So, even though you are not of a fundamentalist faith that holds that divorce is immoral, this idea is widespread in our society and you could easily have picked it up—

probably in your early childhood from your parents, school teachers, or playmates. And the idea that you picked up, simply stated, is this:

"'Only bad people get divorces. I got a divorce. So I must be a bad person. Yes, it must be true. I am a bad person. Oh, what a no-good, awful, terrible person I have been!'"

"Sounds dreadfully familiar;" she rather bitterly laughed.

"I'm sure it does," I resumed. "Some such sentences as these must have started going through your mind—otherwise you could not possibly be as disturbed as you are. Over and over again, you must have kept repeating this stuff. And then you have probably gone on to say to yourself:

"'Because I am such a terrible person who did this horrible thing of getting a divorce, I deserve to be *blamed* and *punished* for my dreadful act. I deserve to be wretched and miserable and desperately unhappy. And that's just what I am—I am even more unhappy than when I was married to that lousy husband of mine.'"

"Right again!" she ruefully smiled.

"So of course," I continued, "you have been unhappy. Anyone who spends a good portion of her waking hours thinking what a terrible person she is and how unhappy she is and how much she *deserves* to be unhappy because of what a terrible person she is (notice, if you will, the circular thinking involved in all this)—any such person will be bound to feel miserable. If I, for example, started telling myself right this minute (and went on doing so for most of the rest of the day, and the next, and the next) that I was no good, a low-lifed heel, a stinker because I never learned to play the violin or to ice-skate or to do some of the other countless things I could have learned to do—if I kept telling myself this kind of bosh, I could quickly make myself feel depressed.

"Then I could also tell myself, in this kind of sequence, how much I *deserved* to feel unhappy because, after all, I had my chance to learn to play the violin and to ice-skate and I had messed these chances up nicely. And what a real worthless skunk, under these circumstances, I am. Oh, my god, what a *real* skunk!"

My patient, by this time, was almost in stitches, as I satirically kept emphasizing my doom. "Again," I said, "I make it sound silly. But with a purpose—to show you that *you* are being just as silly when you start giving yourself the business about your divorce."

"I am beginning to understand what you mean," she said. "I *do* say this kind of thing to myself. But how can I stop? There is, after all, quite a difference between divorce, on the one hand, and violin-playing or ice-skating on the other hand."

"Granted. But has your getting a divorce really been any more horrible, terrible, and catastrophic than my not learning to play the fiddle?"

"Well, you'll have to admit that I made a serious mistake when I married such an irresponsible person as my husband. And maybe if I had behaved more maturely and wisely myself, I could have helped him to grow up."

"O.K. agreed. You did make a mistake to marry him in the first place. And, quite probably, you did so because you yourself were not sufficiently mature at the time of your marriage. All right, so you made a mistake, a neurotic mistake. But does this mean that you should be *punished* the rest of your life by having to live forever with your mistake?"

"No, I guess not. But how about a wife's responsibility to her husband? Don't you think that I should have stayed with him and tried to help him get over his severe problems?"

"A very lovely, and sometimes even practical, thought. But didn't you tell me previously that you *did* try to help him and he refused even to acknowledge that he was slightly disturbed himself? And didn't you say that he strongly opposed your going for any kind of therapy while you were married, let alone his own going for help, too?"

"Yes, that's the way it was. The mere mention of the word *psychologist* or *marriage counselor* was enough to send him into a fit of temper. He'd never think of going or even letting me go for help."

"The only thing you could have done, then, would have been to play psychotherapist to him, and in your state, you'd hardly have been very effective at that. What are you beating yourself down for? You made a mistake in marrying; you did your best to do something to rectify it after marriage; you were blocked, mainly by your husband, but partly by your own feelings of severe upset, on both counts. So you finally got out of the marriage, as almost any reasonably sane person would have done. Now what's your crime? Why do you *insist* on blaming yourself? You think, erroneously, that it's the unhappy situation you're now in which is making you miserable. But is it the situation—or is it what you're telling yourself *about* this situation?"

"I'm beginning to see your point. Although my marital situation never was and still isn't good, you seem to be saying that I don't *have* to give myself such a hard time about it. That's quite a point of view you have there!"

"Yes, I like it myself—and you'd be surprised how often I use it in my own life. But now if we can only make it *your* point of view, not even a poor marriage and an as yet difficult divorce situation will faze you. In fact, if I can really get you to adopt this viewpoint, I can't imagine anything that will ever bother you too much."

"You really mean that, don't you?"

"Mean it, hell—*I believe it.*"

And so, to some extent, did this young divorcée, after another few months of rational psychotherapy sessions. Whereas she previously kept telling herself how far from ideal was her behavior, and what a horror she was for not always achieving this ideal, she now began to substitute constructive problem-solving, internalized sentences for her old self-beatings. In one of her last conferences with me, she said: "You know, I looked into the mirror yesterday morning and said to myself: 'Geraldine, you are a happy, fairly bright, increasingly mature, growingly efficient kid. I am getting mighty fond of you.' And then I laughed with real joy."

What this patient discovered was that her feelings did not derive from her unsuccessful marriage or her divorce but from her *evaluations* of these and other events in her life. When she changed the kinds of thoughts (that is, her internalized sentences) she had been having about herself and her life functions, her emotions changed from depression, discouragement, and unhappiness, to elation, encouragement, and joy.

If human beings theoretically can control their negative thoughts and feelings, but in actual practice they often refrain from doing so and keep experiencing unnecessary misery, the question arises: Why? What are the blockings which prevent them from thinking effectively and emoting on a more pleasant, or at least a less unpleasant, plane?

The main barriers to effective thinking and emoting are these: (a) Some people are too stupid to think clearly. Or (b) they are intelligent enough to think straight, but just do not know how to do so. Or (c) they are sufficiently intelligent and well-educated to think clearly but are too disturbed or neurotic to put their intelligence or knowledge to good use. As we have noted in two of our previous books, *How to Live with a Neurotic* (Ellis, 1956) and *Psychoanalysis and Psychotherapy: 36 Systems* (Harper, 1959), neurosis essentially consists of stupid behavior by a non-stupid person.

Otherwise stated: a neurotic is a potentially capable individual who in some way or on some level of his functioning does not realize that he is or how he is defeating his own ends. Or else he is an individual who (in rare cases) has full understanding of or insight into how he is harming himself but who, for some irrational reason, persists in self-sabotaging behavior. Since we are assuming that neurotics are potentially capable and not intrinsically stupid, we must also assume that they are emotionally disabled because either they do not know how to, or do not care to think more clearly and behave less self-defeatingly.

If so, what can be done? In the next chapter we shall try to be even more specific about how one can recognize and attack neurotic behavior.

Recognizing and Attacking

6   Neurotic Behavior

CLEAR THINKING, WE have insisted, leads to sane emoting. Stupidity, ignorance, and disturbance block straight thinking and result in serious degrees of over or under-emotionalizing. When an individual is severely inhibited or practically foaming at the mouth and when he is obviously *not* stupid, then we usually call him neurotic. Let us, for the sake of still further clarity, consider a couple of examples.

A twenty-two year old male says that he does not want to finish his dental training because he dislikes some of his subjects and has a difficult time studying them. In consequence, he says, he would just as soon be a business man.

When his motivations are probed more deeply, it is soon discovered that he really would very much like to be a dentist but that he is fighting dentistry because (a) his parents are pressuring him to finish school and he loathes their pressuring; (b) he is not getting along too well with his classmates and feels that he is quite unpopular with them; and (c) he doubts that he has the manual dexterity and manipulative ability that is required of a good dentist.

This individual is sabotaging his own desires because he has not insight into, or is ignorant of, his basic, unconscious motivations. He starts with the conscious supposition that he "naturally" dislikes certain of his subjects; and, as a result of some psychological probing and direct interpretation (which is one of the main techniques of rational psychotherapy) he is quickly induced to admit (first to the therapist and, more importantly to

37

himself) that he actually is terribly afraid of being dominated by his parents, of failing to win the esteem of his classmates, and of ultimately failing to be a good dentist. His "natural" dislike for some of his subjects is therefore a highly "unnatural" product of, or rationalization for, his underlying philosophy of "Oh, my Lord, what a weak poltroon I am and will always continue to be!"

When, in the course of psychotherapy, this individual becomes aware of his underlying irrational fears; and when, perhaps more importantly, he is induced by the therapist to question and challenge these fears—to ask himself "*How* can my parents actually dominate me, if I refuse to let them do so?" and "*Why* would it be so horrible if I failed to be the most popular boy at school or the best dentist the school ever turned out?" he decides to return to school and to work through his parental, social, and self-confidence difficulties. This highly intelligent youth thereby stops his irrational (or stupid) thinking and the over-emotionalized (neurotic) reactions (needless fear and flight) to which his low-level thinking is leading.

A female patient had a similar problem but more insight. This twenty-year-old girl knew that she wanted to be a teacher and also knew that she was making no effort to become one because she had no confidence in herself. She also suspected that she was trying to punish herself for some promiscuous sex activity in which she had engaged a year previously. Even though this girl presumably had insight into her underlying motivations, she continued to defeat herself and to behave in a neurotic manner.

What this patient did *not* realize was that her lack of self-confidence and her extreme sex guilt were based on ignorance and faulty thinking. Her lack of confidence was originally instilled in her by her hypercritical older sister, who jealously did not want the girl to think well of herself. Then the patient, working on the false and unquestioned assumption that she had little scholastic ability, began to avoid her school work and thereby to "prove" to herself that she actually had none—thus reinforcing her original sister-instilled lack of confidence.

This girl's sexual promiscuity, moreover, largely stemmed from this same lack of confidence. Feeling that she was worthless and that boys would not care for her, she took the easiest way of winning them by bartering her body for their attentions. Her guilt about her promiscuity was based on the arbitrary notion, largely taken over again from her older sister, that premarital relations are wicked and that promiscuity is a particularly heinous offense.

Even though this girl *seemed* to know why she was sabotaging her desires to teach, she actually had only partial or lower-order insight into her neurotic behavior. She did not consistently realize the falseness and irrationality behind her two basic premises: (a) that she was incapable of doing well scholastically and that all people who do poorly in this area are utterly worthless; and (b) that she was wicked for engaging in premarital sex acts.

A fuller understanding of her self-defeating behavior led to far-reaching changes in her thoughts and actions. First she was induced to question the connection between scholastic success and so-called personal "worth" and to see that she was thoroughly valuable and deserving of happiness *whether or not* she was highly successful at school. Seeing and accepting this view enabled her to work much better in school and to achieve better grades.

Secondly, this patient was helped to challenge the so called wickedness of premarital sex behavior and to understand that although she may have made sexual mistakes (by having affairs with males whom she did not really enjoy as lovers), she was not to *blame* and need not be *punished* for these very human mistakes. By thus surrendering self-blame and punishment, she took away her remaining motives for sabotaging her own endeavors and was thereafter able to work quite concertedly toward her goal of becoming a teacher.

The case of this patient, as perhaps of all individuals who come for psychotherapeutic help, exemplifies the difference between what we call Insight No. 1 and Insight No. 2. Insight No. 1 is the fairly conventional kind of understanding first clearly postulated by Freud (though partly seen by several psychologists and writers before his day): that is, knowledge by the individual that he has a problem and that there are certain antecedents that cause him to have this problem. Thus, the young dentist in training whose case was noted at the beginning of this chapter knew that he had a problem with his career, but thought it was because he disliked certain subjects and not because (as subsequently turned out) he was afraid of social and vocational failure. Not knowing the antecedents of his problem, he could not be said to have any reasonable amount of "insight" into it.

The young teacher in training was in a somewhat different position, since she not only knew that she was failing at her chosen career, but also knew or suspected that (a) she lacked confidence and (b) she was trying to punish herself for her previous sexual promiscuity. Knowing, therefore, some of the motivational antecedents of her ineffective behavior, this girl had a considerable amount of "insight"—or what we call Insight No. 1. Even her Insight No. 1, however, was rather vague: since she *knew* that she lacked confidence but didn't clearly see that this lack of confidence consisted, more concretely, of her telling herself: "My older, hypercritical sister thinks that I am inadequate; it would be absolutely terrible if she were correct and I were inadequate; perhaps she is correct; in fact, I am sure that she is."

This young woman also knew *that* she was guilty and self-punitive about her previous premarital affairs. But she did not specifically see that her guilt and self-punishment were the result of the internalized sentences: "Many people say that premarital sex relations are wicked. I have had these relations. Therefore I must be wicked." And: "It is often agreed that people who do mistaken or erroneous acts should be punished for their sins; I have committed such acts by having premarital sex relations with males for whom I did not really care; therefore I should punish myself for my sins by not really trying to succeed in the career, teaching, in which I would like to succeed."

Although, then, this patient definitely had a good measure of Insight No. 1, she had it in such a vague and indefinite manner, that we could well call it only partial rather than full insight. As for Insight No. 2, she had virtually none. For Insight No. 2 consists of the wholehearted belief that "Now that I have discovered what Insight No. 1 is, and what the self-causes of my own disturbances really are, there is no other way of my eliminating these disturbances than by steadily, persistently, and energetically working to change these self-causes."

More concretely: after discovering that the real causes of her failing in school consisted of (a) her telling herself how worthless she was largely because she accepted her sister's view of her inadequacy and the assumed horror of one's being inadequate, and also consisted of (b) her telling herself how sinful and deserving of punishment she was for having mistakenly submitted her body to several men for whom she had very little liking, this girl, in order to obtain Insight No. 2, would also have to see that the only way out of her dilemma would be to work persistently and energetically at changing these two false beliefs. This, with the help of some thirty sessions of highly active-directive rational psychotherapy, she was finally able to see and to work through.

It is our contention, in other words, that almost all neurotic or self-sabotaging behavior results from some kind of basic ignorance or lack of insight on the part of the disturbed individual. Although it is theoretically possible for human beings to become severely aberrated because of certain biophysical conditions (such as severe hormonal imbalances in their bodies or by being kept sleepless for many nights on end), neuroses caused by these kinds of conditions are rare. Under more usual conditions, the individual's aberrated behavior is caused by his own *ideas*, which may be consciously known to him or which he may stoutly hold without his being aware that he has them.

Thus, as in the two cases cited in this chapter, the individual may know that he resists going to school because he is fighting against parental pressure; or he may unconsciously resist going to school without clear awareness that his rebellion against parental pressure is at the bottom of his resistance. Or she may know that she is punishing herself for some sex guilt;

or she may punish herself without realizing that she is doing so because of this kind of guilt.

In any event, whether or not the individual is conscious of the underlying ideas that are driving him to behave inefficiently and self-defeatingly, these ideas must be, on theoretical grounds, irrational and illogical—else he is not neurotic. Thus, in the instances given in this chapter, if it *were* logical for the young dental student to be so fearful of parental domination and social and vocational failure that he gave up studying and flunked out of school, there would be nothing inappropriate about this behavior and we would have to conclude that he was a bright boy who saw the facts of life and acted in sane accordance with them. And if it *were* rational for the student of education to accept her sister's view of her worthlessness and to keep punishing herself for her sexual deeds, we would have to admit that she was perfectly right about giving up teaching and becoming, say, a prostitute for the rest of her life.

But pronounced fears of failure, feelings of worthlessness, unthinking acceptances of others' views of us, and self-punitive tendencies are virtually never, as we shall keep insisting in this book, justified. Not because they are absolutely wrong or wicked, or because they contradict the laws of god or the universe, but simply because, on good pragmatic grounds, they are inevitably self-defeating and needlessly prevent human beings from getting many of the goods and achieving most of the goals that they desire.

Stated differently: any intense, sustained, and frequently repeated negative emotion—such as a feeling of severe anger, depression, guilt, or anxiety —tends to be the result of a (consciously or unconsciously held) prejudiced, childish, senseless idea and almost inevitably leads to woefully inefficient, self-sabotaging behavior which we call neurosis (or, in its most extreme forms, psychosis). When an individual keeps seriously over or under-emoting and in consequence displays neurotic behavior, there are several palliative or superficial means he can employ to help himself temporarily overcome his disturbance. Thus, he can change his job or his marital status; take a vacation; develop a vital interest in some area; become successful at his professional or avocational pursuits; consume sufficient quantities of alcohol, marijuana, heroin, tranquilizers, psychic energizers, or other drugs; become fanatically devoted to a new church or creed; or try various other diversionary approaches.

Almost any or all of these kinds of diversions will temporarily work. For they essentially induce the individual, who is irrationally attached to some set of neurosis-provoking ideas (which we may call x), and divert him, for the moment, to some other set of ideas (which we may call y). As long as he keeps thinking of y instead of x ideas, he may not feel too troubled.

Unfortunately, this kind of diversion is rarely a solution to the neurotic person's basic problems. For no matter how vigorously or often he may divert himself to *y* ideas, he still underlyingly believes in and has never rid himself of *x* ideas; so that he strongly keeps tending to return to the neurotic behavior caused by *x* ideas.

Take Mrs. Janus, for example. At the age of thirty-eight, she was still a beautiful and talented woman; and when she was not lying in bed all day with a horrible migraine headache (which she frequently was) or fighting viciously with her husband and two teenage children (which she almost always was), she was a charming companion, hostess, and clubwoman. So, to help keep herself calm, unangry, and relatively free from migraine, Mrs. Janus drank heavily, took loads of Miltown, and became passionately devoted to a New Spiritism group which believed in reincarnation and taught that life in this sorry vale of tears is only a prelude to an infinity of Real Lives to come.

It almost worked. Being half crocked most of the time, and intently proselyting for her spiritist views, Mrs. Janus found relatively little time to upset herself, become terribly angry at others, and retreat into her migraine headaches. But then when the liquor lost some of its effectiveness, and life in the afterworld was found somewhat wanting in solving the problems of this world, Mrs. Janus's neurotic symptoms returned full blast. In fact, she became so unable to contain her anger against her associates that even her newly found spiritist friends began to look askance at her behavior and to ease her out of some of the high positions that they were at first delighted to give her. Seeing even this new group desert her, Mrs. Janus became still angrier and began to verge on a complete breakdown.

Came the dawn. And, more by brute force than gentle persuasion, Mrs. Janus was dragged into psychotherapy by her husband who simply told her that unless she did something to really help herself he and the children were packing and leaving. It required only a few sessions of intensive therapy to reveal that what was really bothering Mrs. Janus was her pronounced belief that, because her parents had both been overly strict and highly punitive when she was a child, the rest of the world owed her a completely opposite kind of living. All her close associates, she believed, especially her husband and children, should lean over backward to make life easy for her—and thereby compensate for the unduly hard life she had had during her childhood.

When, in the normal course of human events, Mrs. Janus found that her close relatives and friends somehow did not feel the way she did about their catering to her, she became inordinately angry at them, fully believed that they were unethical and unfair, and did her best to get back at them for their "rank injustices." When everything was going her way—which of course is rare in life—she was fine; but when she was balked or frustrated, she felt miserable and unconsciously tried to divert herself by making life for others equally or more miserable.

Alcohol and Miltown often made Mrs. Janus "feel good" for a short while —at which times all the "injustices" of the world would not seem so unjust. And her spiritistic views, which promised her the best of all possible worlds in afterlives to come, also temporarily diverted her from her injustice collecting. But such diversions, naturally, could not last forever and she *still* underlyingly believed that the world *should* be a kinder, easier place and that her close associates *should* make up for the horrors of her past life by catering to her in the present.

In the course of a year and a half of both individual and group rational psychotherapy, Mrs. Janus was first given insight No. 1: namely, that her extreme hostility and migrainous upsets stemmed from her own behavior, rather than that of others, and that this behavior largely consisted of the irrational philosophy: "Because I suffered in the past, people *should* be utterly kind and ingratiating to me in the present."

After the therapist's helping Mrs. Janus to see the real causes of her neurotic behavior, he then (with the help of the members of her therapy group) led her to Insight No. 2: "Now that I see that *I* am creating my disturbances with *my* often repeated internalized sentences about the 'injustice' of it all, I will just *have* to keep questioning, challenging, and changing these sentences, until I really come to believe that it is *not* unfair, but at the most simply unfortunate, that people do not cater to me; and I will just *have* to get myself to believe, instead, that I can get along perfectly well in life by catering, if I want anything, to myself."

When she began to receive Insight No. 2—that *she* must keep working at changing her *own* philosophy and ways—Mrs. Janus reduced her drinking to a cocktail or two a day, threw away her bottle of Miltown, and became remarkably unangry, with her husband, children, and friends, even when (being fallible humans) they occasionally *did* act unjustly or unfairly to her. The more she accepted reality, and refused any longer to *make* it as grim as she had been making it, the less spiritistic she grew and her belief in reincarnation became a thing of the past. As she said at one of the closing therapeutic sessions: "Why do I have to worry about any highly hypothetical afterlives when I now know how to make *this* life so enjoyable?"

7

Overcoming
the Influences
of the Past

"THIS STUFF ABOUT people making themselves emotionally sick by their poor philosophies of life sounds all very well," many of our critics often say. "But how about the important influences of the past, over which we had no control whatever? How about, for instance, our childhood-imbibed Oedipus complexes or the fact that we may have been severely rejected by our parents? Didn't *these* things make us disturbed to begin with? And how are we to overcome them now, if we are merely to be concerned about changing our *present* philosophies?"

Good questions, these, but fairly easy to answer in the light of our rational-emotive approach to personality change.

Let us take the Oedipus business first. Let us suppose that the Freudians are at least partly right and that some individuals, if not all, have severe Oedipus complexes during their childhood and that they are emotionally maimed thereby. Can we still, by purely rational assaults on such an individual's current philosophies, overcome the pernicious effects of his early family romance?

Indeed we can. Let us, before we give any therapeutic details here, first see what a so called Oedipus complex really is and how it comes about. A young male child, let us say, lusts after his mother, hates his father, is guilty about his sex desires for his mother, and is afraid that his father is going to castrate him. Consequently, he fears older men for the rest of his life and either cowardly refuses to compete with them (as, say, in business) or makes enormous efforts to ingratiate himself with them and thereby gain their favor (as, say, by becoming a passive homosexual who keeps looking for older and more active male sex partners and is afraid to have a normal relationship with a female). Obviously, such an individual has a rather classical Oedipus complex.

Let us even grant, with the orthodox Freudians, that this individual originally acquired his Oedipal feelings because his sexual instincts (his id) are biologically rooted and, whether he likes it or not, they inevitably push him in the direction of lusting after his mother and then, because of his superego (conscience), force him to become guilty about his incest feelings and hate both himself and his father. Even if this is so (and often in our society it seems not to be, since many boys apparently do not lust after their mothers or get jealous of their fathers' relations with these mothers), the question still must be asked: Is the boy's Oedipal *attachment* the same thing as his Oedipus *complex?* And the only sane answer seems to be: No, it by no means necessarily is.

Any so called *complex* is little more than a chain of negative ideas about what may (or may not) be an unfortunate set of facts. Thus, it may be perfectly true that John is physically weaker than Henry and that, compared to Henry, he is in this respect inadequate or inferior. But if John has an inferiority *complex* we mean (a) that he is (or thinks he is) weaker than Henry (and many others) and (b) that he *believes he is worthless or has a relatively low value* because he is (or thinks he is) weaker. While (a) may be an objective statement of fact, (b) is a subjective negative evaluation *about* the fact; and it is (b) rather than (a) which constitutes John's complex.

So with the Oedipus complex. Harold may "naturally" and "normally" lust after his mother and be somewhat jealous of his father's attention to his mother. But if he, while feeling lust and jealousy, does not at the same time *believe that he is worthless or has a relatively low personal value* because of his feelings, he will only have an Oedipal *attachment* rather than a *complex.*

If Harold does have a full-blown Oedipus complex, then we may be pretty sure that, in addition to his lust for his mother, he believes (a) that it is vitally important that his mother, father, and other people approve or love him; (b) that it is a terrible thing for him to lust after his mother; (c) that if his lust is discovered he will be severely disapproved by his parents and others; (d) that if he actually has sex relations with his mother, the crime of incest that he will then be perpetrating is one of the most heinous known to man and will lead to serious legal and other difficulties; (e) that even if he never commits incest or commits it and is never caught or punished for his deed, his mere contemplation of such an act is a horrible offense against his parents and humanity; and that (f) if his father ever discovers his lust for his mother, he may make grim reprisals against Harold, such as castrating him.

Whether Harold's beliefs about his lust for his mother are true or not is somewhat irrelevant, as long as he strongly holds the kind of beliefs just listed. Thus, it may not be true that he vitally needs his parents' or others' approval and that he cannot get along in the world very well without such approval. Nor may it be true that having sex relations with his mother will get him into serious trouble; nor that if his father discovers his incestuous ideas or actions he will castrate Harold. No matter. As long as Harold *believes* these things to be true, he will tend to be seriously upset.

Although, then, Harold's Oedipal *attachment* or *desires* may in large part be biologically based (or may, as the Freudians say, spring from his id), his Oedipus *complex* is not rooted in these desires but in his *ideas* and *attitudes* about the desires. And these ideas and attitudes are largely learned and are likely to differ widely depending on whether Harold has been raised in one community or another, in one kind of family or in a different kind.

If, therefore, Harold wishes to overcome his Oedipus complex and the neurotic symptoms (such as fear of other males) to which it may lead, he does not have to change his biology (which would be almost impossible) but to modify his ideas. He does not have to give up lusting after his mother, but to surrender his notions of how *horrible,* how *criminal* is such lusting.

More importantly, Harold, in order to rid himself of his Oedipus complex, does not have to change or even to understand fully his *past* ideas about his Oedipal attachment, but he does have to acquire Insights No. 1 and No. 2 into his *present* or *still-existing* attitudes toward incest. Suppose, for example, that he once lusted after his mother and, being weak and puny and unable to stand up for himself against the other boys in his neighborhood, was afraid of his father's "castrating" him not because of his committing the horrible crime of incest, but because he felt that he "deserved" to be punished for being so weak and ineffective. And suppose that, later in his life, having grown bigger and taller, he no longer is intimidated by the boys in his neighborhood, and therefore no longer fears his father's "castration" in terms of his original fear of his "undeservingness" or "weakness."

Under these circumstances, if Harold *now* gained insight into his *past* castration fears and Oedipus complex, he would perhaps learn little useful information about himself: since his *original* complex no longer exists in the old form, and the details of its origins might be cold and meaningless potatoes to Harold today. If, however, Harold *still,* to this very day, has remnants of his old Oedipus complex, then we can be fairly certain that he *still* has some of the irrational ideas that originally caused him to acquire this complex, or some new variations on these old ideas; and if we can bring to Harold's attention these *remaining* illogical notions and get him to acquire Insights No. 1 and No. 2 about *them*, then it hardly matters whether or not he fully remembers, understands, or works through his *original* irrationalities (as, in Freudian theory, he is supposed to do in order to be cured).

No matter how we slice it, therefore, if *any* human complex still exists to the extent that it bothers a person in his current life, we can be reasonably certain that he still harbors some senseless ideas in connection with it; and it is these *present* ideas that are most important, whatever the original ideological sources of his complex may have been. This is why so many non-Freudian psychoanalysts—such as Adler, Fromm, Horney, Rank, and Sullivan—emphasize analyzing the patient's present problems, ideas, and relationships, rather than the gory details of his past history, if he is truly to overcome his existing neurosis.

As another case in point to show how an individual's past experiences for all their importance in creating his present difficulties, are hardly insuperable barriers to his understanding and attacking his emotional disturbances, let us take an instance of maternal rejection. Let us assume that a child is continually criticized and rejected by his mother; that he consequently feels himself loathsome and inadequate; that he therefore refuses to try certain tasks; and that he ends up feeling more and more inadequate.

Such an individual will of course be seriously disturbed. But will he be disturbed because of the *fact* of his mother's rejecting him or because of his *ideas* about this rejection and its supposed consequences?

Largely, the latter. For the bare *fact* of maternal rejection is not necessarily noxious, as shown by the observation that in our society not *all* rejected children turn out too badly, and as also shown by reports that in certain other societies children are severely criticized and rejected by their mothers without growing up to be unusually disturbed.

Lili E. Peller writes in this connection, "I have had the opportunity to observe children—Arab children in rural areas of Palestine and Egypt— where there is almost no consideration for their welfare, where they experience the effects of the changing moods of adults; considerations of their wishes and needs are of no importance and they are a nuisance. Should any brutality be spared them by their parents, there are plenty of siblings and hardly-older uncles and aunts to provide it. Yet these children do not become neurotic for lack of love."

What *is* harmful about maternal rejection in our society is not merely the rejection itself (though, admittedly, that is not likely to do a child much good) but the set of *ideas* that almost all of us learn in connection with this rejection. These ideas, which are ubiquitous in our fairy tales and other children's literature and drama, include the notions that (a) one's parents *should* be loving and approving and that it is most unfair when they are not;

(b) if one's mother is not accepting, then one must be worthless and value-less; (c) if one is generally worthless, one will fail at certain important tasks; (d) if one does fail at certain tasks, this is a horrible crime and proves again that one is of no worth; and (e) if, out of fear of failing, one avoids certain tasks and never learns to do them well, this shows that one was apparently incapable of doing them in the first place and is once again proven to be incompetent and valueless.

It is ideas like these, most of which are highly questionable but which are nonetheless widely believed and promulgated in our society, which put the real sting in maternal rejection and make an unpleasant event terribly traumatizing and neuroticizing. Without the backing of these ideas, it is dubious whether maternal rejection would be as crippling as it frequently is made to be.

By the same token, it would seem almost impossible for a human being to be severely hurt by anything but noxious stimuli unless he had traumatizing *ideas* about what was happening to him. For, aside from literally injuring you physically, what can an external person or thing *do* to cause you pain?

A person can of course call you names, disagree with you, show that he doesn't love you, incite others against you, and so on. But, other than physically hurting you in some manner—such as directly assaulting you or indirectly doing something that will deprive you of food, clothing, shelter, or other physical comforts—all that he can do against you is to use some kind of negative words, attitudes, or ideas. But he can only effectively employ these words, attitudes, or ideas through *you*—through *your* letting his sallies affect you.

Suppose that some friend or associate says unkind things about you behind your back; or snubs you to your face; or stirs up others against you; or writes an article labeling you as a blackguard. These are all essentially words or gestures and *no* word or gesture can, in itself, hurt you unless you think it can—unless you let it hurt. If you do not *care* when someone says unkind things about you; if you do not *mind* being snubbed to your face; if you are not *concerned* when someone writes nasty things about you; under these circumstances, how could you possibly be harmed?

Stated differently: there are only two basic kinds of pain that can be inflicted on you: (a) physical pain, such as that experienced through having a headache, a stubbed toe, or a case of indigestion; and (b) psychological or mental pain, such as that experienced through being rejected, losing a loved object or person, being anxious, or feeling angry. Over physical pain, you have relatively little control since you may literally be hurt by an external force (someone punching you or something falling on you, for instance); and, once physically assaulted, you will normally feel pain and unhappiness for a certain period of time.

Even in the case of physical pain, however, you often have *some* degree of control over your discomfort. If you have a headache and keep telling yourself how terrible the pain is, and how unfair it is for you to be afflicted with it, the chances are that your discomfort will be intensified and prolonged. But if you have the same headache and keep telling yourself that it is not so terrible and that this is merely one of those unfortunate events that frequently happen to humans, the chances are your pain may well be alleviated and may even disappear.

Physical pain and unhappiness are not the same thing, even though they significantly overlap. One can be in fairly severe pain and not be too unhappy about it; and one can be in slight pain and be exceptionally miserable. It is not entirely, then, the pain itself which causes us to be unhappy but also our attitude toward it.

Over the second kind of pain, psychological or mental discomfort, we have considerably more control. For it seems to be largely our attitude toward such pain which causes us to be uncomfortable in the first place and to be unhappy about our discomfort in the second place.

Thus, if someone calls you a liar or a knave, you have your choice, theoretically, of taking him or not taking him seriously. If you take him seriously and tell yourself that it is most important what he thinks of you, you shall tend to be pained and made unhappy by his words. If you do not take him too seriously and tell yourself that it does not greatly matter what he thinks of you, you shall tend to be little pained or made unhappy by his statement.

Our being hurt by psychological or mental assaults is also intimately related to our attitude toward ourselves. Suppose someone calls us a liar and, because we respect him and take him seriously, we are pained by his words—or, more accurately, we pain ourselves by our interpretation of his words. If we dislike ourselves and have little self-confidence, we are likely to say to ourselves: "Oh, my heavens! How awful it is for him to think this of me. I'll never be able to convince him, now, that I am not a liar. Oh, what a terrible predicament!"

If, on the other hand, we like ourselves and have considerable self-confidence, we are more likely to think: "Now, how could he call me a liar when I am not one? He must be mistaken, and I can surely show him that he is. Now let me see how I can prove to him that I am truthful, so he will view me with favor again."

Or, in some cases, we might even think: "You know, I believe he's right about my being a liar. I have done some lying and I'd better admit it. Now, that's no way to be if I want people to trust me. So I'd better stop this silly lying and prove to him and others that I can be as truthful as anyone."

Mental or psychological hurts, then, are intimately related (a) to the person or situation that seems to be causing the hurt; and (b) to our own concepts of ourselves. If we are over-concerned about what others think of us and under-confident of our own abilities and "worth," we tend to be easily hurt by outside persons and events. If we are little concerned about what others think and confident of our abilities and "worth," we find it most difficult to experience, or at least to sustain, any severe psychological hurt. No matter how much we like ourselves, we may momentarily be disturbed by something someone has said or done "against" us; but the more we value our own being, the quicker we tend to question how "hurtful" another's word or act really is.

To recapitulate what we have been saying in the first part of this book: Human thinking and emoting are *not* radically different processes but, at points, significantly overlap. Emoting does not occur in a vacuum, but results from excitation of the brain and nerve pathways (especially the fibers of the autonomic nervous system), from perceiving and moving (that is, sensorimotor stimulation), from the influence and the responses to previous emotion, and from thinking.

Sustained emotion, in particular, normally stems from sustained thought. And, since adult human beings usually think in terms of internalized phrases and sentences, or self-talk, they sustain their emotions by talking to themselves or by telling themselves certain kinds of sentences.

In general, negative emotions, such as feelings of depression, anxiety, anger, and guilt are intensified and sustained by such self-propagandizing sentences as "This is awful!" "I can't stand that!" And positive emotions, such as love, joy, and elation, are intensified and sustained by sentences such as "This is fine!" or "I like that!" Because this is so, human emotions can often be radically controlled or changed by determining precisely the kind of sentences lying behind them and then by changing these sentences.

There is no point in trying to control or change *all* emotions, since some are indispensable or pleasurable and others are, at worst, only mildly troublesome. Sustained negative or painful emotions, however, are not usually indispensable and they frequently lead to the most self-defeating kinds of behavior. Physical pain and the unhappiness consequent to this kind of discomfort cannot always be controlled. But psychological or mental pain and its resultant misery generally can be controlled or eradicated, since in human adults it originates not in the external events they experience but in their attitudes toward these events.

No matter what a person's past history may be, or how his parents, teachers, and other early associates may have helped him to become emotionally disturbed, he only remains disturbed because he *still* believes some of the unrealistic and illogical thoughts which he originally imbibed. To become undisturbed, therefore, it is only necessary that he see what his present irrational self-indoctrinations are and that he energetically and consistently work at deindoctrinating and reindoctrinating himself in these connections. His understanding of how he *first* became neurotic may be of some help, but it is most unlikely that it will be truly curative.

Emotional pain or disturbance, in sum, usually originates in some irrational or illogical ideas. The job of the neurotic is to uncover and understand the basic unrealistic ideas with which he is disturbing himself; to see clearly the misinformation and illogic behind these ideas; and, on the basis of better information and clearer thinking, to *change* the notions which lie behind and keep creating his disturbance.

How Reasonable
Is Reason?

8

LET'S FACE IT, man has trouble thinking straight and acting well. No matter how bright and well-educated an individual may be, he invariably finds it easy, horribly easy, to make a dunce of himself. And not once or twice in a lifetime, either. Continually, rather; yes, almost continually.

Is man, then, as the philosophers have for centuries been telling us, truly a rational animal? Yes, he is;—and no, he isn't. He has the most incredibly mixed-up *combination* of common sense and uncommon senselessness you ever did see. And yet, of course, he has done and will doubtlessly continue to do absolute wonders with his mental processes, and he is so far removed from his closest lower-order animal neighbors (the higher apes) in this respect that even most of his moronic brothers are distinctly more intelligent than these brightest of sub-humans.

Yes, man is a highly reasonable, brain-using animal. But he also has distinct biological tendencies to act in the most ridiculous, prejudiced, amazingly asinine ways. He is, quite normally and naturally, inclined to be childish, suggestible, superstitious, bigoted, and downright idiotic about much of his personal behavior, particularly about his relations with other human beings. And even when, as often is the case, he *knows* that he is behaving in a self-defeating, perfectly senseless manner, and knows that he would be far happier and healthier if he acted otherwise, he has such great difficulty achieving and sustaining a level of sound and sane behavior that he rarely does so for any length of time, but keeps instead continually falling back to his puerile ways.

52

Take a typical case in point. Miss Marlo Long, when I (R.A.H.) first met her in my office, was an unusually pretty and highly intelligent girl of twenty-three who functioned very efficiently as secretary to the president of a large corporation and would probably have been headed, were she of the other sex, toward one of the highest positions in her firm. Although she had no more than the usual high school education, she started working for this firm at the age of nineteen and, because of her pleasant personality, intelligence, industry, and efficiency rose quickly from one of twenty girls in a stenographic pool to the most important and responsible secretarial position in her company.

In her love life, however, Marlo was hardly as effective. She met an older man when she was twenty, began living with him after knowing him a few weeks, was shocked to learn that he was still married and had little intention of divorcing his estranged wife, convinced herself that life was no longer worth living under these circumstances, and took a large dose of sleeping tablets. She was discovered by a friend and rushed to the hospital in time to have her stomach pumped and her life saved.

Romantically enough, the young resident physician, Jake Golden, who pumped out Marlo's stomach, quickly fell in love with her and they began dating. She resisted his advances for many months, for she felt that "all men were no good" after her experience with her first lover. This highly intelligent girl, in other words, found it surprisingly easy to make one of the most facile and ridiculous mistakes to be found in any primer of logic—that of absurd over-generalization. Because *one* lover had turned out to be untruthful and unreliable, *all* potential lovers were categorized as being equally prevaricative and irresponsible.

But this was not the worst of it. By extreme patience and understanding, the young medic countered Marlo's over-generalized fears and finally convinced her that he really did love her and wanted to marry her. She reluctantly agreed, but felt rather relieved that their actual wedding date had to be postponed for another year, until after he had finished school and passed his medical boards. Even though she *knew* at this point that Jake was most loving and trustworthy, she also *felt*—that is, strongly believed, in spite of complete lack of evidence—that maybe he did not really care for her the way he kept saying and showing that he did.

In this instance, Marlo's internalized illogic was a little more complicated and more roundaboutly insane. What she consciously was saying to herself was, "My first lover *seemed* to care for me and actually didn't. Now Jake *seems* to care for me—how do I know that he really does?" Here again, in slightly different form, is an example of Marlo's more limited kind of over-generalization, which remained even after she had given up the previous more universal kind (namely, "My first lover was irresponsible; therefore all men are").

But this, as we said a couple of paragraphs back, was not the worst of it. What Marlo was actually, quite unconsciously, saying to herself was this illogical chain of sentences, "The reason my first lover left me was not because of his own irresponsibility but because he finally discovered, what I have known all my life, how worthless a person I am. And since I am so worthless, and since Jake is so obviously a nice person and a thoroughly worthwhile individual, he couldn't possibly care for me as he thinks he does. Just as soon as he finds me out—as my first lover did after a few months—he, too, is bound to see that there's no point in going on with me; and he, too, will then leave me. So it's just as well that we wait a year before we marry, by which time he will have found me out, left me, and thereby avoided any drawn-out nightmare of marrying and divorcing."

So Marlo, this wonderfully bright and efficient girl, "reasoned." And with this kind of illogical thinking, she secretly awaited the breakup of her engagement to Jake, which she was sure would come just as soon as he really found her out.

Then the next logical step in this inordinately illogical chain of thinking occurred. Once Marlo decided that perhaps Jake was to be trusted a little —for, remember, he was still a man—and that she really did love him, she began to become extremely jealous and possessive. If he were ten minutes late meeting her after his working day (or night) at the hospital, she would give him a regular third-degree grilling. If he smiled pleasantly at a patient, nurse, or hospital receptionist, she accused him of being "on the make."

Here again we have an extension of Marlo's previous irrational thinking. Since one man jilted her, this man might do the same. And since Jake really seems to care for her, how can she be perfectly, absolutely sure that she is truly lovable and deserving of his caring? Moreover, since she is still somewhat indecisive about her feelings (because of her general doubts about men, Jake, and herself), how does she know, how can she be *sure*, that he is not still indecisive about his feelings for her?

All kinds of unconscious and semi-conscious thoughts such as these kept going through Marlo's mind and the behavioral result was deepseated feelings of insecurity—which almost inevitably, in heterosexual relations, lead to intense jealousy.

Jake, recognizing Marlo's jealousy as evidence of her own insecurity, nicely put up with her compulsive inquiries and posessive challenges and finally induced her to undertake orthodox psychoanalysis—which Marlo experienced three times a week for the next two years. Most of the analytic sessions were concerned with Marlo's early life and the disclosure of the fact that although she ostensibly loved her father and was his favorite child, she often feared that he would discover how bad a person she was and would reject her in favor of her older sister. Marlo's analyst thought that this childhood pattern was a precursor and a cause of most of her later behavior with her first lover and with Jake. Marlo didn't strongly disagree with him and did feel somewhat better as a result of her analytic sessions; but dredging up the facts of her childhood had no effect whatsoever on her current feelings of extreme jealousy and possessiveness. In considerable disgust and despair, she terminated her psychoanalysis.

By this time Jake was getting discouraged himself and was taking an increasingly dim view of the prospects of his having a happy married life with Marlo. Knowing, however, her suicidal tendencies, he decided to place her under psychotherapeutic care before he broke with her; and he insisted that she try at least a few sessions with me. After she had seen me five times, and we had started working actively at her basic irrational thinking, Jake told Marlo that he was definitely and permanently breaking off his relationship with her and literally left her at my door.

Quite understandably, we had quite a session. Marlo, in spite of some sedation which Jake had given her during their talk that day, was in an hysterical condition as we started the interview. After fifteen minutes largely devoted to my helping her quiet down she said: "Well, I know what I must do now. I must finish that job he delayed for three years."

"You mean commit suicide?" I asked.

"Yes."

"That, of course, is your privilege. And do you mind," I persisted in an almost jocular voice, "telling me why you plan to slit your own throat when you could so nicely stick around and torture yourself for another half a century or so?"

I have found, through considerable experience with people intent on suicide, that the best counter-attack is often to discuss their intent quite openly, forthrightly, and with a certain degree of casual humor—as matters of all kinds are usually discussed in rational therapy sessions. For the rational therapist holds a deep personal conviction that life is—that aliveness is a basis, a fundamental premise of existence from which other behavioral assumptions derive. Consequently, although I think that life can be a most enjoyable process, I grant to others the right to differ and I believe that anyone, including one of my patients, has the privilege of deciding to stop living.

I do not get upset, therefore, when one of my patients threatens suicide, but deal with this usually quite irrational thought in the same way that I and other rational therapists treat a patient's non-suicidal illogical beliefs.

My patients thus see that I know they are serious in contemplating suicide, that I do not deny their right to commit it, but that I very much want them to reconsider some points about living and to see if dying is what they *really* want. Thus far, I am happy to say, I have lost no patients via suicide.

But back to Marlo. "I know it's my privilege," she said, "to take my life. And since I find that it's just not worth going on with it, that's exactly what I intend to do. It's a phony deal. No one can be trusted or depended upon. Things always end up the same."

"How so? Just because two lovers in a row have left you? That's a hell of a big conclusion from a pitifully small bit of evidence!"

"Just the same—it's always the same."

"Hogwash! How can a bright girl like you believe such twaddle? I see very little similarity between your first lover's leaving you because he just didn't want to assume the responsibilities of divorcing his wife and taking on another and Jake's leaving you because, to say the least, you've acted like the most godawful pain in the neck he's doubtlessly ever met among your sex. And isn't the solution—if you really want a solution to your problem of maintaining a secure relationship with a man of your choice—doesn't the solution lie in *your* stopping being a pain in the neck, rather than the males of the world stopping doing you in?"

"But how do I know that Jake didn't plan this, right from the start, just like Thorwald, my first lover, did three years ago? How do I know that he didn't deliberately take everything he could get from me and then leave me just before we were going to prepare for the marriage?"

"You don't know—for sure. But the situation certainly doesn't seem the way you are now setting it up. Not to me, it doesn't! Besides, let us suppose for a moment that your views are accurate, and that Jake really did, just like the first man in your life, plan to get what he could out of you sexually and then leave you waiting at the church. So? That would certainly show that he, just like Thorwald, was a scoundrel. But is that *your* problem? Is that any reason why *you* should splatter your brains over your lovely Persian rug?"

"But if I can't trust *anyone*," Marlo half-wailed, "how can I see any prospect of my ever being happy?"

"Anyone?" I relentlessly persisted. "I can't see how two men in an entire lifetime, so far, equal *anyone*. Let's even say, for the sake of your argument, that both Thorwald and Jake proved to be entirely untrustworthy. Aren't you more than slightly over-generalizing? If you hired two girls in a row to assist you in your work at the office and both of them proved to be quite unreliable, would you necessarily conclude that there is not *anyone* you could possibly ever get who would be more reliable?"

"No, I guess I wouldn't. I see what you mean."

"And even if we may grant—for the sake, again, of *your* argument—that you have had the unusual misfortune of meeting two grade-A blackguards in succession, is this such an impressive record of adversity that you are justified in telling yourself that your whole life process is a fraud and should be forthrightly dispensed with?"

"You seem to dismiss Jake and my losing him as nothing worth considering," Marlo (now quite unhysterically) said.

"Not at all. Could we not more appropriately say that you seem to consider *yourself* and your losing *you* as nothing worth considering?"

"You mean—I am showing, by getting this upset and thinking of ending it all, that I don't consider *myself* sufficiently worth going on with?"

"Well, *do* you? You remind me somewhat, in this connection, of the woman who was asked by the judge who was trying her for speeding, "How come, Madam, that you have five children, ranging in ages from one to eight, when you just told me that the only husband you ever had has been dead for three years.' 'Well, Judge,' she replied, 'My husband may be dead—but *I'm* not!' This woman, obviously, thought life worth going on with even when her husband was irrevocably gone. She liked herself. Do *you?*"

"But how *can* I like myself when, as you can see, no-one else seems to do so, when one man after another keeps rejecting me? Doesn't this indicate *something?*"

"Yes, it indicates something about you—that you believe it is all-important to be accepted by others, particularly by a man of your choice, as a prerequisite for accepting yourself. It indicates that you make your self-liking dependent upon the approval of others, and that you illogically keep telling yourself, 'Because I am intrinsically worthless, and can only consider myself worthwhile if others approve me, and because two men in succession have not approved me sufficiently to take me to the altar, this proves what I was sure of in the first place: that I am intrinsically worthless.' Can't you see the senseless circularity of this reasoning?"

"Mmmm. Let me get that straight now. You're saying that I'm saying and have always said to myself, 'I am only worthwhile and my life is only worth living if and when others, especially a chosen boy friend, truly care for me.' And then, when I find they do not care for me as much as I thought they did, I immediately conclude that 'Yes, of course they don't care. Because, as I said in the first place, I'm worthless, and how could they ever possibly really care for a worthless person like me?' Mmmm. That *is* circular reasoning, if I actually am saying that to myself."

"Well, aren't you?"

"Looks like it, doesn't it? I'll have to give this some more thought."

"That's exactly what we're here for: to give this sort of thing more thought. And to have you think more about it outside these sessions. While you're thinking about, please give a little thought to a further aspect of it, too."

"And what is that?" Marlo asked. She now, incidentally, as are most of my patients after I meet their hysterical outbursts with calm reasoning, and especially after I force *them* to think about the reasons for such outbursts themselves, was so intent on looking at herself in a problem-solving way that one would never have dreamed that, just a few minutes before, she had been almost ready to plunge out of my office window.

"Think, if you will," I said, "of the enormous *demands* you keep making on people, such as Jake in particular, with whom you became involved. Precisely because you do consider yourself essentially worthless, and believe that you *need* their approval to make you "worthwhile," you don't merely, as you mistakenly think you do, ask them to act in a certain way toward you; rather, you demand that they do."

"I demand that Jake approve of me, no matter how I treat him or what I do? Is that what you mean?"

"Yes. To fulfill your own needs for great approval, you expect him to conform rigidly to your preconceived ideas of how a man courting you and intending to marry you *should* behave. And when he does not act precisely the way you think he *ought* to act—and Lord knows you try every possible test in the books to see if he *is* acting this way!—you immediately raise hell with him and call *him* untrustworthy. Finally, by continuing to make your unreasonable demands, and forcing him—yes, actually forcing him—to turn away from you, you 'prove' to yourself how untrustworthy you were sure he was in the first place. Actually, of course, you only 'prove' how unindependent, again, you are of his and others' approval. Another round of circular thinking!"

"I think I need him to bolster me. Then I force him to conform to my so-called needs. Then he doesn't do so, because he finds me such a bother. Then I tell myself, because he finds me such a bother, that this proves that I was no good in the first place and that I need Jake or someone else to bolster me and help poor unworthy me get along in this big bad world. Golly, I really *do* have it in for myself—all along the line—don't I?"

"You do! And until we can help you to trust and honor *yourself* most of the time, how can we ever expect you to be able to trust people like Jake and find them honorable? Until we can get you to see that it is not catastrophic, but merely unpleasant, when you are rejected by a lover, how can we ever expect you to act well enough with such a lover that he will not eventually find you too much bother?"

So Marlo and I continued to talk. And by the end of this session she was not only entirely calm but perceptibly began to show a new kind of thinking about herself, and a concomitant new aspect of self-confidence, that she had never displayed before.

It would be nice to report that, as a result of a good many more therapeutic sessions and hundreds of well-spent hours rethinking things with herself, she is now happily married to Jake. That, alas, is not true; since, in spite of her notable improvements in her attitudes toward herself, Jake had already had it, and only occasionally saw Marlo again. But before another year had passed Marlo had found a new beau, related to him with much more realistic expectations and without undue jealousy and possessiveness, and consummated what still appears to be (three and a half years later, at this writing) a good marriage.

To return to our main theme in this chapter: Because she was a very human human being, Marlo found it very *easy* to mix herself up about her love life, even though in outside affairs she was most intelligent and efficient. To over-generalize; to continue to have unchallenged premises about her own basic worthlessness; to think that she was only normally asking certain responses from her fiancé when she was actually abnormally making unrealistic demands on him—these kinds of elementary errors in logic were the easiest thing in the world for this bright girl to make.

Why? Because Marlo is human. Because humans have ten or twelve years of real childhood during which they are weak, dependent, and unable to discriminate very well between sensible and silly behavior. Because, once having technically outgrown their childhood, they tend to remain affected by it and its experiences for the rest of their lives. Because, no matter how old they may be and how bright about external affairs, they have some difficulty objectively viewing their own behavior and their relations with others. Because they have some atavistic biological tendencies to get anxious or hostile at times, even when such feelings are most inappropriate to their effective present behavior. Because they are literally trained by their families and their communities, from childhood onward, to remain gullible, suggestible, and conformist in many significant ways. Because, being human, they are afflicted with physiological tendencies (not instincts, but what Maslow calls instinctoid tendencies) toward habit patterning, inertia, excitement-seeking, moodiness, negativism, and other action or inaction-tendencies which frequently interfere with calm thinking and concerted planning and which encourage them, even when they see what sane conduct is, to fall back into self-defeating modes of behavior.

Particularly in regard to his social existence man tends to be indiscriminative and unreflective. For it is difficult, and at times almost impossible, for a reasonably intelligent human being consistently to discriminate between sensible and senseless modes of social behavior. If this same human lived by himself on a desert island, he would probably have little trouble in acting sanely most of the time and only occasionally falling back into self-destructive behavior.

But he does not live on a desert island. And, whether he likes it or not and whether or not he has so called gregarious urges, he *must* cooperate with and conform to his social milieu to a considerable degree. Yet, at the same time, he must also, if he is to be truly human and fulfill his own (and, again, probably instinctoid) biosocial destiny, achieve a considerable degree of social independence and individualism—must succeed in expressing and being *himself*.

These two partially conflicting goals of man are perhaps the most difficult thing in the world to achieve to any even near-perfect degree. In fact, anything but a highly imperfect, temporary, and continually shifting kind of resolution of the largely antagonistic goals of being oneself and simultaneously getting along well with others is probably impossible.

Take the relatively simple situation, for example, in which you are sitting around talking to a group of seven or eight friends or acquaintances. Suppose you are fairly bright and well-informed and that most of the other members of the group are on a similar social and educational level. Suppose, also, that you are not seriously emotionally disturbed, neither too shy or retiring on the one hand, nor overly aggressive and Queen-of-the-Mayish on the other. Nor, in general, are you a terribly anxious or unreasonably hostile individual.

Nonetheless, you are in something of an individual-social pickle. If you cajole or force the members of the group to talk about the things in which you are most interested, several of them will probably soon become bored and disgusted with your "hogging the floor." But if you completely go along with what the other members of the group spontaneously want to discuss, the chances are that you will find yourself sitting in dead, somewhat pained silence for a good part of the evening.

If, when a subject about which you have strong views comes up for discussion, you honestly say what you feel about it, some members of the group are very likely to feel hurt, insulted, or angry. If you carefully keep your mouth shut at times, or only very cautiously express some of your own deepest-felt views, you will surely begin to feel frustrated and edgy yourself.

If you most considerately and politely allow other members of the group to have their say whenever they feel the urge to do so, the chances are that some of them may not be equally polite, will monopolize the conversation when you believe you are giving them a moderately short opening in which to express themselves, and will by their behavior probably force you, by the end of the discussion, to remain silent about several things which you think are important and which you very much would have liked to say.

If, however, you are quite uninhibited about breaking into the conversation when you have something pressing on your mind, some of the other group members are almost certain to feel that their toes are being stepped upon and that *they* have not been sufficiently able to express themselves in the course of the evening.

You really can't win—not completely, that is. No matter what you do, there is no perfect solution. Even in this fairly simple group situation, if you behave as *you* really want to behave, some or most of the group members will feel that *their* wants are impinged upon and will tend to dislike you; and if you behave as you feel the group members want you to behave, you will almost inevitably feel that *your* basic desires are frustrated and will tend to dislike some or most of the others. Unless, by sheer accident, your wants happen to coincide with those of all the other members of the group (a highly unlikely occurrence!) someone, you or they, is bound to be frustrated; and anxiety or anger, on your part or theirs, is almost certain to be an *easy* possibility.

Things get much more complicated, of course, if you unduly *care* what other members of the group (or people outside the group) think of your behavior. For if you are quite concerned about having the group members think well of you, you will tend to lean over backward to do what they want you to do, instead of what you want to do yourself; and then you will tend to hate yourself for being a milksop and hate them for witnessing your patsyism. Or else you will do what you mainly want to do—and then worry inordinately whether they still like you for doing it.

Such an inordinate degree of caring for the approval of others is a form of neurosis. But even *without* such neurotic feelings and actions on your part, the careful discriminations that you must make, and continually keep making, between what you would like to do and what it might be better for you to do in group situations tend to be most difficult to make and inevitably lead to somewhat discouraging results. For you *want* to be yourself. And you also *want* other people to be comfortable in your presence and to approve your behavior—quite apart from any neurotic needs for approval that you may have. You are constantly torn, therefore, between two conflicting desires; and there is never—no, *never*—a permanent resolution of this conflict.

All this, mind you, in the simplest kind of a social situation. In a more complicated kind of individual-group relationship, things get even hotter. Thus, in a highly competitive group—such as a classroom where most of the members of the class are trying to get into favorite colleges, or a business office where it is required that the employees, at one and the same time, cooperate with each other to win out over rival businesses and compete with each other to make higher commissions or salaries—it often becomes considerably more difficult to do what one wants to do (a) for one's own individual ends and (b) for gaining and keeping the favor of the other group members.

In almost any social group, therefore, you will find it tough sledding to keep a sane, somewhat middle-of-the-road course and to avoid surrendering your personal tastes, preferences, and expressive tendencies while also avoiding getting into real difficulties with other group members. What your best *reasoned* or most *reasonable* approach will be in such groups cannot be fully calculated in advance and must continually shift, from time to time, with changing conditions in you and in others. Thus, when you first enter a discussion group, it may be wise to keep your mouth shut for twenty minutes or more and let the other group members have something of their say; *then* it may be best to get in your own two cents' worth, even though those who previously held the floor would love to continue holding it; and *then* it may be reasonable to give the others a chance to do more speaking again. But exactly when and where to draw the line between your own active participation and polite acceptance of others' participation is almost never calculable in advance and depends on many different personal and group factors.

Another way of stating what we have just pointed out is to acknowledge that both self-expression *and* social acceptance are to some degree desirable in virtually everyone's life; and that although some form of hedonism, pleasure-seeking, or enlightened self-interest seems to be as good a plan of personal living as anyone has yet devised, enlightened self-interest includes, and cannot possibly sanely ignore, some degree of social interest as well. For if one *only* strove for his "own" good, and ran roughshod over others in the process, the chances are at least 99 out of 100 that those over whom he was riding would sooner or later scotch his "own" good. Therefore, to *some* extent included in his concept of his "own" good must be the good of others as well.

Similarly, if you mainly concentrate on striving mightily for your *immediate* good—if you employ the general principle of short-range hedonism—you will almost inevitably, even if you presently succeed, sabotage many of your potential *future* enjoyments. "Live for today, for tomorrow you may die" is a perfectly sane philosophy—*if* there is a good chance that you will die tomorrow. Most of the time, however, you live to the ripe old age of 70 or 80 these days; and your tomorrows are likely to be miserable if you *just* live for today. At the same time, if you *only* live for tomorrow, your todays are likely to be over-cautiously and drably lived; and again you will in the long run defeat your own ends.

Reason, then, is a hard task-master. It is never *absolutely* good or certain as a standard of conduct and drawing the exact line between *what is* reasonable and what is not, even in the best of circumstances, is often difficult. When taken to extremes, moreover, rationality can quickly become highly irrational. For several reasons:

1. As we have previously pointed out, *some* degree of emotionality seems to be necessary to human survival and it would probably be unreasonable, meaning self-defeating, for us never to have strong, rather prejudiced reactions—such as our "irrationally" wanting to kill, and perhaps viciously lashing out at, someone who has (accidentally or deliberately) stepped on our toe.

2. Human tastes or preferences, which are frequently quite "irrational" or "groundless", may add considerable pleasure and interest to life. It is, in a sense, "unreasonable" for an individual to be obsessed with collecting stamps, or making his girl friend or wife happy, or listening to music ten hours a day. But many people derive enormous, harmless enjoyment from these kinds of "irrational" or "emotional" pursuits. "Pure intellect," if this ever really existed, would be highly efficient but equally pleasureless. "Affects" (one of the older names for emotions) are designated that way because they *affect* us—influence us to obtain pleasure (as well as pain). Without any kind of feeling or emotion, human existence might persist but it would be incredibly dull.

3. Reason, when carried to extremes, sometimes becomes inefficient and self-sabotaging. If every time we tied a shoelace or ate a piece of bread, we had to stop and reason whether this was the "right" or "best" thing to do or way to do it, our reason would become more of a hindrance than a help and we would end, perhaps, by being highly rational—and unhappy.

4. A totally reasoned-out life would presumably be a mechanical existence—a life that was too cold, unfeeling, and machinelike. It would, as the critics of rational therapy often go to great lengths to point out, undermine the creation and expression of much that is dear to sensitive human beings, particularly in the realm of art, literature, music, and other modes of esthetics.

All these accusations against extreme rationality have some validity. But they are also something of straw-man objections which themselves are often taken to irrational extremes. When boiled down to their essences, they often consist of the objector's fear of the unknown. Even though his present, highly irrational state of being is distinctly uncomfortable and anxiety-ridden, he at least *knows* the limits of the pain he receives from it. Not knowing, of course, the degree of discomfort he might obtain if he were living a rational life, and (quite irrationally) fearing that it might even be greater than his present discomfort, he dreams up strawmen horrors about rationality in order to give himself an excuse for not attempting to attain it.

Or again: knowing that his present irrational state is producing unpleasant behavioral results, but also knowing that thinking and acting more logically will be a very difficult state to achieve and will require considerable expenditure of time and effort, the presently neurotic individual lazily (usually meaning fearfully or rebelliously) spends more effort thinking up arguments against rationality than in experimentally trying to apply it to his life.

One of my (R.A.H.'s) patients, for example, kept resisting my rational approach to his severe problem of anxiety and compulsive eating and frankly admitted that he was resisting therapy.

"Are you afraid," I asked, "that if you reconstruct your life along the ways we have been discussing, you will become a kind of rational machine-monster?"

"Well, in a sense, yes," the patient replied.

"All right. Now let's look at your fear of becoming machine-like as a result of therapy just as we would examine any of your other anxieties. What evidence is there to support your concern? Name a person you know who seems so rational that he doesn't appear to enjoy life and seems to be a logical machine, as you have been implying?"

"Well, I don't know, exactly. But I must admit that at times you seem a bit, you know, that way yourself. You do seem awfully efficient. And you never get upset about things. Even when I break down and cry or rant it doesn't seem to affect you. And that seems strange and, well, maybe a bit heartless to me."

"And this proves that I am coldly and dreadfully incapable of enjoying life, or being happy?"

"Not exactly. But I am afraid that *I* might be unhappy if I became so calm and objective, like you."

"Ah, but that's quite a different thing, isn't it? Here you are, almost as miserable as you can be, with your extreme anxiety and compulsiveness; and here I am, as you just described me, never getting upset about things. Obviously, if your description of me is accurate, I can't be very unhappy. And yet you are afraid that if you become relatively calm, like me, you will magically become unhappy, or at least incapable of being happy. Is that right?"

"Yes. Somehow, that's the way I feel."

"You mean, really, that's the way you *believe*. But I still ask: what is the evidence for your belief? Have you experimentally tried, even for a few days or weeks, being as calm as I? Have you, in the course of such a trial, proven to your own satisfaction—or shall we say, your own dissatisfaction? —that you would then be even worse off, more unhappy, than you are now?"

"No, I can't say I have."

"Then why don't you, quite experimentally, try? After all, you can always return to your present miserable state, you know, if this kind of honest trial fails. If, somehow, you try being more rational and start turning into an IBM-like zombie, you can always reintroduce whatever degree of non-rationality or irrationality you care to get back into your life. You sign no contract to go on *irrationally* becoming more and more coldly 'rational,' if that's how your experiment in logical thinking actually starts turning out. So far as I can see, however, since you haven't even *tried* rationality yet, and since you are indubitably miserable being your dear old present irrational self, you are setting up a bogeyman as an excuse against the dangers, or what you consider to be the dangers, of changing yourself."

"You mean people like me actually are so afraid to change their ways that they dream up exaggerated and false objections to doing so?"

"Precisely. Without even trying a thing, they set up so many theoretical, and often highly fanciful objections to it that they never give themselves a chance to learn whether it would be satisfying for them or not."

"You mean like homosexuals, for instance, who never give themselves a chance to find out whether they could enjoy girls, because they convince themselves in advance, out of sheer childish prejudice and fear, that they never could enjoy them?"

"Right. I'll never forget how my associate, Dr. Albert Ellis, handled this very problem you're raising when he was speaking to a large audience at the American Psychological Association some years ago. He had been contending that homosexuals are necessarily disturbed because, when they fixatedly and exclusively go for members of their own sex, they are obviously under-lyingly afraid of or rebellious against members of the other sex. A psychologist in the audience objected;

" 'But, Doctor Ellis, isn't it possible that some people are *naturally* prejudiced, by their own tastes, against some modes of sex participation? If, for example, an individual has a natural prejudice against eating oysters, would you consider him abnormal or neurotic?'

" 'Not necessarily,' Dr. Ellis replied. 'But if I encountered some one who was "naturally" prejudiced against eating oysters, without once having looked at them, smelled them, or tasted them, I would certainly consider *him* neurotic. For how else would he, except by sheer irrational prejudice, then acquire his "natural" taste? So with homosexuals: when I find as I frequently do, that they have *never* tried kissing or having sex relations with a girl, and they are *still* convinced that doing so would be highly unpleasant, I can only suspect that they are woefully fearful of or angry at females. And *this*, their fear or their anger, is their sickness, not their homosexual behavior in itself.' "

"So you think that my sickness, right now, is not so much my being irrational, but my refusing to even try rationality and then insisting that, if I did try it, it would make me into a mechanical-like, unemotional zombie?"

"Exactly. Why don't you try it and see?"

And this patient did try thinking more logically about his compulsive eating and did seriously begin to question and challenge his many crippling anxieties. Several weeks later, after making considerable progress in these directions, he enthusiastically reported:

"Not only have I stopped eating when I'm not really hungry, as I was doing when I came to see you; but I've actually started a real diet for the first time in years and have already lost eight pounds. I'm sure I'll be able to keep it up, too, now that I see that my eating was mainly a device to divert myself from my real central problem, which was, and still seems to be—though at last I'm beginning to make some inroads there, too!—my unwillingness to face the hazards of life myself, without falling back on the help of my parents, my wife, and even my children.

"The main thing I wanted to tell you, Dr. Harper, is something a little on the side. And that is that as my compulsive eating and some of my fears of standing on my own two feet kept going down, that mechanical-like feeling that I told you I was so afraid of getting a few weeks ago just hasn't materialized at all. Just the opposite! I'm so darned *more* emotional, in a good way, and enthused about my life now that I practically go to the office singing every morning. In fact, this very morning I *did* find myself singing, for the first time in years, on the way to work. And I stopped for a moment, when I saw what I was doing, and said to myself, 'Holy cats! That son-of-a-gun Harper was right. If singing on the way to work is an example of how mechanical this rational therapy stuff is going to make me, I think I'd better get some even heavier doses of that rational thinking and learn to warble like a nightingale!' Mechanical-schmechanical—I'm beginning to like being this kind of a robot!"

As this patient began to see, a thorough rational approach to life does not mean a one-sided, monolithic kind of rationality. The definition of rational, as employed in modern social science and in the relatively new field of game theory, is: showing reason; not foolish or silly; sensible; leading to efficient results; producing desired effects with a minimum of expense, waste, unnecessary effort, or unpleasant side effects.

Human reason, therefore, includes and decidedly makes allowances for emotionality, unthinking habit performance, and whatever else is needed for an effective, anxiety-minimized existence. Rational living is not, according to our definition, an end in itself; but life is truly rational only when it is experienced for the purpose of making the liver less unhappy and more satisfied with his existence.

Rationality, as we use the term, is never perfectionistic or absolutistic.

Although we consider ourselves to be highly rational, we are not, in the sense in which the word is often used in philosophy, dedicated rational*ists* (Ellis). Rational*ism* is the theory that reason or intellect, rather than the senses, is the true source of knowledge. This we do not believe: since, like almost all modern scientists and logical empiricists, we believe that knowledge ultimately stems from and must be directly or indirectly related back to our perceiving—to the observations of our senses of touch, smell, sight, hearing, and tasting.

If rational thinking is not considered as an Absolute Good, or an end in itself, but more *reasonably* deemed to be a means toward the end of maximizing human well-being—and particularly of minimizing anxiety, depression, hostility, and other highly emotionalized blocks to well-being—then it is difficult to see how one can possibly be *too* rational. Extreme, exaggerated, or over-rationality is a self-contradiction. As soon as reason is taken to ridiculous, self-defeating extremes, it no longer, of course, is reason. Rather, it is then anti-reason.

A truly rational approach to life cannot ever lead to the mechanization or under-emotionalizing of man. Rational means, we repeat, sensible, efficient, *un*self-defeating. And human emotion, sensitivity, creativity, and art are normally as rational (that is, as harmlessly satisfying and pleasure-producing) as they could possibly be. As shown in the case cited a few pages back, when an individual, be he an outstanding philosopher (such as José Ortega y Gasset) or an average man, fears that he will become *too* rational when he uses his thinking ability to regulate his own life, he is either ignorant of the definition of rational employed in this book or else he is defensively afraid of or rebellious against giving up his present irrational and self-defeating ways. In which event his *rationalizing* blocks his being truly *rational*.

Although rationalizing, in a philosophic sense, means to make rational or to make conform to reason, in a psychological sense it means to devise superficially rational or seemingly plausible explanations or excuses for one's acts, beliefs, or desires, usually, without being aware that these are not one's real motives. Psychologically, therefore, rationalizing or excusing one's behavior is virtually the opposite of being rational about it.

Similarly, although to intellectualize, in a philosophic sense, means to reason or to think, in a psychological sense it means to *over*emphasize intellectual pursuits such as mathematics and to consider them superior to other pursuits such as popular drama or music. To intellectualize also, psychologically, has come to mean to think about one's emotional problems in such a detailed and compulsive manner as to deny their true existence and to avoid rather than to attempt solving them.

Although, therefore, the principles of rational therapy and rational living, as their names imply, strongly favor a highly reasoned approach to human life, they do not favor a rationalizing or intellectualistic approach, as these terms are often used in modern psychology. To reason one's way out of one's emotional difficulties (which, according to our theory, one has previously *un*reasoned oneself into) is highly sane and sensible. But to rationalize or intellectualize about one's self-defeating, neurotic behavior is to help perpetuate it endlessly. We will have no truck whatever with rationalization and intellectualization; and if our opponents, as they often do, accuse us of advocating rationalized and intellectualized "solutions" to human ills, that (alas for them) is *their* problem.

The Art of Never Being Desperately Unhappy

9

ANYONE WHO TRIES to give you a rule by which you can always be happy is either a fool or a knave. And yet we unhesitantly declare: We can teach you the art of (virtually) never being unhappy.

Do we contradict ourselves? Seemingly so; actually not. Happiness, or a positive feeling of pleasure, joy, or elation, is usually a by-product of what you do, and cannot intelligently be sought in its own right. What you, as a unique human individual, do, and how much pleasure you get from doing it largely depends on your personal preferences—which are not easily predictable or changeable. You may adore a walk in the country; or you may hate it. You may become ecstatic over going to bed with your spouse; or you may look upon doing so as an odious chore. Who are we, then, to tell you what will probably bring you joy?

We legitimately may, of course, tell you what makes *us* happy or what brings *someone else* joy, but we cannot predict, except by putting you through actual experiences or trials, what will make *you* highly satisfied. We can be quite vague, if we are cagy enough, and tell you that something general, such as absorbing work or vital interest in a cause, will probably make you happy. But *what* work or *what* vital interest will do the trick for you we cannot honestly say. Only you, in the last analysis, by a process of your own trial and error, can sensibly answer that question.

If we can't tell you how to be happy, can we tell you how not to be unhappy? Paradoxically, yes. Because while human beings differ enormously in what brings them positive contentment, they are remarkably alike in

69

what makes them miserable. And we, as psychologists who have worked with many miserable people, can tell you almost to a T just what you are doing to make yourself unhappy—and how to stop doing it.

Are we contending, you may ask, that *all* unhappiness is illegitimate and unnecessary? No, not quite. Merely that almost all human pain, suffering, misery, and discontent are superfluous. Almost? Yes. The only—and we mean the *only*—sustained unhappiness that we accept as legitimate or justifiable is that which is the direct result of physical pain. All other sustained, intense, and repetitive unhappiness, we contend, is needless.

"Oh, come now!" you may protest. "You don't mean to say, Drs. Ellis and Harper, that if my mother dies, or my wife leaves me, or I lose a fine job that I want very much to keep—you don't mean to say that even *then* I don't need to be unhappy?"

But we do mean exactly that. No matter *what* happens to you, with the exception of prolonged, intractable physical pain, we do not think it necessary for you to remain unhappy for more than a very short while. For a minute or two, yes, and in a mild sort of way for that minute or two: that we'll concede. But if for more than a short time you are intensely depressed because some dreadful or seemingly dreadful thing has happened to you then you are indubitably, without a shadow of a doubt, illegitimately unhappy.

"Really? You're *really* serious about that?"

Yes—really, we most certainly are. Because, we insist, what is generally called mental, emotional, or spiritual unhappiness is nothing but a state of mind, an arbitrary definition; and because it is brought on by your telling yourself silly, illogical, self-defeating sentences, you can bring virtually all of it to a swift halt by telling yourself intelligent, logical, self-reconstructive sentences.

"Really? *Really!!?*"

Yes, really. But before you split a gut in your incredulity, perhaps we had better do a little solid defining of the terms "happy" and "unhappy." Then perhaps you may not think us so crazy as we at first seemed to be.

The dictionary loosely and generally defines the term *unhappy* as: sad; miserable; wretched; sorrowful. We believe that this definition tells only half the real story. What unhappiness, or at least acute unhappiness, actually seems to consist of is: (a) a feeling of sadness, sorrow, irritation, annoyance, or regret at not getting what one wants or at getting what one does not want; and (b) a second and more important feeling of terrible injustice or great anxiety *because* one has not got what one wants and has experienced feeling (a) in connection with not getting it.

We distinguish, in other words, between normal and relatively mild feelings of frustration or loss on the one hand and abnormal and deepseated feelings of pain or anguish *at* one's feelings of frustration or loss on the other hand. We think that it is humanly normal to be moderately *dejected* at the loss of a desired or loved person or thing; but abnormal (albeit statistically most common) to be *depressed* at the same loss. We also hold that it is perfectly sane for a man or woman to be moderately *annoyed* by a frustrating set of circumstances; but by no means sane for the same individual to be inordinately *angry* at the same set of frustrations.

Whereas dejection is an expectable response to a distinct loss, depression is, in addition, intense *dejection about being dejected.* Similarly, as was pointed out in the book, *How to Live with a Neurotic,* it is perfectly proper, in many instances, for a human being to be annoyed at not getting what he wants, when he becomes *annoyed at being annoyed* he tends to fall into an overly-reactive, neurotic pattern of behavior.

If by unhappiness, then, is meant intense, prolonged, or quite frequent feelings of mental or emotional discomfort, and particularly of any of the many forms of anxiety and anger, then we believe that this kind of unhappiness is unnecessary for human beings to experience. And that they need never—well, practically never—be unhappy in this manner if they understood what they usually do to create their own anguish and if they stopped doing these things. If human beings conducted their lives with consistent intelligence, they would have many different kinds of experiences; would enjoy some and dislike others; would keep seeking the experiences they enjoy and calmly avoiding those they do not enjoy; and, finally, when they could not avoid certain unpleasant experiences—such as the death of someone they dearly love—would still calmly accept the fact that life holds certain inevitable unpleasantries and frustrations and that that is too bad— but it is not terrible, atrocious, or catastrophic.

Having said this, let us immediately emphasize that we do not believe that any human being can, for any length of time, be *perfectly* or *completely* or *ecstatically* happy. The frenetic search for a perfect *anything,* in fact, almost inevitably dooms the searcher to severe frustration and violent unhappiness. And humans are just not the kind of animals who can be perfect in virtually any ways—especially perfectly happy. Because of their normally fluctuating and often rhythmically pulsating physical and psychological experiences, they are subject to literally hundreds of irritations, pains, ills, diseases, states of ennui, conditions of tension, and other discomfort-producing situations. Many of their mental-emotional handicaps, as we endeavor to show in this book, can be largely overcome or diminished. Largely, but not completely.

Sustained negative emotion, for example, can almost always be tackled and appreciably conquered. But it can be effectively tackled largely because it is sustained and because there is sufficient time to think about it, track it back to its origins, and contradict the thinking which one (consciously or unconsciously) employed to create and sustain it. Evanescent negative feelings, on the other hand, cannot as easily be tackled, simply because they are fleeting and may not be around long enough to analyze and unravel.

Even the battle against sustained psychological pain is never entirely won. When you are unhappy because of some silly idea and you analyze and eradicate this idea, it rarely stays away forever but instead keeps recurring from time to time and has to be re-analyzed and forcibly subdued repeatedly. You may have the ridiculous notion, for instance, that you cannot live without some friend's approval and may be making yourself immensely miserable because you believe this rot. Then, after much hard thinking, you may finally scotch this notion and convince yourself that it is quite possible for you to live satisfactorily without your friend's approbation. Eventually, however, you are most likely to discover that, quite spontaneously, you from time to time revive the groundless notion that life is valueless without the approval of this—or some other—friend. And once again you have to go to work to beat this self-defeating idea out of your skull.

Let us hasten to note that the task of depropagandizing yourself from your own self-defeating beliefs usually becomes easier and easier if you persist. If you consistently ferret out and contradict most of your mistaken philosophies of life, you will soon begin to find that their influence is weaker; and, eventually, some of them almost entirely lose their power to harrass you. Almost. For the day may well come when, if only for a brief time, the same idiotic thought with which you once drove yourself crazy again returns and has to be forcibly reanalyzed and overcome.

Some of the major ideas that cause severe emotional disturbance, then, are exceptionally powerful; because, biologically, humans tend to think in these particular silly ways; and because, socially, they live in the kind of communities that encourage them to think irrationally.

Take, by way of illustration, the idea of the necessity of outstanding success or achievement. Quite possibly, there is some innate tendency of many or most humans to try to be outstanding in their accomplishments: to strive to be the fastest runner, or the best gardener, or the highest mountain climber. As White has ably shown, the drive to master other people and things is most deep-seated in normal people. And, considering what advantages such a drive may well have for individual (though not necessarily group) survival, it is easy to conceive it as being partly inherited.

To this possibly innate tendency, we need only add the deliberately taught competitiveness which most (though not all) communities inculcate in their citizens and the result will easily be the overwhelming achievement drives which we actually witness in the majority of people reared in most cultures. Under these circumstances, it is easy to see why, if a person reared in a competitive society becomes unhappy because he cannot live up to his own perfectionistic demands for success, and if he begins to think about and question his own (and his society's) standards, he will thereby be rationally challenging and fighting against characteristics or attitudes which are deeply ingrained in his "nature," and which he will have considerable difficulty changing or eradicating.

Difficult, however, does not mean impossible. Of course, it is difficult for people to think and to act rationally in an irrational world. Of course it is hard for them to reason their way out of circumstances in which they have been unreasonably bogged down for many years. All right, so it's difficult. But it's also difficult for a blind man to learn to read Braille, a victim of polio to use his muscles again, or a perfectly normal person to swing from a trapeze, learn ballet dancing, or play the piano well. So it's difficult! But it still can be done.

Many critics of a rational approach to living also object that it is "unnatural" to expect a human being to be consistently rational—that this is simply not the nature of the beast. And these critics are not entirely wrong. For it is to some extent "unnatural" for people who are born and reared with many irrational tendencies to make consistent use of their reasoning powers to overcome these tendencies.

However—and let us not for a moment forget—it is also "unnatural" for people to wear shoes, employ contraceptives, study foreign languages, drive cars, and do hosts of other things that they were obviously not born to do, and that in many instances contradict their early upbringing. So it is "unnatural." The real question is: How sane is the individual who rigidly sticks only to perfectly "natural" behavior?

I shall always remember the young and potentially attractive female who was referred to me (A.E.) by her boy friend because she refused to take practically any care of her body or her physical appearance and was, at the age of 23, already showing serious signs of overweight, flabbiness, and esthetic decrepitude. When I asked her why she didn't take better care of herself even though her boy friend (whom she said she loved and very much wanted to marry) was quite displeased with her appearance and kept threatening to leave her if she did not do something about it, she said:

"But would that really be honest? Should I *pretend*, with lovely clothes and makeup and stuff like that, that I'm more beautiful than I really am? Would that be being true to myself—or to him? Wouldn't he know, actually, that I didn't look the way I looked on the surface, and wouldn't he resent me all the more? If he can't accept me this way, without the elegant clothes and makeup routine, if he can't accept me the way I *am*, what kind of love does he really have for me anyway?"

I did my best to show this girl that, quite apart from her boy friend and his opinion of her looks, there might well be several reasons why she herself would want to look neater and take care of her body. Reasons of health, for instance; and of her own esthetic feelings when she looked in a mirror; and of the vocational advantages in the profession for which she was training.

To no avail. She kept returning to the themes of how artificial, how unnatural, how dishonest it would be for her to try to appear to be what she really wasn't. I came within a hair of irrationally angering myself and telling her what she could do with her goddam feelings of "integrity"—such as getting herself to a nunnery and be done with it.

Reason, however, prevailed. I reminded myself for the twentieth time that she was not a louse but merely a very mixed-up, defensive girl who, out of severe underlying fright, stubbornly held to her untenable, self-contradictory position because she desperately felt that she *could not* let go of it. I also told myself that even if I failed utterly to change her self-sabotaging philosophies, *my* value as a human being was in no way at stake: I would merely have one more good, if alas unsuccessful, try under my belt; and I might even learn something from my "defeat." So back I went to the therapeutic fray.

"Look," I said, "you're too intelligent a girl to really believe this kind of hogwash that you keep handing yourself and handing me."

"What do you mean, hogwash?" she asked rather belligerently.

"Just what I said, h-o-g-w-a-s-h. And you know, to some extent, what I mean already. I can see by the somewhat phony way in which you lift your eyebrows. But, to be more explicit, what I mean is this. You keep saying that you cannot do anything artificial and unnatural to make yourself look better, because that would be dishonest, that wouldn't be cricket. Right?"

"Yes, that's just what I keep saying—and what, whether you think so or not, I mean."

"Perhaps so; but I'm not so sure. Just let's take your argument, for a moment, to its logical extremes, to see whether it will hold up. You won't use makeup or proper clothing because that's unnatural, you say. All right. How about drinking glasses, knives, forks, spoons, and other eating utensils. Aren't *they* unnatural?"

"Well, in a sense, yes. But not in the sense I mean."

"You mean not in the *non*sense you mean. But what 'sense' are you talking about? What *do* you mean?"

Of course, she couldn't tell me. She reverted to saying again, in a vague and circumlocutory manner, that it just wasn't *right* and *natural* to make herself look well or physically healthful; but that, somehow, it was still right and natural for her to use knives, forks, and spoons. I saw she was getting nowhere, so I interrupted:

"Look: why do you keep handing me this nonsense? Why don't we try, instead, to discover why you are *not* being consistent in your use of the words *right* and *natural,* and why you keep insisting that helping yourself with one device, such as wearing glasses, is OK, but that helping yourself with another device, such as suitably tailored clothes, is not OK. As I said before, you're a very bright girl. Now surely there must be *some* reason why you are being so inconsistent. What is it?"

She at first kept insisting that she was *not* being inconsistent. But I wouldn't buy that and kept showing her how inconsistent she was. I talked as if her inconsistency was a fact, not a debatable question, and said I would only discuss with her *why* and not *whether* it existed. She finally seemed willing to discuss the whys of her self-contradictions; so I said:

"Don't think that I am trying to convince you that there are only abnormal or pathological reasons for your inconsistency. This, alas, is a trick of many psychotherapists of different orientations, who practically insist that *everything* a patient does must be for the wrong reasons. In rational therapy, however, we make it a habit to look for some of the *normal* reasons why people may be doing the wrong things and thereby defeating their own ends."

"So if I am inconsistent about refusing to use artificial aids to improve my looks, you think that I may have some normal, as well as abnormal, reasons for being so?"

"Right. Let's take a fairly obvious normal reason. You said before that if your boy friend cannot accept you the way you *are,* without artificial aids, what kind of love does he really have for you? Well, that's at least partly true, isn't it? For if he *only* loves you because of the things you do to make yourself look beautiful, his love will tend to be decidedly superficial and probably unenduring; and you may well say to yourself: Who needs that kind of love?"

"Yes—who needs it?"

"Right. Therefore, it is perfectly sane of you to question how far you should go to make yourself look beautiful, so that he may possibly love you for your looks. And *that* reason for your refusing to use artificial beauty aids, while at the same time using eyeglasses or forks and knives, is a normal reason. But when you take this same reason and exaggerate it, so that you refuse to use beauty aids for your *own* esthetic and health satisfactions, you are turning to abnormal reasons for what then becomes a gross inconsistency in your behavior. And we must then look for possible abnormal reasons for your self-inconsistency."

"Such as?"

"Such as your terrible underlying fear that if you did try to keep yourself looking well, you might still fail, since you may believe that you really *are* ugly, no matter how you fix yourself up; or that you might succeed in looking well and still fail to marry your boy friend since he might dislike you in spite of your good looks."

"But isn't it true that I *may* not be goodlooking to my boy friend, no matter what I do? And that I *may* look fine to him and still ultimately be rejected by him?"

"Oh, certainly. Of course those things are true. It's always true that we may do our very best to win someone's approval or to achieve some goal, and that we may nonetheless fall on our faces and miserably fail to get what we go after. So what?"

"But wouldn't that be a terrible thing for me, if I dieted, and wore the right clothes, and otherwise fixed myself up and *still* lost my boyfriend?"

"It most certainly would not be a terrible thing—unless you insisted on making it so. It would be inconvenient, of course, or frustrating, or a sad thing for you to lose your boy friend. But why would it be *terrible?* Would you die of it? Would the ground open and swallow you up? Would you be unable to get another boy friend or to do other enjoyable things in life even if you did not have another suitable male replacement?"

"I don't know. I don't know what I'd be able to do if I really lost John."

"That's exactly the point: *that's* your sickness. You believe, quite wrongheadedly but still most definitely, that it *would* be terrible to lose John, that you *wouldn't* know what to do if you lost him. And by having this belief, by *translating* a nuisance and a frustration into a terrible catastrophe, *you actually bring that very catastrophe about*. By *believing* you can't live successfully without John, you make certain that you really *can't*."

"And because I believe it would be terrible to lose John, and know that I may lose him no matter what I do with myself physically, I deliberately shy away from doing much to keep him—is that what you mean? I give up on getting him in advance, so that I will not suffer the torments of the damned later on?"

"Exactly. You quite sanely want John—because we'll assume that he's a great guy and is pretty well suited to you. Then you insanely tell yourself that because you want him you *must* have him, and would be destroyed if you did not. Then you 'logically' give up trying for him in advance, so as not to be hurt later. Or, more specifically, you set up exceptionally difficult rules of the game—that is, your refusal to try any beauty aids on the supposition that if he still loves you in spite of these almost impossible rules, he will later love you forever and never leave you."

"But is that so crazy?"

"Yes—because it practically never will work. It's like being afraid that your maid will bring back the wrong groceries from the store and therefore demanding that she have a Ph.D. degree in home economics before you hire her. What are your chances of ever finding anyone with a Ph.D. in home economics who will be willing to work as your maid for a regular maid's salary?"

"I see what you mean. I'd have no chance of finding such a maid, however desirable it might be to have one. And similarly I have practically no chance to win the love of my boy friend if I keep making these unreasonable demands on him?"

"Right. So instead of changing *his* characteristics, so as to retain your own neurotic demand for absolute love from him, would you not better think carefully about and work hard to change your own sick needs for total love security?"

"Hmmm. I never saw it that way before."

"But that's what emotional disturbance is: not seeing that you are taking an initially normal wish for approval (and a desire to be approved for less superficial characteristics than good clothes or a trim figure) and turning these into an abnormal demand for approval and a refusal to do anything to win it. Think about this some more and I am sure that you will see it more clearly."

And she did think about it some more; began to diet and take care of her appearance; and started to get along much better with her boy friend.

The main point of this case, as with so many other cases of disturbed individuals, is that it is both normal *and* abnormal, natural *and* artificial for human beings to be reasonable or unreasonable. We are, we humans, intelligent *and* stupid, thinking *and* suggestible; and therefore, although it is easy, almost automatic, for us to strive to be rationally behaving animals, it is just as easy for us to fail, at least in part, to reach our goal. Rational living, like all aspects of life, is a process, an ongoing attempt, an experiment; it is hardly a product or a final result.

Stated differently: human adults are predisposed to act, at times, in immature, childish manner. That is one of the essences of their humanity: fallibility. Because they are what they are, they find it exceptionally easy to be, on many occasions, unthinking, prejudiced, and consequently severely over or under-emotional.

But the fact that human beings find it *easy* to be childish does not mean that they *must* be. They *can* teach themselves to be fairly consistently mature, thinking, reflective. If they do, they will never reach the state, in all probability, in which they are completely, consistently happy; nor ever the state where they are never in any way unhappy.

They can, nonetheless, finally, with much work and effort, train themselves to be never—well, practically never—intensely miserable for any sustained period of time. What more can one reasonably ask?

Tackling
Dire Needs
10   *for Approval*

SEVERAL POWERFUL, IRRATIONAL and illogical ideas stand in the way of our leading anxiety-free, unhostile lives. One of the greatest of these—which we shall label Irrational Idea No. 1— is *the idea that it is a dire necessity for an adult to be loved or approved by almost everyone for virtually everything he does.*

"But," you may quickly interject, "do not most psychologists and psychotherapists keep insisting that human beings *need* approval and that they cannot possibly be happy unless they get a good degree of it?"

Yes, they do. And they are wrong; or, at least, careless in their formulations. Humans almost always *desire* approval and almost all of them would be considerably less happy and effective if they received *none* of it. In modern society, moreover, most people could hardly survive at all if they did not get *some* approval or (at a minimum) lack of disapproval from their fellows. For otherwise who would rent or sell them living quarters, provide them with food, or furnish them with clothing?

Nonetheless, adults do not really *need* the love or approval of others. In its strict definition, *need* is derived from the Middle English word, *nede*, the Anglo-Saxon, *nead*, and the Indo-European term, *nauto*—which mean to collapse with weariness (seen also in the Gothic term, *naus*, or corpse). Its main meaning in English is: necessity; compulsion; obligation; something that is requisite for life and happiness.

Since it is quite possible for a human being to live in isolation for many years without dying or even feeling terribly unhappy, and since it is also

absurd

?

79

possible for him to live in a social group for several decades without becoming disturbed because all or most members of his group do not approve or love him, it is obvious that some persons do not *need* to be accepted by others. Indeed, there even seem to be a few individuals who do not *want* to be approved by others. But almost all of these are probably being defensive and *do* want some kind of approval from their fellowmen even when they are contending that they do not.

Scientific and personal observations seem to sustain the hypothesis that virtually all humans who are raised in social groups do want, prefer, or desire acceptance and caring from some of their fellows and that they will tend to be happier and more productive people if they obtain some measure of the approval they seek. But wants, preferences, and desires are still not needs or necessities. We would *like* our physical and mental cravings to be fulfilled; but we do not really *need* them to be.

Considerable confusion in regard to human needs has arisen in psychological writings because the requirements of children and adults have been confounded. Children, for fairly obvious reasons, actually need approval and love, especially from their parents, if they are to thrive healthfully and happily. Not that they will necessarily wither away if they are disapproved or unloved; for as Orlansky (1949), Peller (1938), Sewell (1955), and other recent psychological and sociological writers have shown, they will not. But they are *literally* dependent on the adults around them, and cannot ordinarily be sufficiently provided with food, clothing, shelter, health-protection, and other necessities of life if no adult *cares* for them or in some manner loves them.

Children, again, cannot too easily protect themselves against the verbal criticism of others. If their companions and caretakers keep telling them that they are wrong and worthless, they cannot too easily say to themselves: "Oh, that's just *their* opinion," or "Who cares what *they* think? *I* know I'm *not* worthless." Consequently, children suggestibly *accept* the negative views of others about themselves and are often seriously psychologically maimed by their own acceptances of these views.

Adults, however, are not children and *need* not act as if they were. If others around them do not sufficiently care for their physical and health-demanding needs, they can usually manage somehow to shift for themselves and do something about begging, borrowing, or stealing adequate subsistence. And if others savagely criticize or reject them, they can stop and ask themselves, "*Why* did Jones say I was worthless? What was *his* motive in saying so? Is *he* an accurate observer?"

Even when adults agree that perhaps Jones is right about his criticisms of them, they can still protect themselves against his attack by saying to themselves several self-preserving sentences, including:

1. "Well, maybe Jones finds me pretty bad, but Smith and Rogers seem to like me well enough. So I can associate with them if Jones won't have me."

2. "Perhaps both Jones and Smith don't like the way I do things; and perhaps they are right when they say I am inefficient for acting in this manner. But I *still* think my way is best and most enjoyable for me and I would rather be enjoying myself than be efficient in the ways they would like me to be."

3. "Maybe Jones and Smith are correct in showing me that I'm a woefully bad tennis player, and maybe I would better, for my own good, learn how to play better. In case, however, I never become the best tennis player in the world, that still is no crime and I need not consider myself worthless—but merely a poor tennis player."

4. "Perhaps Jones and Smith are quite right about my not understanding music. Why not admit to them, then, that I am wrong, and see if they will help me understand it better, so that I may enjoy myself more with it."

In many ways such as these an adult may accept the disapproval of others, make allowances for it, do something about it, and consequently come off relatively unscathed. He may never learn to *like* disapprobation or negative criticism; but he may definitely learn to *tolerate* it and to *use* it for his own good.

Earl Thames was an unusually intelligent man of forty-five. A great deal of his energies, as he indicated when I (R.A.H.) saw him for psychotherapy, had always been devoted to gaining the love of others.

His widowed mother had praised him, indulged him, and led him to believe that he was so special and wonderful that he deserved the very best in life. Because he had considerable ability and charm, it was not difficult for him to get the same kind of admiration from his classmates, teachers, and (later on) business associates. *At first!*

The trouble came later. After first winning their approval, Earl would find that people—of course—had other things to do in life than to continue telling him what a lovely, lovely fellow he was. Their initial enthusiams for him would naturally wane. Whereupon, feeling desperately rejected, he would come around waving some new accomplishment, witticism, or kind sacrifice to try to jog their tiring devotions. These sacrifices at the altar of love, when they worked at all, also had short-lived effects. In time, people became too tired or busy or (eventually) plain bored with Earl to give him the sort of effusive appreciation that his mother had endlessly bestowed. When he noticed this, Earl would go into a rage, roundly condemn his associates for their stupidity, inhumanity, lack of sensitivity, and run off to acquire a new and presumably more appreciative set of friends.

Between the ages of 25 and 40, Earl didn't do so badly with his field-running and managed to go through three wives and innumerable business and personal associates. Then mama died, leaving him a considerable fortune, and he began to fail worse than ever in business and to drink heavily. He ran through most of his money in highly speculative deals, approval-seeking philanthropies, and bad management associated with his drinking sprees. In the past, when other people withheld approval or things went wrong in any way, he always had mama to help him and reassure him that he *was* a perfectly wonderful boy. Now he had nothing but the anesthetic provided by alcohol.

When a physician who specializes in the treatment of alcoholics referred this patient to me for psychotherapy, Earl put on one of his typically brilliant charm dances for me. Even when desperately seeking help, he knew not how to relate to anyone in any other way. Believing fully and intensely that he *must*, that he absolutely *needed* to be loved, admired, applauded, approved by each new associate, he applied the same standards to me as to the others and did his boyish handsprings in precisely the same manner that he had been doing them for almost forty years.

Some psychotherapists that I know would doubtlessly have reacted to Earl's help-seeking dance just the way he wanted, and could have mightily striven to give this pitiful middle-aged man who "needed" love exactly what he "needed." For the next five to ten years they might well have coddled and suckled him to make him feel "really" wanted and approved, on the theory that they would thereby finally get him over his desperate demands for approval and enable him to stand on his own two feet. I doubt whether they would ever have succeeded; for Earl, as many other sick people like him, was a bottomless pit who would accept all possible degrees of extended loving and caring and still keep himself open for more.

My psychotherapeutic view and reaction was radically different. Feeling that Earl "needed" love like he needed a hole in his head, and that giving him more approval and affection would only have served to reinforce his silly notion that he did have such a dire "need," I gave him nothing of the sort. Instead, I calmly and quickly told him the facts of life, very strongly insisted that he did *not* need approval and that he *was* able to live without it, and ruthlessly exposed to him the sad results of his campaign of the last two decades to con others into caring for him.

Earl fought like the dickens. He quoted psychological scripture to indicate that he did need approval. He got the physician who referred him to pressure me for not treating him gently enough. He kept threatening to leave therapy and go back to the bottle. He pulled every stop in the organ to show me what a heartless cur I was and how I would, doubtless, delight in exploiting helpless widows and orphans. No sale. I was adamant; and on one occasion said:

"It's no use. It won't work. Maybe I am the heartless dog you keep accusing me of being. Maybe I beat my wife every night and take candy from little babies. But that's my problem. Your problem is that you still think you *need* love when, like most of us, you *want* it. And you think you need it because you're such a helpless slob, who can't take care of himself, without it. Well, you *are* a helpless slob, let's face it. And you're one *because* you believe you are and *because* you think that love and love alone will save you from slobbery worse than death.

"Well, it won't. I wish I could really get someone in your own life—not me, but someone you live with— to love you the way you want to be loved: just to show you that it *won't* work. For you'd still, under those circumstances, feel you were a slob. And, not having done anything for *yourself* in life, you'd never have shown that you *could* help yourself and you'd still feel helpless.

"But the hard and cold fact is, whether you like it or not, that you're probably never going to get anyone to love you the way you want them to. And even if you did, you'd then become woefully afraid that he or she might later die, or leave you, or love you less than before—so you'd still be terribly anxious and upset. No, there's only one possible thoroughgoing solution to your problem. And that is, of course, that you give up the idea that you *must* be approved or loved by others in order to deem yourself worth while in your own right. And if you refuse to give up this idea, you'll merely go on drinking, running your affairs into the ground, and doing other things that terribly anxious people inevitably do.

"So it's your choice. Either keep thinking that you must be loved—and defeat yourself royally. Or start believing that, however nice it is to be approved by others, it is *not necessary*—and then have a chance to rebuild your bollixed-up existence. It's your life—choose!"

Earl was a difficult patient; and it took many more sessions and many more attempts at forcing him to choose between his dire need for love and effective living. It was hard work, but we (he and I) made it. At last report, two years after I first saw him, he is no longer an alcoholic, is managing his business affairs well, and for the first time in his life has found a feminine partner whom *he* loves rather than one who merely cares *for him.*

Was not Earl Thames an extreme case of an individual who needed to be loved and approved? Yes, somewhat extreme. But he sharply and accurately illustrates the love-need theme that runs through the lives of millions of people. Even when these people experience this need in a less extreme form it can cause them considerable misery.

Why is it illogical for anyone to insist that he be approved by all those who are important to him? For several reasons:

1. To try to be loved by virtually everyone you consider important sets

up a perfectionistic, unattainable goal. Even if you get ninety-nine people to love you, there will always be the hundredth, the hundred and first, and so on.

2. Even if you demand love from a limited number of people, you cannot usually win the approval of all of them. Some of those whose love you seek will, because of their own limitations, have little ability to love anyone. Others will disapprove of you for reasons entirely beyond your control (such as the fact that your eyes are brown instead of blue). Still others will be prejudiced against you for all time because of some initial mistake you made with them, or for various other reasons.

3. Once you are over-concerned with being loved, you inevitably will begin to worry about *how much* and *how long* desired individuals will approve you. Granted that your second cousin or your boss cares for you, does he really love you *enough?* And if he does, will he *continue* to love you tomorrow and the day or year after? With thoughts like these, your anxieties about being loved are bound to be endless.

4. If you are always to be loved by those you seek, you must be always distinctly lovable. But who is? Even when you usually have lovable traits (such as a sweet disposition) how can you retain them at all times for all people?

5. If you could, theoretically, always win the approval of those whose love you "need," you would have to spend so much time and energy doing so that you would have little time left for other pursuits. Striving ceaselessly to be approved means living your life for what *others* think and want you to do rather than for your *own* goals. It also usually means your playing the patsy and buying other's approval at the expense of selling your own soul and losing your self-respect. The more you desperately need others' love, the less you will tend to do what *you* really want to do in life.

6. Ironically enough, the greater your need for being loved, the less people will tend to respect and care for you. Even though they like your catering to them, they will tend to despise your weakness and to cease to find you admirable. Also, by desperately trying to win people's approval, you may tend to annoy and irritate them, to bore them to distraction, and again become less desirable to them.

7. Being loved, once you achieve it, tends to be boring and onerous, since the individual who loves you often makes inroads on your time and energy. Actively loving someone else is a creative and absorbing act. But the dire need to be loved seriously blocks loving and minimizes its experiences. Perversely, it is probably the most loving-destroying of all activities, since most individuals who demand intense and sustained love from others have little time and energy to devote to being truly absorbed in the growth and development of those on whom they make their demands.

8. The dire need for love is almost always a coverup for feelings of severe worthlessness. The full sentence that the individual who has this overwhelming need is usually telling himself is: "I must be loved because I am a worthless, incompetent individual who cannot possibly get along in this world by fending for myself; therefore I *need* to be succored and cared for by others." In desperately seeking to be loved, this individual frequently covers up his underlying feeling of worthlessness and does nothing whatever to tackle them: namely, to prove to himself that he *can* be self-sufficient and self-caring. The more he succeeds in his seemingly benign but actually nefarious purpose of being greatly loved, the less he will tend to cure himself of his terribly sick notion that he *cannot* be himself and get much of what *he* really wants in life.

In view of the foregoing reasons, it would seem that the intelligent or rational-creative approach to life should not include the goal of being madly or inordinately loved by practically everyone you consider desirable; but, instead, that of trying to love yourself and to become vitally absorbed in people, things, and ideas outside yourself.

Respecting yourself and being devoted to people and things outside yourself are to a considerable degree reciprocal aims. For if you really love yourself and are not overly-concerned about what others think of you, you will have so little time to spend in worrying or being "self-centered" (which really means other-directed) that you will be virtually forced to find absorbing interests on the outside. By the same token, if you throw your energies into outside activities and actively devote yourself to other people and things, you normally will tend to be little concerned about what others think of you and, hence, to like yourself.

Put somewhat differently, a person who is devoting himself enthusiastically to long-range hedonism—that is, to activities that he considers desirable and enjoyable from a long-term perspective—cannot help respecting himself: because he *is* what he really wants to be and is not falsely being what someone else thinks he should be. To *be* is essentially to be *oneself:* to do what one *likes* (without ultimately defeating one's long-range ends).

Our patients and associates frequently ask: "I can see that concentrating on loving myself rather than on desperately needing the love of others is a more realistic orientation. But how is this going to help me love other people? As I become less and less concerned about whether others approve of me, won't I find it more and more troublesome and unnecessary to give a damn about others—to relate lovingly to them?"

The answer is: No, for several reasons. First of all, if you direly *need* love, you will tend to be so preoccupied with obtaining it that you have as much chance to love yourself or others as a dope addict has to relate freely and self-confidently to the person who supplies him with drugs.

Secondly, if you surrender your dire need for love, you will still retain, in most instances, a strong *desire* for acceptance by others. People often wrongly assume that to say one does not direly need to be loved is the same thing as saying that being loved is for the birds. Not at all. You can easily enjoy and keep attending well-written and beautifully-acted plays even though you do not *need* to do so to go on living. Why can you not, then, *enjoy* and *seek* love relationships without believing that your life depends on them?

Thirdly, when you are free from your own *demands* that you be loved, you are in a much better position *to* love. You can see more clearly the lovable traits of others; stop hating them when they do not immediately respond to you; learn what you really enjoy in a love relationship; be able to risk committing yourself to loving, even when you know that a given relationship may not work out perfectly; and feel unanxiously free to experience and experiment with loving and to throw yourself more wholeheartedly and intensely into love relationships because you realize that although you may lose your beloved you can never lose *yourself.*

Another question that frequently is asked is: "Granted that loving is generally more rewarding than desperately trying to be loved, should I therefore try to give up all my desires for approval and recognition?"

Answer: Certainly not. Complete self-sacrificiality or the total surrender of your own desires for approval can be just as sick as your being obsessed with winning the esteem of others. Again for several reasons:

1. It is perfectly normal and pleasant for you to *want* to express your own unique conceptions of the world to others and to *want* them to be pleased with some of your expressions. You would hardly be a _human ani-mal_ if you did not derive some kind of satisfaction from relating to others, including liking them *and* wanting them to like you.

2. Wanting to be accepted to some degree by others is one of the main essences of desire; and human beings who are entirely free from desire again do not appear to be entirely human. According to the Hindu classic, the Bhagavad-Gita, the strongest individual is one who "is indifferent to honor and insult, heat and cold, pleasure and pain. He is free from attachment." This may be, for a few select individuals, a worthy ideal; but it is doubtful whether many humans could ever attain it. To lean so far over backwards to get rid of your psychological pain that you also eradicate all your pleasure does not seem too rational to us. By all means try, if you will, to eliminate your extreme, unrealistic, self-defeating desire; but not desire itself.

3. From a practical view, if you ardently want various good things in

life—such as material goods or more leisure—you simply have to win the approval or respect of *certain* people, such as your parents, teachers, or bosses. Even then, though you may wisely eliminate your inordinate or overweening demands that others love you, you must sanely retain, in any social group, *some* wishes to be accepted (and not actively interfered with) by other group members.

Granted that having an inordinate need to be loved by others will only serve to defeat your own ends, and that having *some* wish to be accepted and approved by your associates and loved ones is eminently sane, the question arises: How can you somehow manage to attain a middle-of-the-road policy and fulfillment in this respect?

First and foremost, by admitting that you do have a dire need to be loved in many instances; by making a continual effort to *observe* this need in operation; and by then continually *challenging, questioning,* and *contradicting* it.

A good illustration of combating one's own inordinate love needs came up recently in a group therapy session. Three young women in the group brought up the fact, during this session, that they were woefully unhappy because their husbands did not love them every minute of the day; and whenever they discovered this fact again, one of them habitually became depressed; the second became very angry at her husband and the whole world; and the third young wife started looking around for possible lovers.

All these girls, after talking over their problems with the other group members, admitted that they had a tremendous need to be loved. One of them asked the group: "All right. Now what can I do about this to get over my love needs and keep myself from becoming depressed when they are not always being met?"

One of the males in the group quickly chimed in: "Oh, that's really very easy. All you have to do is to see what you're doing to keep annoying your husband, and to get him not to love you, and then stop doing these things. Then he will really appreciate you and care for you much more than he does—especially if you are being nice to him when he is not being so nice to you."

"Oh, no," chimed in the second of the three girls, who was getting angry whenever her husband didn't show great love for her, "that won't solve the problem at all. If she or I or any of us only tries to be nicer to those who are not loving us, even if we succeed in winning more love from them we don't do anything for *ourselves*. We still go on *needing*, or thinking that we're still needing, their love. And just as soon as they don't give it to us again, we're right back in the soup, just where we started. So that plan won't work at all."

"Right," said the girl who had asked the question. "I've tried that many times, and often have succeeded in getting Johnny to show more love for me by being very nice to him. But it doesn't last. He still doesn't love me *all* the time. And then I go right back into my dive. I agree with Phyllis that that plan won't work at all."

"I can see what you mean," said the male who had answered the first girl. "I guess I was wrong. Getting a better technique to induce people to love you won't do the trick. You've got to not need them."

"What do you mean?" another male member of the group asked. "How can you not need others?"

"That's a good question!" smiled the first male. "I'm not sure I can answer it."

"Well, let me try," said the second girl. "You have to stop telling yourself that you *do* need others—isn't that it?"

"Can you be more specific?" asked still another group member.

"I think I can," she replied. "Let's see. I told you before that whenever my husband looks at me cross-eyed, I tend to shrivel up and die-like and then I get very angry at him. And sometimes, as Mabel said in regard to her husband, I even start looking around for other men, though I know I'm not really going to do anything about them. But I was really wrong when I said that 'whenever.' It *used* to be 'whenever.' It used to be that I'd *always* die at first, and then be terribly angry when Jim gave me a dirty look or otherwise indicated he didn't love me at that exact second that I wanted to be loved. But now it only happens once in a while. It's really much better now."

"And what did you do to make it better?" asked the first girl.

"Oh, yes. I nearly got lost there. That's what I started out to say. I used to go through hell every time Jim wasn't right there with the ever-lovin' spouse bit. But then, when he obviously wasn't caring much of a damn for me at certain times, and I was beginning to feel my gorge rise, I started saying to myself: 'All right. So he doesn't love me dearly right at this minute. So what? Is the world going to come to an end? Do I really *need* his adoration and devotion every second of the day? Of course I don't! Sure, it would be *nice* if he were always there, whenever I felt like his loving me up, or something. But why can't I live without it when he isn't there? Goddam it, I can!' And I found that I could. Not always, unfortunately. As I said before, I still at times get angry as hell when he isn't right there to pat me on the head when I think I need it. But much less often than I used to get. And, by God, I intend to make it still much less often in the future!"

"In other words," said the first male, "you now keep challenging and questioning your dire need for love, not all of the time, but at least often enough. And that's the way you keep reducing it."

"Yes," she replied. "It's one heck of a hassle. But I keep challenging and questioning."

And so it can be with you. If you do have a dire need to be loved; if you accept the fact that you have it; and if you keep challenging, questioning, and contradicting it, it will ultimately, and often quite quickly, start decreasing. For remember: It is *your* need; and only you can keep sustaining it.

Other methods you can use to combat and minimize your inordinate love needs include the following:

1. Ask yourself what *you* really want to do in life, rather than what *others* would like you to do; and keep asking yourself, from time to time: "Am I doing this thing or refusing to do that because *I* really want it that way? Or am I, once again, unthinkingly trying desperately to please others?"

2. In going after what you really want in life, take risks, commit yourself, don't be afraid of making mistakes. Don't be needlessly foolhardy; but convince yourself that if you fail to get something you want, and people laugh at or criticize you for your failure, that is *their* problem. As long as *you* learn by your errors, what difference does it really make what *they* think?

3. Focus on loving rather than on being loved. Try to realize that vital living hardly consists of passive receiving but of doing, acting, outgoing. And just as you can force yourself to play the piano, do Yoga breathing exercises, or go to work every day, you can also often forcibly commit yourself to loving other human beings. In so doing, your dire needs to be loved will almost inevitably decrease.

4. Above all, stop confusing being loved with personal worth. If human beings have any intrinsic worth or value, they have it by virtue of their mere existence, their *being*, rather than because of anything they do to "earn" it (Hartman; Suzuki; Tillich). No matter how much you may be approved by others, or how much *they* may value you for their own benefit, you do not add an iota of value to your *own* "worth" because of their approval. You are "good" or "deserving" just because you *are;* and if you can really believe this most important of human truths, you will find it virtually impossible to be desperately in need of others' approval. Just as importantly, too: If you can rid yourself of your dire need for approval, you will find it relatively easy to accept yourself as "worthwhile" merely because you exist, because you *are.*

To underscore this last point about human worth, consider the case of Herbert Flisch, a forty-year-old successful business man who recognized, after eight sessions of rational-emotive psychotherapy, that almost every single one of his actions for the past four decades had been motivated by his dire need to win the approval of his wife, children, friends, and even employees. At his ninth session he asked:

"Do I understand you correctly to mean that if I stop trying to win everyone's approval and do what *I* think I would like to do (and what would not at the same time defeat my own ultimate ends) that I'll then love myself because I'll consider myself more worthwhile?"

"No," the therapist replied. "Those of us who have been working to develop this system of rational psychotherapy have come to realize that *worthwhileness* is just as illegitimate a concept as its counterpart, *worthlessness;* and that, in fact, just as soon as you tend to think in terms of personal 'worth' you must almost automatically tend to think, at the same time, in terms of personal 'worthlessness.'

"Thus, if you consider yourself 'worthwhile' today because you function effectively, make wise decisions, or think bright thoughts, there is a good chance that you will decide tomorrow that you are 'worthless' because you then function less effectively, make some unwise decisions, or think dull thoughts."

"But *wouldn't* I be worthless if I never functioned effectively?" asked the patient.

"No, absolutely not. Even if you were mentally deficient or hopelessly disturbed and never functioned well, you would then be extrinsically 'worthless'—meaning that *others* might not find you a suitable companion or employee—but intrinsically, to yourself, you would be just as 'worthwhile' as any other more efficient individual. You would be, that is, if you believed you would be. But if you believed, as you obviously do, that to be inefficient is to be 'worthless,' then you would obviously feel and in a sense *be* 'worthless'—or be what you believed you were."

"So I am worthwhile if I think I am—no matter how inefficiently I may actually perform in life?"

"Yes—except that, as I said before, the very concept of 'worth' is a dangerous one, since it always implies the concept of 'worthlessness.' It is like the concept of heaven—which also implies the concept of hell. In fact, the way we usually employ the terms, to be worthwhile really means pretty much the same thing as to be angelic or heaven-directed; and to be worthless means to be demonic or hell-directed. Doesn't it?"

"In a way, I guess it does. I can see what you're driving at," said the patient.

"Moreover, if you have the concepts of 'worth' and 'worthlessness,' even if you avoid extreme self-designations in using these concepts you will tend to become preoccupied with varying *degrees* of 'worth.' Thus, you will tend to say to yourself: 'Today I am *very* worthwhile; yesterday I was *fairly* worthwhile; I hope and pray tomorrow I can be *more* worthwhile than I am today.'

"This kind of concept of 'worth' (and, hence, lack of worth or less worth) carries with it irrational and undesirable aspects of guilt, self-disrespect, self-blame, shame, disappointment, anger, hostility and other negative emotions. The counter-concept, that a human individual is neither 'worthwhile' because he is effective nor 'worthless' because he is ineffective, but that he just *is* —this concept, difficult as it seems to be for anyone raised in Western civilization to see and accept, is perhaps the only way of doing away with the notion of intrinsic 'worthlessness' and self-blame."

"I'll have to give this some more thought," said the patient. "But it does seem to have something to it. However: how does it tie in with self-love?"

"It has a most important tie-in with self-acceptance or self-love. For if you view yourself existentially, as you *are*, you will almost automatically accept yourself. Not because you are efficient, 'worthwhile,' or anything else. But just because you *exist*, because you are *alive*. You will then try to do the things that you *enjoy* rather than those that you *do well* though the two, of course, may overlap."

"You mean that I may then enjoy myself more and love myself and my existence for its being more enjoyable. But that I still will not be more 'worthwhile'—only more alive, happier?"

"Right. And you will not blame yourself or punish yourself whenever—being an imperfect human—you do something wrong or unwise. You will accept yourself *with* your foolish thoughts, feelings, perceptions, or actions, and use the learning that you get as a result of these unwise acts to help you enjoy yourself more and behave more rationally in the future. What greater love of self (and through love of self, potential love for other human beings) could you then have?"

11 \ Eradicating Dire Fears of Failure

IF HUMAN BEINGS were only overwhelmed with a dire need to be loved by virtually everyone to whom they are attracted, they would have sufficient woe to last them a lifetime. If they wish to be even sorrier creatures by far, they can easily add one more idiotic notion to their existences: namely, Irrational Idea No. 2: *The idea that one should be thoroughly competent, adequate, and achieving, in all possible respects.*

Several of our recent patients beautifully—and tragically—exemplify the extreme fear of failure and of incompetence that is ubiquitous among members of our society. Patient A is a brilliant and talented woman who became very proficient in solo activities, such as writing and composing music, but refused to take part in any group experiences, for fear she would not be as good as the other group members. In her writing and composing, moreover, she rarely put anything down on paper, but restricted herself to composing in her head: so that she need rarely take the risk of committing herself fully.

Patient No. 2, an exceptionally bright matron, was so afraid that she would not be able to hold a suitable conversation with the guests at her own house parties that she usually clammed up and said virtually nothing during the whole evening. At other people's gatherings, however, where she did not have the responsibility of being hostess, she conversed very well.

Patient No. 3, a twenty-five year old physicist, never realized satisfaction from his first orgasm when he had sex relations, since he was concentrating only on how to prove to his partner how capable he was sexually. If he had a second orgasm on the same evening he could enjoy that immensely—because he now felt that his adequacy was already proven.

Patient No. 4, a thirty-year-old teacher, was terribly afraid that if she went out on a date with a man someone might insult her and her date would not defend her adequately from such an insult. If this happened (which, of course, it never did) she was certain that she would be horribly humiliated and would sink through the floor.

Patient No. 5 was afraid to think for himself during the therapeutic sessions: because *that,* like so many other things he had tried, might end in failure and he might not think too well. Therefore, he did not work at his therapy.

These are typical examples of literally hundreds of individuals whom we have seen, who are incredibly fearful that they will fail at some task or goal, and who usually manage to avoid trying for what they want because they construe failure as the worst of all possible crimes. And we see so many of these people not only because we are therapists to whom they come for help, but because the world is full of them in every walk of life. Just glance around you and you will soon see.

The notion that the value of a human being is directly proportional to his accomplishment, and that if he is not thoroughly competent, adequate, and achieving he might as well curl up and die, is highly irrational and self-defeating, for several reasons:

1. It should be obvious to any thinking individual that *no one* can be perfectly competent and masterful in most respects. Even Leonardo da Vinci doubtlessly had many weak points and certainly the rest of us mortals do. Trying to be outstanding in *one* field of endeavor is difficult, since millions of other individuals frequently compete with you in the same area; and the goal of being *generally* successful in life is a perfectionistic ideal that almost always dooms you to serious disappointment.

2. Achievement is not, except by arbitrary definition, related to your intrinsic worth. If you *think* you become "better" or "greater" because you succeed at something, you may temporarily be happy in such an achievement. But you actually do not change your intrinsic value one iota by your successes; nor do you lower your I-ness by your failures. You may become happier, more efficient, or "better off" by achieving this or that goal; but being "better off" does not mean that you are a "better person." As we must keep insisting in this book, you are "good," "worthwhile," or "deserving," if you want to use these very poor terms, simply because you exist, because you *are,* because you have aliveness. To raise your "ego" by material or other achievements really means *falsely* to think yourself "better" than you previously were. Most of what we call "pride" in accomplishment is actually false pride: the silly belief that you are worthless unless you are accomp-

lished, and the equally silly belief that because you are now accomplished you are "worthy."

3. Although accomplishment may bring you real advantages, fanatic devotion to the bitch-goddess success usually involves considerable discomfort. Those who are hell-bent on achievement commonly push themselves beyond their limits of physical endurance; tolerate or invite painful conditions that they would avoid if they were not so determined to succeed; and rarely give themselves sufficient time to relax and enjoy what they are doing, nor time to lead well-rounded existences. They also may literally kill themselves with over-work.

4. The frantic struggle for achievement usually reflects one's dire need to excel *others:* to show them that one is as good as or better than they are. But you are *not* other people; and you will never be yourself if you keep trying to be as good as or better than they. What have they really got to do with you as far as comparisons go? If they are inferior to you in various ways does that actually make you by one whit a better *person?* And if they excel you in this or that activity, does that make you a louse or a no-good-nik? Only by magical notions in your own head are others related to your you-ness or to your intrinsic value. And thinking magically that they are thus related will only serve to make you hopelessly other-directed and pathetically divorced from what *you* really want to do with your life.

5. If you inordinately strive for success and are terribly afraid of failing, you will almost inevitably concomitantly fear taking chances, making mistakes, doing the wrong thing, or doing what you would really like to do in life. By insisting on outstanding or perfect achievement, you will leave yourself the pitifully narrow choice of (a) making mistakes and being unhappy about them or (b) refusing to try to do many things for fear of making mistakes and being unhappy about them. Having an unrealistically high level of aspiration foredooms you not only to failure but to fear of failing—which has more pernicious effects than failure itself.

One of the most common and most gruesome illustrations of the fear of failure being worse than failure itself is well illustrated in patients with impotency and frigidity problems who often come to see us. As we have noted in our previous writings, *The Art and Science of Love* and *Creative Marriage,* the original cause of failure in the case of an impotent male or a frigid female can be one of a wide variety of events— such as, fatigue, illness, worry about some unrelated problem, lack of attraction to the sexual partner, or fear of pregnancy. Not infrequently, however, the main cause is a deep-seated feeling of inadequacy on the part of the sexually incompetent person which takes the form of the thought: "I shall probably fail because I am such an inadequate individual that I could not possibly succeed in this difficult and important task."

Whatever the original cause of a particular erectile failure in a man or orgasm inadequacy in a woman, the anxious individual who first fails is likely to have many subsequent failures because he or she *fears* failing. Thus, an impotent male keeps saying to himself something like: "Oh, my God! I failed the last time and I am afraid that I will fail again this time. And it will be awful, embarrassing, dreadful and calamitous if I show my mate that I am impotent again!"

Anyone, of course, who approaches a sexual relationship with such a catastrophizing philosophy is extremely likely to find himself impotent. First of all, he is focussing on his fears about his sexual inadequacy rather than on sexually satisfying stimuli. Secondly, and worse still, he is specifically indoctrinating himself with the idea that he probably will *not* be able to respond to sexual stimulation. He is thereby filling himself with dread about the very situation to which he wants to respond in a relaxed, erotic, enjoyable way. The effect is the same as if he sent ice water instead of warm blood to the erectile tissue of his penis; and this organ, naturally, shrinks from the dreadful situation he has produced.

How can this vicious circle be broken by the application of rational thinking? Let me (R.A.H.) cite an example from my files. I was consulted awhile ago, by a thirty-four-year-old office manager who kept losing his erection with his wife, and to whom I described some of the causes of impotency which have been discussed in the past few paragraphs. My patient said:

"I know that my fear of failure is causing me to be impotent, but how can I *help* being afraid? I *don't* want to fail. And I *do* think failure is awful. I do feel inadequate for sure when I am trying to have intercourse with Janie and can't even make an entry. I do think it is terrible, so how can I tell myself that it *isn't?*

"But let's look at *why* it is terrible," I replied. "You have already told me that you can satisfy Janie with manipulation of her clitoris and that she seems relaxed and happy after achieving orgasm by this means. Is that right?"

"Yes, that's right. But what about *me?* Where do I get *my* satisfaction?"

"Just a moment; we'll get to you soon enough. Anyway, whatever is dreadful about this impotency business, as you see it, relates to your failure to have complete satisfaction through intercourse? Is that it?"

"Well, that's not quite all. I don't like to have Janie think of me as impotent. And, darn it, I don't like to think of *myself* that way."

"Ah, so that's a little more than your merely regretting the loss of your own satisfaction, isn't it? What you seem to be telling yourself is: 'Here I am missing out on all the fun and satisfaction of sex and it is an awful pain in the neck.' And that is a true sentence, since you *are* missing out on a good thing. But then you're also adding the highly false sentences: 'Janie will doubtlessly think that I'm a pansy or something. And maybe I am a goddam latent homosexual! And wouldn't it be terrible if I were! What an awful mess I am.' Isn't that what you're saying to yourself, something along those lines?"

"That's about it."

"Well, if that's it, isn't the solution to your problem fairly obvious?"

"—Uh—well, I guess so. Stop saying the false sentences and keep telling myself only the true ones. Is that right?"

"Exactly right. Stop telling yourself how awful, how dreadful it would be if you failed sexually, and how that would make you into a homosexual— which again would be a frightful thing. And go back to the true sentence— that you are missing most of the joy of sex—and work on correcting this sentence by focusing on your wife and how pleasurable it is to be with her, instead of how terrible it is to be impotent or to prove what a pansy you are."

"But what will I tell Janie, while I'm working on this? Shall I discuss it with her too?"

"By all means. The next time you and Janie decide to get together sexually, tell her something like this: 'Look, dear. The psychotherapist I went to see about my problem told me the trouble is strictly in my head. It consists of nonsense that I have been feeding myself. He says that what you and I need to do is to take a more indirect approach to this sex business at first. We would do better to forget coitus as the ultimate end and largely concentrate on having *fun* with each other sexually. The idea is for us to have a pleasurable experience and not care whether I do or don't have an erection. You caress me in any way that seems fun to you and me, and I'll fondle you in any way that seems enjoyable to both of us. And, as we've been doing already, I'll make sure that you're always satisfied one way or another. Then, he says, if we stop worrying about whether or not I'm going to get a good erection, my body will almost certainly take care of itself and soon I'll be more potent than I've probably ever been before. But the main point is: whether or not I do achieve anything in coitus, we can still enjoy the experience immensely. And if we concentrate on that, most of our problem will be solved.'"

"Well I hear what you're saying and it sounds good. But it also sounds just a little bit crazy. Aren't we just kidding ourselves, Janie and I, if we say that we don't give a damn whether or not I get an erection?"

"No, not really. As Janie has already demonstrated, she, like practically all women, can have an orgasm even when you are *not* showing great prowess sexually; and I am sure that you, too, can get a great deal of enjoyment even when you are not realizing your potential. Many of my patients, in fact, keep having enjoyable relations even though they do not always have actual coitus. Granted that both you and Janie may well enjoy yourself *more* if you are fully potent; but you can still satisfy each other when you are not.

"The main point is that if you stop focusing on the *necessity* of copulating well with Janie, and look upon doing so as a highly *desirable* thing instead, the chances are at least a hundred to one that you soon will be perfectly potent and will be able to have completely satisfactory intercourse. But remember this: You must not take this approach insincerely and try to fool yourself that you believe it. It is not likely to work if you falsely say to yourself. I will pretend to have fun in other ways since it will help me to get an erection with which I can then have coitus, because it will be terrible if I cannot eventually have coitus. You must really *convince yourself*, really believe that it is *not* terrible if you never have coitus—merely that it is undesirable and inconvenient."

"So I must really show myself that even though I *want* coitus I don't *need* it. I must convince myself that having *fun*, not copulating, is the main thing in my sex relations with Janie."

"Right. If you focus on trying to have fun, you will almost certainly be able to copulate. But if you focus on copulating, you may well not be able to have any fun."

After this talk the patient had sex relations with his wife that very night, had a long talk with her along the lines suggested by the therapist, and simply tried to enjoy himself rather than to achieve potency. For the first time in years, he not only did enjoy himself, but was able to maintain an erection for twenty minutes and to have the most effective copulatory experience of his life.

The idea that one should be thoroughly competent, adequate, and achieving in virtually all respects boils down to the notion that one should be superhuman rather than human; and that is palpably a ridiculous dictate. This inane idea, however, is remorselessly propagated in our homes, schools, books, newspapers, movies, advertisements, songs, TV shows, and every other medium of mass communication. Other cultures, too, have taught their people that they should excel in various ways; but none, perhaps, to the enormous degree to which we teach this nonsense to *our* people.

What, instead of believing this kind of balderdash, should the thinking individual believe, and how should he act in regard to competence and achievement?

First of all, we should say, the rational person should fully understand that the only absolute requisite for a reasonably happy life is that he must *do* rather than that he must *do well*. This is not to say that it is never *desirable* for an individual to do well. Often, it is; since by doing well you gain more of the goods, services, and favors in life than you gain by doing poorly. And that is fine. But not *necessary*.

Enjoyment, then, rather than accomplishment is the more sensible goal to seek in living. Often, the two are related: the better you play tennis, the more you are likely to enjoy the game. But if you enjoy *only* what you do well, then you are fairly obviously saying to yourself (a) "I like this activity because it is my natural cup of tea," and (b) "I like it because I am proving how much better I am than others in performing it."

While (a) is a perfectly legitimate sentence, (b) is not. The "ego-raising" that you obtain from proving superior to others at any activity is actually *false* pride, which stems from the notion that you are no damned good *unless* you better others' performances. This kind of "ego-raising" will last only so long as you succeed in what you are doing, and in the last analysis demands perfect performance and absolute superiority over others.

The truly rational and sane person, therefore, mainly enjoys himself because he is *playing* the game and only incidentally because he is *succeeding* at it. Artistically, he is interested in bettering his own *performance* but is little obsessed with out-performing *others*. He accepts the fact that he may do well under *some* circumstances, but hardly under *all*; and that even when he is accomplishing what he set out to do, he practically never will be a *perfect* achiever. He frequently has high but not unrealistic levels of aspiration. And if he fails to achieve what he would like to achieve he is disappointed but not desolate, he regrets his failure but does not view *himself* as worthless.

Because the thinking individual approaches the problem of achievement in a rational manner, he is more likely to do well at what he wants to do than the person who desperately *needs* to succeed. For he will learn to welcome his mistakes and errors, instead of being petrified by them, and he will *use* them to better his future performances. He will realize that *practice* more than anything else, makes perfect, and that, being a fallible human, only continual practice will help him to eliminate his errors and to better his performances. He will also, not being afraid of error, be risk-taking and committable; and will consequently *try* many tasks that he otherwise would avoid trying and would, of course, never succeed at because he didn't try.

If, then, you would like to succeed at some project, profession, or artistic endeavor, and are willing unblamefully to accept yourself (and others) in case you make an honest attempt and fail, you will try to do *your* best rather than *the* best, and you will not falsely invest your "ego" in your try. You will honestly strive to win mastery over your material, and perhaps over yourself; but you will not try to demonstrate that you are a better *person* than others.

A twenty-five-year-old physicist came to therapy because he constantly felt that he was failing. His feelings of failure were all the more remarkable because, objectively viewed, he was doing very well in his work and appeared not only normal but supernormal. Not only had he obtained his Ph.D. at an early age but in addition to his academic achievements had played on the college football, baseball, and basketball teams. He was tall, muscular, and good-looking; and, at the age of 25, was well on his way to becoming one of the country's leading physicists. Here was an individual who had almost everything—and was, nonetheless, terribly unhappy.

"The whole trouble," said the patient at one of his early psychotherapy sessions, "is that I am really a phony. I am living under false pretenses. And the longer it goes on, the more people praise me and make a fuss over my accomplishments, the worse I feel."

"What do you mean you are a phony?" asked the therapist. "I thought that you told me, during our last session, that your work has been examined at another laboratory and that some of the people there think your ideas are of revolutionary importance. They are certainly not the kind of scientists to be fooled by pretenders in the field."

"Oh, that data and my interpretations are probably sound enough. But I have wasted so much time. I could be doing very much better. Just this morning I sat in my office, stared into space, and accomplished nothing at all. I do this often. Also, when I actually work on my problems I often do not think with the clarity and the precision that I should. Just the other day I caught myself making a mistake that a college junior wouldn't have made. And in trying to write the paper that I am working on for the next meeting of my regional professional organization I am taking many hours to do what I should be able to knock out in an hour or two at most."

"Aren't you being just a little bit hard on yourself?"

"No, I don't think so. Remember that book I told you I was writing for popular consumption, why, it's been three weeks now since I've spent any time on it. And this is simple stuff that I should be able to do with my left hand while I am writing a technical paper with my right. I have heard Bob Oppenheimer reel off stuff extemporaneously to a bunch of newspaper reporters that is twice as good as what I am mightily laboring on in this damned book!"

"Perhaps so. And perhaps you're not quite as good—yet—as Oppenheimer or a few other outstanding people in your field. But that's not the point. The real point, it seems to me, is that you have the most ridiculous perfectionistic standards for judging yourself that I've heard in, well the last few months. And I hear about perfectionism practically every day in the week! But here *you* are, at just twenty-five, with a Ph.D. in a most difficult field, with an excellent job, much good work in process, and what well may be a fine professional paper and a good popular book also in progress. And just because you're not another Oppenheimer or Einstein quite yet, you're savagely berating yourself."

"Well, *shouldn't* I be doing much better than I am?"

"No, why the devil *should* you? As far as I can see, you are not doing badly at all. But your major difficulty—the main cause of your present unhappiness—is your utterly perfectionistic criteria for judging your performance. You pick the *one* physicist, such as Oppenheimer, who is truly outstanding at communicating his views to the public, and you lament that you are not doing as well as he. And you compare yourself, at one relatively uncreative time in your life, with your most furiously creative periods. Studies have been made of the creative process—of creators such as Oppenheimer, Einstein, Newton, and Rutherford—and they demonstrate beyond dispute that it is an uneven kind of activity. Nobody, and I mean *nobody*, just steadily creates. In fact, it has also been shown that during those periods in which the creator putters, stares out of the window, and apparently just wastes time, he may be dredging up and recombining ideas on which he later will focus his full attention and which may turn out to be among his very best creations."

"That may be so. But that does not prove that *my* periods of staring out of the window are truly creative."

"Right you are, it doesn't prove that. But let us suppose that you do waste a fair amount of time staring out of the window. Why is this horrible? Why must you be so perfect, so everlastingly productive?"

"Well, I need to produce. I need to utilize my genius fully—that is, if I am not a phony."

"Why? What's the hurry? What's the compulsion? Suppose you do have great talent—are a potential Newton or Einstein. Are you obligated to work perfectly, like some unimaginably wonderful brain machine that turns out the maximum number of brilliant ideas before it ever stops running? It would be nice, perhaps, if you did, and might well advance human knowledge. But why *must* you? If you *enjoy* fulfilling your creative potential to the hilt, fine. But is this self-berating, this constantly pushing yourself to your absolute utmost limits—is this *enjoyable*?

"So you don't think I owe it to myself or to mankind to make use of my potential productivity?"

"No, I don't. If you owe anything to yourself, it is to enjoy yourself fully, not just for the moment but for most of your life. And if perfect, maximum productiveness on your part *were* the best manner of long-ranged enjoyment, that would be glorious. But *is* it? Or would you be far wiser—and perhaps even in the long run more creatively productive—if you worked *somewhat near* your potential capacity, if you were *reasonably* productive, instead of your striving for *perfect* achievement? And would it not be better, for both you and society, if you strove for *your* fulfillment as a scientist, rather than, as you fairly obviously are, to outdoing *others?*"

It was a hard, tough therapeutic battle. But ultimately the patient agreed that he was compulsively achievement-bound and that he could more wisely follow a more moderate approach to mastering his chosen field. As he reported at one of the closing therapeutic sessions:

"I always used to try to do the best I could, as if my life depended on it. Now I still try to finish each of my projects in the best way I know how—but *not* as if it were a crime if I failed. If my *best* isn't quite good enough now, that's too bad: but I *accept* it as my best. I work more efficiently and enjoy my work more since I stopped giving myself hell. If I can enjoyably accomplish what I want to do today, I'll do it. If somehow I can't finish it today, I always remember, now, that there is a tomorrow. And if some of the things I want to do *never* get finished, that's just too bad. As you once said to me, I'm no goddam god or angel; and for a change I now really accept my mortal limitations."

Was, through this kind of therapy, potential genius lost to mankind? Not at all. Since he has begun enjoying himself at his work, this young physicist has made even more outstanding contributions than before and is already considered to be one of the top young men in his field. Instead of being less productive, he is in many ways more so; and the only things that seem to have been lost are his perfectionism and unhappiness.

We most definitely are not opposed to mastery and achievement drives. People with excellent brain cells are normally impelled to use their heads to create new, original, superior artistic, scientific, industrial, and other products. Long may they be so impelled! Maximum happiness, in their cases, is almost synonymous with creative striving. As long as they do not insist on an utterly perfectionistic never-a-wasted-moment philosophy.

As we often say to our patients: There are several good reasons why a man may choose to climb the highest available mountain. He may, for example, enjoy climbing; delight in the challenge this difficult peak presents; or want to thrill to the view from the top. But there are also bad reasons for climbing the same mountain: especially, to look contemptuously down on the people below.

How
12 \ to Stop Blaming
and Start Living

THE ESSENCE OF mental disturbance can be designated in a single word: blaming. If any human being would stop, really stop, blaming himself, others, or unkind fate it would be virtually impossible for him to be emotionally upset about anything. And you can probably omit "virtually" from the preceding sentence.

But we do, all of us, tend to be severe blamers. And we specifically tend to hold tenaciously to Irrational Idea No. 3: *The idea that certain people are bad, wicked, or villainous and that they should be severely blamed and punished for their sins.* This idea, which is the working hypothesis for a considerable portion of human behavior and interpersonal relations, is thoroughly invalid and irrational for several important reasons:

1. The idea that certain people are wicked or villainous springs from the ancient theological doctrine of free will. And although it is probably not accurate to say that man has *no* free choice whatever, modern psychoanalytic findings have fairly conclusively shown that he has exceptionally little free will in the sense that this term is usually employed in theological discussion. As Fenichel, Freud, Jones, and other analytic writers have indicated, and as many psychological experiments during the last fifty years have proven, humans learn or are conditioned to behave in certain ways from their earliest childhood years; and, once they are significantly oriented in a given "good" or "bad" direction, and unconsciously hold philosophies of living that drive them to follow certain behavioral pathways, it is most difficult (although not impossible) for them to change. In these circum-

stances, blaming an individual for his wrongdoing is to unfairly attribute to him a perfect freedom of choice of behavior which he simply does not have.

2. The idea that people are "bad" or "wicked" as a result of their wrong-doings is based on a second erroneous notion: namely, the concept that it is easy to define "good" and "bad" or "ethical" and "unethical" behavior and that any reasonable person can readily see when he is acting "right" and when he is "wrong." The last century of philosophic and psychological discussion has again demonstrated that morality is a relative concept; that it differs widely according to places and circumstances; that people in a *given* locality rarely reach a unanimous decision as to what is truly "good" or "bad;" and that most people, when even they theoretically "know" or accept certain standards of "good" conduct, easily and unconsciously rationalize their own behavior and find "good" reasons for doing the "wrong" things. To excoriate humans for their difficulties in defining and accepting "good" behavior is therefore unrealistic and unjust.

3. Even when standards of "wrongdoing" are fairly well agreed upon, it is senseless to blame people for not following these standards. For the main purpose of ethical principles is to induce wrongdoers to say to themselves: (a) "I have done a wrong or immoral act" and (b) "Therefore, how am I going to correct myself and not repeat this kind of act in the future?" But blaming human beings for their mistaken behavior almost invariably induces them to say quite a different set of sentences: (a) "I have done a wrong or immoral act" and (b) "What a louse I am for doing this act!" (Ellis).

Once the individual accepts the concept of blame and devalues himself as a human being for having done a wrong act he will tend either to consider himself worthless and inadequate (instead of merely mistaken or unethical); or will (rather than devalue himself) refuse to admit that he was wrong in his original act; or may even refuse to admit that he committed the act at all. Otherwise stated: by believing in blame and punishment for sin, the individual will tend to feel worthless, become obsessively-compulsively obsessed with his wrongdoing, deny that his act was wrong, or repress knowledge of his wrong deed. In any event, he will practically never get around to the relatively simple act of *correcting* his behavior, because (due to self-blame) he is preoccupied with either punishing himself or refusing to admit that he was ever wrong in the first place. Blame or guilt, then, instead of alleviating wrongdoing, often leads to further immorality, hypocrisy, and evasion of responsibility.

4. Anyone who accepts the philosophy of blaming himself for his errors will tend to be so afraid of making further errors that he will forego experimentation, risk-taking, and commitment to life.

5. Blaming yourself or others for your "sins" leads to an evasion of sane

morality. Normally, you should be a moral individual, who does not needlessly harm his fellows, not because you will be a louse or a "sinner" if you
are immoral, but because in the last analysis you will harm yourself and
your loved ones. If you gratuitously interfere with the rights of others, they
or their friends or relatives will tend to retaliate against you or your friends
or relatives; and even if you personally escape scot-free, you will thereby
help set up an anarchistic, unjust system of living under which you would
normally not want to live. Out of enlightened self-interest, therefore, you
should be as moral as possible in accordance with the rules of your community; and you should not be unthinkingly moral because some arbitrary
or definitional god or convention says that you should be.

6. Blaming an individual means to confuse his wrong *acts* with his sinful *being*. But no matter how many evil acts an individual performs, *he* cannot be intrinsically evil for the very good reason that he could, today or tomorrow, change his behavior completely and commit no additional wrong
deeds. Just as a man who continually fails is never really *a* failure (but
simply one who *so far* has frequently failed), one who has often been wrong
or immoral is never *a* sinner. A person's (good or bad) acts are the *results*
of his being but they are never that *being* itself. His intrinsic value, as we
must keep repeating throughout this book, has nothing essentially to do
with his extrinsic value, or his worth to others. To call a man a criminal, a
blackguard, or a villain implies that because he has in the past committed
wrong acts he *must*, by his very nature, continue to do so in the future; and
this is simply untrue. And once we label a person as *a* sinner, we appreciably
help to give *him* the conviction that he is hopeless and that he cannot stop
doing the wrong thing in the future. Wrong –

7. To blame another person (or oneself) inevitably means to become
angry or hostile toward this other—to feel that he *should* not do what he did
(instead of, sanely, that it would have been *better* if he had not done it; but,
let's face it, he did commit his wrong deed; now how are we going to help
him not commit it again in the future?) Feelings of anger are invariably re-
flections of one's own grandiosity. One essentially says, by feeling angry,
(a) I do not like Joe's behavior and (b) because I do not like it, he *shouldn't*
have acted that way. The second sentence here is actually a grandiose non
sequitur: because there really *is* no reason why Joe *shouldn't* have acted the
way he did, merely because I do not like the way he acted. I am being unrealistic and god-like when I believe that *my* (or anyone else's) preference
regarding Joe's behavior *should* make Joe act differently from the way he
has acted.

It would certainly be *nice* if Joe acted the way I wanted; but there is still
no reason why he *should*. Consequently, my anger against Joe really results
from *my* grandiose interpretation of his act and not from his wrong act

itself; and I am being at least slightly insane in expecting Joe to act in any way different from the way in which he actually did act. I can legitimately *like* him to act differently, but not *expect* him to do so. And I would better start putting my own thinking in order if I have such unrealistic expectations.

8. Blaming oneself or others not only leads to anger, as just noted, but to many unpleasant consequences of hostility. Even if I am quite right about Joe's acts being wrong or immoral, my belief that he *shouldn't* be (humanly) wrong and my subsequent anger will hardly serve to stop Joe from acting badly again (in fact, it may give him an incentive to continue acting wrongly just *because* I hate him and he hates me back); but it will almost always stir up my guts, cause me to have unpleasant feelings, lead to possible ulcers or high blood pressure in my case, and deflect me from the real problem: which is how can I calmly and effectively induce Joe not to act badly again. Fist fights, duels, capital punishment, international wars —in fact virtually every violent aspect of man's inhumanity to man that you can think of—have frequently resulted from one individual's grandiosely and unhelpfully blaming another individual whose actions he (perhaps quite rightly) considers wrong. And just as two wrongs never make a right, anger against a wrongdoer is probably the most pernicious manner of trying to correct him.

9. As pointed out in one of our prior books, *Sex Without Guilt* (Ellis), anyone who roundly blames another human being for what he (often arbitrarily) considers to be this other's wrong behavior inevitably will tend to turn his blaming standards on himself and will end up with considerable self-loathing. Lack of forgiveness toward others breeds lack of self-forgiveness, with consequent perfectionistic attitudes toward one's own failings and incompetencies. To devalue another as a human being because he has made some serious mistakes is to devalue the whole human race, including one's own humanity. Man's inhumanity to man begins and ends with irrational blame and anger.

An illustration of blaming and self-blaming tendencies may be seen in the case of Mr. and Mrs. James Smart, who came to therapy largely because of their mutual hostility, and who were seen together during most of the therapeutic and marriage counseling sessions. Mr. Smart was a newspaper man who had gained a national reputation by his accurate and objective reporting of inter-racial tensions and struggles in his home town, in the South. He was offered an important job with a large metropolitan daily, which meant a considerable advancement in both prestige and pay. After talking over the offer with Mrs. Smart (who expressed fears and misgivings, but no definite objections), he accepted.

Mr. Smart came to the big city ahead of his family to find a house; and here the trouble began. For twice the amount they had invested in their home in the small Southern town from which they came, he found that they would only be able to obtain inferior quarters in the North. Not having any considerable savings, he rented a large apartment "to give them a place to live while they hunted for a home."

The rest of the story will probably be familiar enough to those who make good salaries but reside in cities where the living costs are high. Smart's considerable increase in income was soon fully consumed by the high rent, higher costs of food, clothing, and other expenses; and by the recreational activities and meals away from home which seemed necessary to give Mrs. Smart and the children a relief from their close living quarters in an apartment which hardly resembled the "barn of a house" to which they had previously been accustomed. There were, in short, no savings accumulated which could be used to purchase a suitable house.

On top of these family living problems, Mr. Smart was increasingly disappointed with his new job. He had administrative responsibilities for which he was poorly prepared and in which he lacked interest. His superior on the new newspaper put up a front of being a liberal newspaper man of the old time tradition but in practice whenever his employees tried to report the news fearlessly he began to jump and tremble for fear that some large advertiser would be alarmed and would withdraw his support.

By the time Mr. and Mrs. Smart came for psychotherapy, they were in despair. Family and professional happiness seemed to be lost forever. Mrs. Smart was blaming her husband for being stupid about his profession and for not caring about her and the children. Mr. Smart was blaming himself for misjudging his new job and for managing the living conditions so poorly. He also felt that his wife was highly uncooperative, sexually frigid, and a poor mother.

One of the early sessions with this couple ran as follows:

Mrs. S: And just to make things worse, Doctor, as if they weren't bad enough already, he's even taken to staying out after work and drinking. He can't be a *good* newspaper man any more, so he has to *act* like one by sitting around at the bar and telling the boys how well he could have covered the Battle of Bull Run.

Mr. S.: There's more bull running around home these days than anywhere else. Why should I come home to hear you read that same old speech about what a louse I am?

Therapist: I think you've both made it quite clear what kinds of complaints you have against each other. Now, just for the sake of discussion let's assume for a moment that you, Mr. Smart, have been making some absolutely inexcusable, selfish, and malicious mistakes.

Mrs. S.: I didn't say 'malicious.' I don't think he thought enough about it to have any malice. But I'll go along with the other adjectives.

Mr. S.: I'll say she will! And a few other choice invectives, if you can think of any. She has no difficulty at all in dreaming them up by the thousands.

Therapist: O.K. Let's grant for the time being that your husband, Mrs. Smart, has made some real horrible mistakes. We *could* make a number of fairly legitimate excuses for him. We could point out, for example, that he couldn't possibly have known, with his past experiences, how bad things would be in this new city, and that therefore his mistakes were only normal. But let's waive all these extenuating circumstances and just plainly state that he made a series of stupid errors—and that he's still making them, including the drinking with the boys. All right: so what? So he's made mistakes. Now what's the possible value of your savagely denouncing him for his errors? How helpful are you being by your denunciations?

Mrs. S.: Well—but—! Do you expect me to give him a medal or something for acting like such an idiot? And then for making things worse with this weak-livered running away from the problem into the demon alcohol? Do you expect me to comfort him, like a good wife, and to cheer him on to *more* mistakes along the same order?

Therapist: No, not exactly. Though you might be surprised, if you really tried it, how well your satirically-made suggestion might work. But let's not ask you to go to *that* extreme. The real point is: granted that your husband has made serious mistakes, what good will *blaming* him do? Has your blame made him commit fewer mistakes? Has it made him feel more kindly toward you? Has it made *you* feel happier in your own right?

Mrs. S.: Well, no. I can't say that it has.

Therapist: Nor will it ever, in all probability. For the more you blame your husband—or anyone else, for that matter—the more defensive he will usually become and less *likely* to admit his errors, least of all to you. As we saw a minute ago: when you were criticizing him, his main line of defense was to be sarcastic to you. And this is a normal human tendency: to protect yourself against blame by blaming back the one who is attacking you.

Mrs. S.: Oh, he's pretty good at that, I must admit!

Therapist: Yes, but who isn't? And the point is: the more he is blaming you back, after you keep jumping on him, the less he is going to face the real problem at hand: which is—"Now let's see. I did badly this time; how can I change my ways and do better next time?" Moreover, the more he *accepts* your blame, and beats himself down the way *you* are trying to beat him down, the less he will be *able* to cope with the real problem, even if he faces it. For he will keep saying to himself: "My wife is right. I *am* no good. How could I have been so stupid? What a perfect fool I was! She's absolutely right. And how can such an idiot get out of this mess that I've gotten myself into? She's right: I'm just about hopeless. No use trying to do the thing over again, I'll just mess it up even worse. I might just as well drink myself into a stupor and forget about the whole horrible business since I'll never be able to resolve it anyhow."

Mr. S.: You're hitting it right on the head! That's exactly what I have been saying to myself. And who wouldn't—when his own wife keeps telling him, over and over, what a hopeless fool and an incompetent louse he is?

Therapist: Right. Who wouldn't? Almost everyone in this society would. And they'd all, every one of them, be one hundred per cent wrong.

Mr. S.: Wrong? But you just said that it was natural for me to feel that way when my wife kept beating me down like that.

Therapist: Yes—*statistically* natural, in that the great majority of husbands would do exactly what you have done. But that still doesn't mean that they would be *right* in doing so, or that they'd *have* to do so.

Mr. S.: But what else could I have done? What would you expect me to do?

Therapist: I would *expect* you to do nothing other than you did. But I would *hope*, once I induced you to acquire a new idea or two, that you would not do what you did, accept your wife's blame and use it to belabor *yourself* with, even though the majority of husbands *would* do exactly that.

Mr. S.: And what is this new idea or two you're talking about?

Therapist: Mainly the idea that you don't *have* to accept anyone's negative views of you and use them against yourself—even when these views contain some amount of truth.

Mr. S.: But how can you help accepting them in those circumstances—when you know you're wrong?

Therapist: Very simply. By following what we call the A-B-C theory of rational therapy. A, in this case, is the fact that you've done badly and that your wife is castigating you for your mistakes. And C is the fact that you're accepting her blame and are taking her critical arrows and sticking them in your own heart. You look at A, what seems to be her justifiable blame, and at C, what seems to be your own justifiable self-castigation, and you say to yourself: "Well, A naturally leads to C. Why shouldn't I blame myself if she's right about blaming me?"

Mr. S.: Well, *doesn't* A lead to C in this case? Shouldn't I admit my mistakes and blame myself for them? How else will I ever change?

Therapist: No, A does not automatically lead to C as you think it does. Rather, A leads to B—which is your interpretation of A. And B is based on your general philosophy of life, which you (as well as your wife) have learned in this silly society, to the effect that one *should* be blamed for doing the wrong thing, for making mistakes. Therefore, when your wife verbally rips you up at A, you *interpret* her criticism as being accurate and good at B, and then *you* accept it at C and do great damage to yourself, by considering yourself hopeless, taking to drink, and so on.

Mr. S.: But I still say: *Isn't* she right in criticizing me at A?

Therapist: No. She would be right if she calmly, objectively called to your attention at A the fact that you are making the wrong moves, committing errors. But that is *not* what she is doing by her criticism. She is *first* calling your wrongdoing to your attention and *then* saying: "But you *shouldn't* be doing wrong, you louse! You have no *right* to be acting so stupidly." And this is ridiculous: for every human being has a right to be wrong. And even though it may be highly *undesirable* for him to make mistakes, it is only human for him to do so, and he is *not* a louse.

Mrs. S.: So I should just calmly call my husband's errors to his attention and try to help him do better in the future. Is that it?

Therapist: Right. His mistakes are past. Now the question is: What can be done about improving the present situation? What are some of the realities that both of you can face to make the future different from the past? What can both of you learn from your errors? What can you do now that will make life more enjoyable for you and your children?

Mr. S.: I'm beginning to see what you mean. And I guess that one thing I can do is to stop acting like an ostrich by sticking my head in the corner bar.

Mrs. S.: If that's a promise, I'll match it with one of my own. I'll stop blaming you for your past mistakes—including what I thought was the mistake of dragging us in here to confess all our woes to the Doctor. I'm glad I came. The Doctor is right: it *is* understandable, now that I look at it that way, how you could have made this move, and got the wrong apartment, and made those other mistakes. I guess I haven't exactly been an angel myself.

Mr. S.: Wow! I wish I had brought along a tape recorder to get down that historic statement! That admission has made more history than Bull Run ever did. But you're right: I can see now that it is understandable how I could have made those idiotic moves. And how you could have been so un-angelic, too! Hell, if we'd only spend some of this self-blaming and blaming-the-other time in looking at our real problems, I'm sure we'd get much farther with them.

Therapist: You see. Turn off the heat of blaming and you are already feeling better about yourselves and each other. Now let's see if we can't get both of you to do less and less blaming and more and more problem-solving in the future. In which case you'll still be left with some real hassles, but none of them should be insoluble.

Which proved to be quite true. Months later, after Mr. Smart had managed to secure another job in a middle-sized city, purchased (with his wife's full consent) a small house, and cut his drinking almost to zero, the therapist received this letter from Mrs. Smart: "James the First is reigning benignly and supremely in his new job. If you didn't see his syndicated series on Jim Crowism in the North, let me know and I'll modestly mail copies of the articles to you. Home is wonderful—just like home. All the kids and Jim and I have made a lot of fine friends. The children like their school. I like the house and the neighborhood. And, though we are probably prejudiced, we all seem to like each other. What was that you said about blame? Never heard of the word. Thanks and love."

What can you do to catch your blaming yourself and others and to tackle and challenge the irrational assumptions behind your blaming? Several things:

1. Whenever you become depressed or guilty you should recognize that you must, on some level, be blaming yourself, and should immediately try to track down the specific sentences you are telling yourself to create this blame. Generally, you will be saying to yourself: (a) "I was wrong in doing this (or not doing that)" and (b) "I therefore am no good or worthless for being wrong." And you must change these sentences to: (a) "Perhaps I was definitely wrong about doing this (or not doing that)"; (b) "This is what human beings are— frequently wrong"; (c) "Now how do I find out exactly what was wrong about my behavior and calmly go about correcting it *next* time?"

2. Resolving to correct your misdeeds in the future will frequently not suffice, any more than resolving to be a good pianist will make you one. You can only play the piano, or diet, or correct your past errors in the future by *work* and *practice*—by literally *forcing* yourself to follow a new path. Thus, if you want to be moral, you must literally force yourself to be honest, responsible, and non-injurious to others. And you must convince yourself that although it is often easier *in the short run* to be dishonest, irresponsible, and injurious to others, long-range self-interest and happiness will be achieved only by your own moral behavior.

Rational morality, in other words, is not achieved by saying to yourself: "I have done wrong; I am a blackguard; therefore I must stop my misdeeds in the future." It is only achieved by saying: "I have done wrong; I will keep defeating my *own* ends and helping create the kind of a world in which *I* do not want to live if I continue to do wrong; therefore I would better change my ways." And to surrender self-blame you require not only Insight No. 1—"I am looking upon myself as a louse because I was propagandized to do so by my parents, teachers, and others."—but also Insight No. 2—"If I am to stop looking upon myself as a louse, I must *work* at challenging the assumptions I have derived from my past propagandization by others and must keep *acting* against my self-defeating beliefs."

3. You should learn to distinguish between *responsibility* and *blame*. You are often responsible for your poor behavior, in the sense that you actually *did* it and theoretically *could have* not done it. But because you are responsible for your activities does not mean that you are a worthless person for performing them—that you are to blame for them.

4. You should try to distinguish between behavior which is *actually* and that which is *seemingly* wrong. Having premarital sex experience, for example, is *said* to be wrong by many religious and community groups. But do *you* think that it really is? Do *you* believe that you are actually needlessly, definitely harming anyone, including yourself, when you have such relations on a voluntary basis?

Do not merely unthinkingly *accept* a given act as wrong or immoral; but *determine*, as best you can, whether it is truly so in *your* eyes. If you *have* to conform to certain laws, even though you do not believe in their value, then (in order to avoid bringing down certain community penalties on yourself) do your best to conform to them. But if there are certain customs, rather than laws, which you disagree with and that you are not forced to conform to, then by all means stand up against them or quietly flout them in some instances—as long as you do not too badly defeat your own ends by your rebellion.

5. When you find that you are angry at or hostile to others, admit your own grandiosity and perfectionism. If you merely dislike or are annoyed or irritated at others' actions, that is quite legitimate: since you are then *preferring* that they should act differently and being frustrated or disappointed when they don't. But anger means you are telling yourself: "I don't like what Dick is doing; and therefore he *shouldn't* be doing it," instead of: "I don't like what Dick is doing; now let me see how I can persuade him or help him to act differently." The thing to do, in these circumstances, is to tackle your *own* grandiosity and to force yourself—yes, force yourself—to accept Dick the way he is, at least temporarily, and thereby to undo the blame and anger that *you* are creating.

If, by employing the foregoing techniques and others that you can devise to supplement them, you keep challenging and contradicting your self-blaming and other-blaming tendencies, you will not end up as a saint or a pollyanna. You will still, on many occasions, thoroughly *dislike* your own and others' behavior. But you will have a much better chance of changing what you dislike instead of boiling in your own juices. To err is human; to forgive is to be sane and realistic.

How to be Happy
Though Frustrated

13

NINETY-NINE AND NINE-TENTHS per cent of the people in this world seem to be inextricably wedded to a thoroughly false notion: that they must be unhappy when they are frustrated. Even most contemporary psychologists believe the famous Dollard-Miller hypothesis: that frustration necessarily leads to aggression. And they are all, these millions of lawmen and thousands of psychologists, almost one hundred per cent wrong.

The frustration-aggression hypothesis stems from Irrational Idea No. 4: *The idea that it is terrible, horrible, and catastrophic when things are not going the way one would like them to go.* This idea is false for several reasons, including these:

1. Although it is indubitably unpleasant or unfortunate when you do not get what you want out of life, it is rarely catastrophic or horrible unless you *think* that it is. When things are going badly, you have the choice, as a human being, of saying: (a) "I don't like this situation. Now let's see what I can do to change it. And if I can't change it, that's tough but not necessarily catastrophic." Or you can say: (b) "I don't like this situation. I can't stand it. It's driving me crazy. It shouldn't be this way. It's simply got to change, otherwise I can't possibly be happy." The second of these chains of sentences will, sure as shooting, lead you to be miserable, self-pitying, depressed, or hostile. The first set of sentences will lead you to be undelighted and regretful but not necessarily dejected or angry.

2. Although children are frequently not able to tolerate any amount of frustration, there is no reason why adults cannot calmly do so. Children are

112

almost entirely at the mercy of their environment. They cannot easily look ahead to the future and see that if they are *now* frustrated they may not *perpetually* be. Children, moreover, cannot be expected to be old enough or bright enough to be *philosophic* about their frustrations. Not so adults. Adults, if they are not mentally deficient, *can* see an end to their present frustrations; *can* change their own environments in most instances; *can* philosophically *accept* their existing life handicaps when these cannot, for the nonce, be changed.

3. If you make yourself—yes, *make* yourself—terribly upset and unhappy about your frustrations, you will almost invariably block yourself from effectively removing them. The more time and energy you expend in lamenting your sorry fate, ranting against your frustrators, and gnashing your teeth in despair, the less effective action you will be able to take in counteracting your handicaps and dealing with those who may be frustrating you. Even if you are correct in your surmise that it is unfair and unethical for others to block your wishes—so what? So it is unfair and unethical. Who said that people *shouldn't* be unfair and unethical—however nice it would be if they weren't?

4. In the case of inevitable and unchangeable frustrations—when your parent or mate dies, for instance, and you cannot possibly bring him or her back to life—it is particularly senseless upsetting yourself because you are deprived of something you want very much. So you are deprived! Will your wailing and moaning bring back your loved one? Will your ranting at unkind fate really make you feel better? Why not, instead, maturely accept the inevitable, however unpleasant it may be?

5. Whether you like it or not, you simply *must* accept reality when you cannot change it. Reality *is;* and if it is unfortunate and frustrating, that is bad; but it is still not necessarily catastrophic. As long as *you* are still alive and in reasonably good health, you are the master of your fate, you are the captain of your soul. Reality may block and defeat your ends. Sometimes it can even kill you. But it cannot, while you are still alive, truly defeat *you.* Only *you* can defeat yourself—if you believe that what is *shouldn't* be, that because you are beset you *must* be unhappy.

Let us look at a few illustrative cases. Mary Manahan kept coming to see me (A.E.) for session after session, always complaining that her husband didn't love her, that he never gave her the things she wanted, and that he was therefore a no-good son-of-a-gun. Her complaints, from what I could see, were at least half-justified; for Tim Manahan was hardly the best husband in the world and most women who might have been married to him would have complained bitterly about his inconsideration and neglect. But even after admitting this to Mary, I still refused to buy her complaints. Then, as I had expected, she turned her anger on me.

"But look here," she exclaimed, "you've seen Tim for yourself and you admit that he's often unkind and inconsiderate to me—especially now that I'm pregnant again and in need of additional help. How can you say that I've got no right to complain?"

"Oh, I didn't say that at all," I calmly replied. "You have every right in the world to complain, if you want to—just as you have every right in the world to commit suicide, if that is what you want. The only point I am really making is that if you *do* keep complaining, as you have been doing for the last several weeks, you might just as well cut your throat—for that is what you really are doing. You are just raising your own blood pressure all the time. And what good will *that* do you and your unborn child?"

"But you don't seem to understand. It's *his* fault that I'm unhappy. *He's* the one that's acting badly, not me."

"True: he's acting badly. But you're acting even worse. All the more reason, since he is doing you no good by his behavior, that you should not do likewise. And, compared to the harm *you're* doing yourself, he's acting almost like an angel. For *you're* the one who's really killing yourself, not him."

"But how can I stop him from acting the way he is? That's the real problem, as I see it."

"Yes—as you see it. But the problem as I see it is, first: How can you stop *you* from acting the way *you* are? Then maybe you'll have a chance to help change him."

"What do you mean? How will my acting differently change him?"

"Very simply. You say that your husband loves you much less than you want him to and acts much worse than you would want him to act. And with these statements I agree: since I can see for myself, by talking to him, that he doesn't love you too much or act too well with you."

"See! Even you agree that he treats me badly."

"Yes, even I agree. But that's not the point. The point is that the worse you treat *him*, because he treats you so badly, the worse still he will tend to treat you. And the more you beat him over the head for *not* loving you, the less he will tend to love you. If you really want him to treat you better— which you say you do, but make no efforts to arrange—then you should obviously love him more and treat him less critically—especially when he is being nasty and inconsiderate. For if you can give a human being love and kindness when he does not, by his actions, merit it, he will clearly see that you must *really* love him. And if, in those circumstances, he does not love you more and act better toward you, nothing, I am afraid, will do the trick of winning him more to your side."

"But he was the one who started to treat me badly wasn't he?"

"No matter. If he treats you badly, then you criticize him for treating you badly, he will only, as he has done, end up by treating you still worse. In fact, he'll probably forget that he *did* treat you badly in the first place, and claim that he treats you badly now *because* you're criticizing him."

"That's exactly what he does contend."

"See! So you can't win, the way you're playing the game. But if you play it differently, and return his lack of love with *increased* love and kindness, then at least you've got a chance to win some real love from him."

"But is that fair? Should I *have* to do it that way, after how he's acted."

"No, it's not fair. So it's not! The question still is: What are you going to do, other than berating your husband, to win more love from him? When are you going to stop all this it's-not-fair nonsense and do something to make your life *fairer?*"

As usual, it was a tough go with this patient, and several times she almost quit therapy in disgust. But, by sheer power of persuasive logic, I finally won, and she did try several weeks of giving her husband more love and less criticism even though he was being his usual inconsiderate self. A near-miracle then ensued; and just four sessions later Mrs. Manahan had quite a different story to tell:

"I don't know how you figured out Tim so well," she said, "but you hit it right on the nose. For ten days he was the biggest louse in the world, refused to help me with any of the heavy work around the house, stayed out late at the office almost every night, and even hinted about taking up with one of his old girl friends again. But, even though it at first killed me, I gritted my teeth, said (just as I've heard you say to me so many times) 'All right, so he's being his usual crummy self. It won't kill me. I don't like it, but I don't have to cry in my beer all night about it.' And I didn't say a word to him, went out of my way to make things nice for him, and instead of withdrawing sexually decided to extend myself more than usual. Well, you should have seen the quick change! He now comes home early every night, sometimes actually brings me flowers, is so solicitous of my condition that I can hardly believe it, and is practically a different person. Quite a change from just a couple of weeks ago! I really have to hand it to you, Doctor. Just as soon as I begin to *work* for the love I wanted from Tim, I began to get it. Much better than crying all the time over how frustrated I was!"

Myra Benson was another good example of how a changed philosophy of living helped a disturbed human being get over a deep-seated feeling of frustration and pain. Myra came to see me (R.A.H.) after her boyfriend of the last two years had broken off their relationship and become engaged to a much wealthier girl. She was desolate, insisted that life was not worth living any more, and that she could never possibly replace him. I was duly sympathetic, but more than a bit adamant and insisted that she was telling herself rot, that within a few months or a year or two she would doubtless be attached to some other man just as intensely as she had been to this one.

"But you don't seem to *understand*," Myra wailed. "He has *left* me. I not only loved him, but had my whole future planned in and around him. *Nothing* has meaning any more. Everything I try to do, everywhere I go, everything I even try to think about is just plain empty without him." And she dived, for the twelfth time that session, for her wad of Kleenex tissues.

"So that is too bad," I said. "But it has clearly happened. Your relationship with him is ended. No doubt about it. Ended; finished; over with. What good is crying about it? Your crying certainly won't bring him back."

"I know. But you don't—"

"Yes, I don't seem to understand. But I *do* understand; and it is you, in all probability, who don't. You don't—or, rather, I should really say you *won't* —understand that it *is* over, and there's not a damned thing you can do about it right now to start it up again. And what you especially don't or won't understand is that the only sane thing to do, at the moment, is to start thinking about what else and *who* else can be interesting and enjoyable to you. No use repeating over and over that 'life is empty without Robert'— thereby *making* it as empty as you're saying that it is. If I began telling myself life was empty without old Calvin Coolidge, and repeated this often and grimly enough, I'm sure that I could feel sad as hell about old Cal— and about old worthless me, who just couldn't get along without good old Cal."

"You're making fun of me!"

"Yes, I guess I am making fun of you a bit—which is a darned sight better than what you're doing: making mincemeat of you. And don't think that I'm just making up this stuff about feeling sad years later. Why, just the other day I had a 54-year-old man in here who literally began to cry when he talked about his mother. Know how long his dear old mother had been dead? Twenty-five years. Only yesterday to him. Genuine emotion? Deep love for dear old mother? Absolutely. But the poor guy had kept it alive for 25 years by regularly saying to himself: 'Mother is dead. How awful, how dreadful. What a fine, wonderful, self-sacrificing woman she was! And now she's dead—gone forever. Poor mother! And poor motherless me! How awful!' "

"Well, you'll have to admit," and Myra smiled a little through her tears, "that I'm not quite as bad as that yet."

"No—not yet. But you probably will be if you keep feeding yourself this hogwash about how indispensable Robert was to your life and how you can't go on without him. If you want to follow the noble example of my 54-year-old patient and his dear departed mother (and me, of course, with my dear departed Calvin Coolidge), I am sure, in fact I have every confidence, that you can go on telling yourself for the next 25 years or so what a stinking, horrible, catastrophic shame it is that Robert has left you and rendered your poor, poor life infinitely barren. You can do it, all right, if you just keep telling yourself such nonsense. On the other hand, if you decide that instead of sitting around in feebleminded grief you'd like to develop an interesting and enjoyable life—this you can do by saying different kinds of sentences to yourself and learning to believe and act on them."

"You are certainly a hardboiled and hardhearted person. You make fun of my genuine bereavement by comparing it with a sick old man's sentiment for his mother and your cynical fiction about grieving for Calvin Coolidge."

"Yes, I make fun because I have found from long experience in helping people that they find it exceedingly difficult to leave my office and start catastrophizing with the same consistency and intensity if I have ridiculed their prolonged disturbance. For you to feel badly for a little while about Robert's desertion may make *some* sense. And it especially makes sense if you want to examine as critically and objectively as possible—with my help—what are some of the things you did or didn't do to contribute to Robert's leaving you. But for you to sit around and tell yourself how hornswaggled bad it is, how devastatingly catastrophic that you no longer have your dear Robert—that makes no more sense than my two examples. So Robert deserted you. The problem is: What can *you* do to enjoy your life *without* him? Stop crying over how unfair reality is to you. It is as it is. Let's see what you can *do* to make it *better*."

As I proceeded to hammer away at Myra Benson's irrational preoccupation with her loss, she began to substitute other self-verbalizations for the ones with which she had been making, and keeping, herself depressed. She soon began to develop new interests, activities, associations. Life ceased to be empty. Not that *it* had intrinsically changed; but *she* began to interpret it differently. And that made all the difference in the world.

[handwritten marginal note: "not good enough"]

What, more specifically, are some of the paths that a sane individual can take when he is faced with real life frustrations, including possible injustices and more than his share of accidental misfortune? Here are some major ways of coping with actual difficulties and unpleasantries:

1. When faced with a frustrating set of circumstances, you should first determine whether it is truly handicapping in its own right or whether you are not essentially *defining* it so. Is your less than perfect appearance *really* preventing you from going with desirable members of the other sex—or are *you*, because of your silly *need* to be the best looking person in town sabotaging your own dates? Is your parents' opposition to your having a certain career *truly* preventing you from following this career—or are you giving up much too easily, failing to plunge ahead despite their opposition, and perhaps using them as an alibi to cover up your own possible fear of fail-

ure? What, when your own negativistic definitions are canceled out, actually *is* inhibiting about this or that frustrating circumstance in your life? Challenge, question—*see.*

2. If the frustration that you face is truly considerable and there is no way in which you can presently significantly change or control it, then you would better gracefully and realistically *accept* it. Yes: not with bitterness and despair, but with dignity and grace. As Epictetus noted two thousand years ago: "Who, then, is unconquerable? He whom the inevitable cannot overcome." Schopenhauer, many centuries later, put the same thought in this wise: "A good supply of resignation is of the first importance in providing for the journey of life." Sydney Smith put it this way, "If it be my lot to crawl, I will crawl contentedly; if to fly, I will fly with alacrity; but as long as I can avoid it, I will never be unhappy."

3. Ask yourself, whenever frustrations and annoyances beset you, "Who says that I *should* not be so sorely beset? It would surely *be nice* if I were not in this fix. But I *am* in it. Tough! Will it kill me to be as frustrated as I am? Probably not. Will it plague and bother me? All right—so it will plague and bother me! All the more reason, therefore, why I should not plague and bother myself—should not make myself *annoyed at being annoyed.* Then I'll just have two frustrations for the price of one!" Convince yourself, in other words, that frustrations and irritations are the *normal* lot of man; that virtually no one lives without encountering many of them; that they are not ordinarily catastrophic; and that you have the thinking power to survive quite well in spite of their existence.

4. The greater your loss or frustration is in life, the *more* philosophic you must force yourself to become in regard to it. Almost all modern members of civilized communities (unlike, among other peoples, the Ancient Spartans) seem to believe that the greater the loss is or the more attached they are to the lost object, the more unhappy they have to be about it. Hogwash! The greater your loss or frustration is, the more you will tend to *regret* or *dislike* it. But regret and dislike need not equal dire unhappiness. When the former is translated into the latter, the unhappy person is saying to himself: (a) "I cannot be with my dearly loved person or have my ardently desired object, and this is regretful," and (b) "Because I cannot have what I dearly want, this is terrible, horrible, catastrophic, and totally unfair and it just *shouldn't be.*" While the first of these sentences may well be sensible and true the second one is arrant nonsense and can be objectively observed and philosophically challenged and uprooted.

5. When you are bothered by real life handicaps, such as physical pains that cannot for the moment be eradicated, you will do well to practice sensation-neglect or distraction. Thus, you can either try to ignore and forget about the painful or annoying sensations; or you can deliberately think

about or do something else. If, for example, you have a headache, you can try to forget about it instead of continually telling yourself: "My, what a terrible headache this is! How can I stand it if it continues?" Or you can deliberately try to think about something pleasant (such as the good time you had the day before or the picnic you are going to have next Sunday); or you can participate in some distracting activity, such as chess, reading, or painting. Since it is not at all easy to put a painful stimulus out of mind while you are still being assailed by it, the second plan, that of deliberately trying to distract yourself with other, more pleasant stimuli, is usually more effective.

Although the use of distraction is admittedly palliative, and does not solve any basic problem permanently, it sometimes produces most beneficial results where all other anti-unhappiness techniques fail. Years ago, I (A.E.) was impressed with its possibilities when I discovered that I could eliminate most of the pain of drilling or other dental work by deliberately focusing, when my dentist was hacking away at my teeth or gums, on recent pleasant experiences (especially sexual experiences) that I had undergone or by composing songs in my head while sitting in the dental chair. I taught this technique to several of my patients who dreaded visiting the dentist and all of them who have used it reported good results in relieving pain.

Wallace J. Gardner and his associates have published a report in *Science* emphasizing the psychological and physiological effectiveness of playing music and noise into headphones worn by dental patients and showing how, in 90 per cent of dental operations, sound stimulation has been the only analgesic agent required.

The use of distraction to alleviate psychological problems may have undesirable side effects: since the individual thereby may merely temporarily soothe himself rather than permanently eradicate his disturbances. Acts of aggression against others, sex diversions, alcohol, marijuana, heroin, and even tranquilizers may be over-effective in making the individual "feel good" for the moment, and thereby believe that he does not have to do anything else to eliminate his basic anxiety and hostility. Abreactive and cathartic techniques employed in some types of psychotherapy (such as those used by some psychoanalytic, Reichian, and experiential therapists) may also nicely divert the patient from his underlying problems and give him considerable immediate gratification. Distraction, therefore, has its distinct dangers. But used judiciously, especially to combat physical pains and annoyances that cannot for the moment be undermined at their source, it has real advantages.

In the main, however, there is no easy path to dealing maturely with frustration. The hardest paths of all, the extreme renunciation of life philosophies of the Christian martyrs, certain Buddhist sects, and various other religious fanatics, are probably too difficult for most humans, and are suspiciously redolent of masochism and crackpotism. A more moderate degree of accepting the inevitable frustrations and unpleasantness of life is, however, indispensable for unanxious and unhostile living.

Ted Byrd may serve as an apt illustration of the desirability of acquiring a self-disciplined philosophy in regard to frustration. When I (R.A.H.) first saw Ted as a patient he was one of the best injustice-collectors I had ever met. With apparently some reason, since he *had* been rejected by his father and mother during his childhood, and been sent off to camps and boarding schools from the age of eight. He was the youngest of five children in a wealthy family and there seems little room to doubt that he had been unwanted from birth onward. His four brothers and sisters, who had been much more welcome than he, had gone on to considerable success in their lives (at least so far as I could tell from his story); but he had been a drifter, a job-loser, a drunkard, and a bitter resenter of the world and its treatment of him.

Ted, who had done a great deal of reading about psychotherapy, particularly in some of the highly fictionalized and dramatized case histories which masquerade as non-fiction, expected me to place him on the sofa, sympathetically listen to his tale of woe for the next few years, and encourage him to express and act out his deep-seated hostility for his parents and other family members. I fooled him, however, by immediately plunging into a counter-attack on his injustice gathering.

"So your parents didn't love you," I said. "They rejected you and treated you shabbily. All right: granted. But what the devil are you so angry about *now?* As a child, to be sure, you had a real rough time of it. But now you're a big boy—remember? So why *go on* feeling sorry for yourself about what you didn't get during your childhood? Why not do something constructive, interesting, and enjoyable with your *present* life? What fun are you getting out of sitting around and telling yourself what a dirty shame it was that you were treated in a rejecting way by your parents when you were eight years old? Since you are now—chronologically at least—a big boy, let's see if we can't get you to think some big-boy thoughts."

Ted was visibly taken aback. "But surely you know—" he started. "Surely you, as a psychologist, realize that it isn't that easy. I think, even with my limited understanding of your field, I can fairly accurately say that it is generally agreed that—well, with rejection in the formative years and that sort of thing, it is agreed that a person never does get over his need, his desperate need, to be loved. Unless, perhaps, by long-term analysis. I think that is what I need. The kind of stuff I've read about in Robert Lindner and Theodor Reik, for example. Where the patient, over a long period of time, lives out and works through his past hatreds and frustrations, and really sees what it is that's bothering him. Isn't that what you do, that kind of psychoanalysis?"

"No, not any more. I used to do something of the sort years ago, when I too was impressed by the kind of books you are citing. But the more patients I saw and the more I put them through active re-livings of their past experiences, and violent re-hatings of their parental figures, the more I saw that it just didn't work. They loved it, all right, and had great times re-enacting their early frustrations and hostilities. But they just didn't get better. So in the last few years, in association with Dr. Albert Ellis of New York, I've been using a radically different approach to psychotherapy. And though it doesn't seem as dramatic or as gratifying as what I used to do, it certainly works a hell of a lot better. My patients used to love me like crazy under the old therapeutic system. Now, believe it or not, I actually get them to love *themselves*."

"Well—uh, I can see what you mean. But don't you really think that in special cases like mine, where there has been so much rejection by my parents and so much negative emotion stored up about it in the past, that I'm one of those who have to work this through, on a long-term analytic basis, before I can possibly come to the more rational kind of approach that you and Dr. Ellis—and quite rightly, I am sure—emphasize?"

"No, I don't think anything of the sort. It is of course *possible* that orthodox psychoanalysis would help you, over a long period of time, to work through your feelings of rejection. But it is more possible that it would not. For, after years of dredging up the minute details of just what your parents said and did to you at the age of two and three, and just how you reacted to their words and deeds, you would *still* have to reconstruct your *present* philosophy of rejection and frustration and stop telling yourself the nonsense that, after thirty years, you are continually repeating to yourself."

"What kind of nonsense do you mean?"

"The kind you have told me about for the first twenty minutes of this session and what you are still obviously upholding; namely, that rejection, especially by one's parents, is a horrible thing, and that unless you can express yourself angrily against it, and somehow induce the world to give you the living which you still think it owes you, life is not worth living and you might as well drink yourself to death."

"But *isn't* rejection a terrible thing and *isn't* it pretty awful to be frustrated?

"Yes—to a child. A child who cannot think straight and fend for himself. But you *can* think straight and fend for yourself—and you're not trying to do so in any manner, shape, or form. You've brilliantly avoided, all your life, changing your own attitudes toward frustrating circumstances, and have only tried to change the circumstances themselves—or else run away from them: leave an unpleasant job (instead of trying to make it pleasanter) or drift from one place to another (instead of trying to make the best of the place where you are). And you're *still*, right this minute, trying to avoid facing frustration by inducing me to put you lazily through several years of abreactive psychoanalysis, which will give you more time to wallow in your bitterness instead of doing something to change it and will allow you the continued luxury of hating others instead of looking them in the eye and eradicating your own needless feelings of hatred."

"So you think I'm still avoiding instead of facing the basic issues of my life."

"Well, aren't you? So you want to look closely, oh, so closely! at what your parents did to you thirty years ago and how *that*, what they did, made you what you are today. But you don't want to, not for a minute, look even moderately closely at what *you're* doing, day after day, to make yourself feel so blocked and deprived."

"What am I doing, if I may ask?"

"Why don't you look and see? That's what you really should be here for: to look, with my help, at the silly sentences you keep telling yourself that *now* make you and keep you sick—instead of trying to look at the sentences your poor, disturbed parents said to you years ago."

"Sentences that I am telling myself?"

"Yes, sentences like: 'Oh, how awful it is to have been rejected by my parents and to have been discriminated against in favor of my brothers and sisters. How can I possibly amount to anything in life when those lousy parents of mine treated me in that despicable fashion?' Can't you see what a ridiculous non sequitur you're setting up in those internalized sentences—making *their*, your parents', past actions magically influence *your* present behavior? And sentences like: 'Lord, how difficult it is to stand on one's own two feet and battle the frustrations of the world. It's unfair that life should be this way!' Can't you see how that kind of self-repeated nonsense is adding to instead of easing the very real annoyances that life often has to offer you?"

"Hmm. You take quite a different tack from those psychoanalytic books I've read. According to them, you're all wet and your lecturing won't go deeply enough into my problems or help me solve what basically ails me."

"O.K.—if you want to live by those books, that's your prerogative. And if you want to go for a long-term, 'deep' psychoanalysis, I'll be glad to send you to one of my associates who still believes in this sort of thing and will be delighted to put you through the paces for the next seven or eight years. But, in the final analysis, you'll still have to do things the hard way, if you really are to change your ways, and revamp *your* (and not your sainted parents'!) philosophy of living."

"So if I really buckle down to work *now* and forget for the most part what happened to me in the past, and what dirty dogs my parents were for treating me the way they did, you think that I can work through my problems relatively quickly and still deeply understand myself?"

"Correct. There is nothing deeper in life than a man's facing his own fundamental philosophy—however or whenever he originally acquired it— and challenging the basic assumptions by which he lives. Your philosophy, in a nutshell, is: 'I had it hard in the past and suffered more than the average lot. Why, therefore should I have to suffer any more deprivations and annoyances today? Why can't I merely revel in my justified hatred for my parents for the rest of my life and thereby feel better and magically change the world so it goes more my way?' A very lovely philosophy—but totally ineffective. When are you going to start growing up and building a more realistic, less self-defeating way of looking at life?"

"You're a hard man, Dr. Harper. But I'm beginning to think that your kind of hardness is what I actually need. You know, now that you make me think of it, it all did seem just a little too easy, a little too good, when I kept reading how John Smith or Joe Blow, after years of lying on the sofa, suddenly saw the light, admitted that all his life he had really wanted to replace his father in his mother's bed, and then quickly lost his neurotic symptoms. Yes, I guess I have been, as you say, going for magic and that I wanted you or some other analyst, with esoteric mumbo-jumbo, to cure passive, little old me, while I did not a damn thing to lift a finger in my own behalf. You're right: that would be just the kind of thing, a psychoanalytic process like that, to *keep* me from changing, to give me a great excuse not to change myself, for years and years. I have a friend, Jim Abramsky, who's been using it that way for hell knows how many years. He goes religiously to his analyst, four or five times a week, and keeps calling him up on the phone whenever he gets into the slightest bit of trouble. But he still drinks like a fish. And whenever I ask him how he's doing in his analysis, he says: 'Fine; really fine. We're going deeper and deeper all the time. Real deep. One of these days we're going to hit rock bottom and then I'll know what's at the base of it all and I'll be no longer blocked up like this.' But I can see now, from what you've just said, that there *is* no bottom for someone like Jim. He really doesn't *want* to get better—for that would require real work and real change on his part."

"You're probably right. As long as he keeps going religiously for his analysis, he has the best excuse in the world *not* to get better—not to look at his own nonsensical self-sentences and work his guts off at changing them. But that's *his* problem. What are *you* going to do about your self-reiterated balderdash, about your crummy philosophy of life?"

"I don't want to promise you anything, Doctor Harper, for I've made many promises to myself and others before, and damned if I haven't goofed on all of them. But I can tell you this and mean it: for once, I'm going to try, really try. I'm going right home and fire out most of those 'deep' psychoanalytic books that I've been solacing myself with for such a long time and I'm going to look much more deeply at myself—or, as you keep putting it, at my own sentences. I guess I've had enough of this self-pitying, this look-what-a-horribly-neglected-child-I-was sort of jazz to last me for the rest of my life. I think I'll try it your way for awhile and see what happens."

And Ted Byrd did try, for the next six months, looking at his own sentences and seeing what his own (rather than his parents') nonsense consisted of. His drinking decreased considerably; for the first time in his life he thought in terms of staying in one place; and, at the age of 36, he went back to school and started to prepare himself for the one profession, electronic engineering, that he had toyed around with for many years but never seriously pursued. He is still at this present writing, not entirely out of the woods. But though the average amount of frustrations and annoyances are his daily and yearly lot, his attitude toward them has changed enormously and his bitter rantings against the injustices of his past and present world have almost entirely ceased.

Controlling
Your Own Destiny
14

MOST PEOPLE ARE consuming so much time and energy trying to do the impossible—namely, to change and control the actions of *others*—that they wrongly believe that they cannot do the one thing that is most possible—to change or control their own thoughts and acts. They firmly hold and rarely challenge what we call Irrational Idea No. 5: *The idea that human unhappiness is externally caused and that people have little or no ability to control their sorrows or rid themselves of their negative feelings.*

This idea is nonsensical for several reasons. First of all, outside people and events can do nothing, at worst, but harm you physically. All the emotional or mental "pain" they "cause" you is actually created by your taking their criticisms or rejections too seriously: by your falsely telling yourself that you cannot *stand* their disapproval or cannot *live* without their acceptance.

Even physical injury that comes to you from without—as when a flower pot accidentally falls and breaks your toe—will often cause you relatively little trouble if you philosophically *accept* the inconveniences of your injury and stop telling yourself, over and over again, "Oh, how awful! Oh, how terrible this pain is!" Not that you have complete control in this regard: for you don't. Some externally caused injuries are bound to cause you considerable pain and discomfort, no matter how philosophic about them you may be. As Bertrand Russell once remarked: "Any man who maintains that happiness comes wholly from within should be compelled to spend thirty-six hours in rags in a blizzard, without food."

Nonetheless, you *do* have considerable ability to minimize, though not entirely eliminate, the pain of physical injuries. And you have virtually complete ability, if only you would use it, to eradicate your emotional and mental pain.

Not that controlling your self-created upsets is easy. On the contrary, as we keep emphasizing, hurting yourself, giving yourself a terribly rough time, taking others' words and actions and insisting on depressing or exciting yourself about them—these are exceptionally easy things for you to do once you have been born and raised in a social community. But—as we keep forcing to the attention of our patients—however easy it may be for you to hurt yourself emotionally, it is easier in the long run, and much more rewarding even in the short run to force yourself *not* to do so.

Take, for example, the statement that our patients are commonly making: "Jerry said that I was stupid and he hurt me very much by saying that."

"No!" we immediately interrupt. "*Jerry* couldn't possibly hurt you by saying that you were stupid. Nor could Jerry's *words* hurt you either. What you actually mean is that you hurt yourself, once you heard Jerry's words, by saying to yourself something like: 'Oh, how terrible it is for Jerry to call me stupid. I'm not stupid and he *shouldn't* be saying that I am.' Or: 'Oh, how awful! Maybe I really am stupid and he sees that I am. And how perfectly dreadful it would be if I were stupid or if he thought I were!' And, of course, it is not Jerry's words but *your* phrases and sentences that make you 'hurt.' For you could easily say to yourself: 'Jerry thinks I'm stupid. Either he's wrong, in which case he must have some serious lack of discrimination or emotional problem. Or he's right, in which case I would better try to act less stupidly or accept the fact that I am not too bright and get along as best I can with my stupidity.'"

Our patients, again, frequently remark: "I can't stand it, when things go wrong."

And, once more, we quickly interrupt: "What do you mean you can't stand *it?* It doesn't really exist—is just a figment of your imagination. What you really mean to say is: 'I can't stand *myself* when things go wrong—because I falsely tell myself that things *shouldn't* go wrong, or that *I'm* no good for letting them go wrong. But if I stopped telling myself this nonsense, then I could fairly easily stand—though never perhaps like—the frustrations of the world and could respect myself for being able to accept these frustrations.'"

Still again: when human beings say that they are unable to control their feelings, what they invariably mean is that *right now*, at this very moment, they have upset themselves in such a manner that their autonomic nervous system (as shown by over-activity of their sweat glands, visceral reactions, heart beat) has temporarily gone out of kilter and that they cannot *immedi-*

ately control it. True. But if they expended some *time and energy*, and forced themselves to look at the internalized sentences with which they upset themselves, and by means of which they temporarily drove their autonomic nervous reactions beyond their normal limits of controllability, they would soon enough discover that they can *eventually* bring their feelings under control again—and sometimes in a surprisingly short length of time.

A case in point is that of Rick Schule, who spent the first several weeks of therapy insisting that he could not possibly control his frequent and deep-ranging feelings of depression because, before he knew it, they were well upon him; and then he was so quickly overwhelmed and depressed that he did not *feel* like doing anything to combat his low state of being.

"I understand all that you say about looking at the sentences that I am saying to create these feelings of depression," Rick said on one occasion. "But I don't see how this is really possible in my case. For one thing, you must realize that I *unconsciously* bring on my depressed feelings. So how can I possibly consciously see them, before they arise, and thereby stop them from occurring?"

"You can't," said the therapist. "At least not at first. The best you can do, at first, is to observe your depressed states after they have already arisen, and then to see, by theoretical analysis and inference, that you must have brought them on by telling yourself some nonsense. If you look for this nonsense, you are certain to find it—because you could not possibly have become depressed without its being there."

"So if I become depressed, for whatever unconscious reason, I can stop myself, right in the midst of the depression, and tell myself that I must be bringing on my depressed mood. And I can then look for the exact sentences with which I am bringing it on."

"Exactly. It will be difficult for you to do this, especially at first; but nonetheless you can do it. Take a recent instance of depression, for an example. When was the last time you can remember?"

"Mmm. Let me see. Well, how about yesterday. I got up late, since it was Sunday, read the newspaper, listened to the radio awhile, and then suddenly felt myself becoming very listless and depressed."

"Hadn't anything happened other than your reading the newspaper and listening to the radio up to this time."

"No, not that I can recall. Let's see if there was anything else. No—Oh, yes. Nothing really. But I thought about calling my girl friend and I decided against it."

"Why did you decide against it?"

"Well, I usually see her every Saturday night. But this time she had another date. I didn't like it, of course; but since I'm far from deciding to marry her myself, I couldn't very well tell her not to. Anyway, I thought of calling her on Sunday, to see if I could see her later that day. But—" Rick hesitated.

"But—?"

"Well—. Well, you see, I wondered if she were still with her date of the night before, and whether she would be embarrassed if I called just then, and—."

"Oh! It's fairly obvious what you were telling yourself to bring on your depression—isn't it?"

"Mmm. I see what you mean. I was telling myself, 'Well, what if she still has her date there? And what if she's spent such a pleasant time with him all night that she just doesn't want to see me any more? What if he was much better, in bed that is, with her than I am? Jesus, what an awful thing that would be!"

"Yes: quite obviously. What an awful thing it would be if he proved to be a better lover than you, and she gave you up as her steady boy friend for him. What a stupid jerk that would make you! Isn't that what you were telling yourself?"

"I guess you've got it, right on the nose. That's exactly what I was saying to myself. And I was afraid to call her—afraid I'd find out what the score was. Afraid she'd no longer think I was any good—and that that would prove I really wasn't. No wonder I got depressed!"

"Yes—no wonder. But the real point is, can you see how, even though you 'unconsciously' gave yourself such a hard time and depressed yourself, can you see how you can bring those 'unconscious' thoughts to consciousness, how you can quickly ferret them out and see exactly what they are?"

"By just asking myself like this, like we've just done. By seeing what sentences I say to myself, just as you keep showing me. By 'unconscious,' then, I really mean those things that I don't look at too closely, but that I nonetheless tell myself. Is that right?"

"Exactly right. That's what almost all of us mean by unconscious. Occasionally, perhaps, we have truly unconscious thoughts—or thoughts we repress because we are ashamed to look them in the face, and that we therefore sort of deliberately forget and cannot easily bring to consciousness any more. That was one of Freud's great discoveries: the existence of repressed thoughts and feelings. Unfortunately, however, he went much too far, and started believing, after a while, that virtually all unconscious thoughts are repressed ones and are not easily accessible to conscious review again. But he was mistaken in this. Most of your so-called unconscious thoughts are quite available to consciousness—if you dig for them a bit."

"So if I unconsciously depress myself, I can usually find out pretty quickly what I told myself to bring on this depression—and can then undepress myself again?"

"Yes—though, as I said before, this will often be difficult. For once your depression sets in, as you noted a while ago, you don't *feel* like undepressing yourself again; you almost *want* to stay depressed. And unless you combat this feeling, and actively go after your underlying sentences with which you created your depression, you will of course stay quite miserable. So you have, in a sense, a choice of evils: remaining depressed indefinitely; or forcing yourself, against your own feeling, to combat the depression by seeing what you did to create it. A tough choice, I'll admit. But if you keep taking the lesser of these two evils—combatting your negative feelings, that is—eventually the time comes when your basic philosophy of life matures and you depress yourself much more rarely to begin with and have an easier time getting yourself out of your vile mood when you do unconsciously put yourself in one."

Rick listened thoughtfully. The very next session he came in highly enthused. "Well, Doc," he said, "looks like I made it this time. I got myself into one of those old unconscious depressions again, but I also got myself out of it."

"Good. Tell me about it."

"Well, it was this way. I told you about my girl friend last week, and her going out with another fellow. I saw her again this week and before I knew it, I heard her saying: 'Rick, get that frown off your face. What are you so gloomy about. You're not going to die.'

"Jesus Christ! That hit me right in the solar plexus. I realized, right away, that I was still brooding over what had happened the previous week and that my glum mood was showing. Which suddenly depressed me all the more. Within the next five minutes, I felt like taking the rope.

"Fortunately, however, I heard your words ringing in my ears: 'When you start to get depressed, ask yourself what it is you are saying to yourself to make yourself depressed.' 'O.K.,' I said to myself, 'what the hell *am* I saying to make me depressed?' And I got it, as you might expect, right away. I was saying, first of all, 'Here she's seeing me again, but how do I know she really wants to? Maybe she'd rather be out with that other guy that she saw last week. Boy, what a terrible thing that would be if she did want to be with him instead of me!' And then, once she made those comments on that frown being on my face and how gloomy I was, I started saying to myself: 'Well, that finishes it. Not only does she like this other guy better than me, probably, but she thinks I'm a killjoy even when I'm with her. After this sort of thing, she'll never want to see me again, for sure. And that will prove, once and for all, what a jerk I am.' "

"You certainly were giving it to yourself good, weren't you? A fine double dose!"

"You can say that again, Doc. That's what I was doing for fair. But for once I caught it—yes, I really caught it! 'Look what you're saying to yourself!' I thought. 'Just as the Doc pointed out. Boy, what malarkey! Suppose she does like this other guy better than you—what does that really prove about you? And suppose she doesn't like my gloomy face. Does that show that I'm a hopeless idiot and that I'll never make it again with her? Now why don't I stop telling myself this junk and do my best to be my old pleasanter self again. Then I can see if she really wants me rather than this other guy. And if she wants him rather than me, that's tough: but it's not fatal. I'll live.'

"Well, would you believe it, Doc? Within no more than five minutes— maybe even less—I actually stopped that depression *cold*. Every other time I've got like that I've gone into a real doozy of a miserable time, with sick headache and all. But not this time! Within no time at all, I was actually smiling and joshing the pants off my girl. And we finally had just about the best day we ever had and she told me that she just didn't want to see the other fellow at all again since being with me was such fun. You know, Doc, I'm even thinking of marrying her now. But the main thing is me: you said I could control my darned depressions, and blast it if I can't. That's the best thing that's ever happened to me."

Thus did one person learn to observe his own thinking and, at times, control his negative emotions. Other techniques that can be used to this same end may be noted as follows:

1. When faced with actual physical injury, deprivation, pain, or disease, you can attempt either to eliminate or to rectify your painful circumstances, or, if they are not rectifiable to accept them philosophically and try, as best you can, to ignore or distract yourself from them. Instead of telling yourself: "Oh, what a frightful thing is happening to me," you can instead say to yourself (and others), "It is too bad that I am in this unfortunate situation. So it is too bad!"

2. When faced with non-physical assaults from without, then you can first question the motives of your attackers and the truth of their statements; and if you honestly think that their attacks are warranted, then you can try to change yourself to meet their criticisms or accept your own limitations and the consequent displeasure of others that sometimes accompanies such limitations.

3. When you are, for any reason, overwhelmed with anxiety, anger, depression, or guilt, you should always realize that it is invariably *not* outward people and events that are causing you to feel these negative emotions, but your own illogical internalized sentences. Even in the midst of these feel-

ings, you can still generally look objectively at your own verbalizations, ferret out the irrational links in their chains (the *shoulds, oughts*, and *musts* which you have illegitimately woven into them), and vigorously question and challenge these irrationalities.

The main point, in sum, which you must note and believe in this connection is that *you* are in your own saddle. You can never expect to be deliriously happy at all times in life. Freedom from all physical pain is never likely to be your lot. But an extraordinary lack of mental and emotional woe may be yours—if you think that it may be and work for what you believe in.

Conquering Anxiety

15

OUR PATIENTS AND our associates often try to confound us on one special point, where they feel that our technique of rational-emotive therapy comes a cropper and sadly begins to bog down. "You may be quite right," they say, "in insisting that most human difficulties are caused by the illogical sentences we tell ourselves and that we can overcome our difficulties by changing these sentences. But what about anxiety? How can we possibly control or change that by challenging and questioning our own assumptions? That's one human trait you'll never be able to change very much, no matter how rationally you approach it."

But these critics are wrong. Anxiety *is* approachable and controllable by straight thinking. For anxiety, basically, consists of Irrational Idea No. 6: *The idea that if something is or may be dangerous or fearsome, one should be terribly occupied with and upset about it.*

This is not to say that real or rational fears do not exist. They certainly do. When you are about to cross a busy intersection, you would be insane not to fear the possibility of getting hit by a moving vehicle; and you would be equally crazy if you were not to some extent *concerned* about your safety. Fear of this sort is not only a natural and somewhat instinctive human tendency, but also a necessity for self-preservation. Without your being, in any circumstance whatever, duly fearful or concerned about your safety, it is unlikely that your days on this earth would long continue.

Nonetheless: fear is not anxiety. Anxiety consists of *over*-concern, of *exaggerated* or *needless* fear. And it most frequently, in this society, is not re-

132

lated to physical injury or illness but to mental "injury" or "harm." In fact, probably 98 percent of what we call anxiety in modern life is little more than *over-concern for what someone thinks about you.* And this kind of anxiety, as well as exaggerated fear of bodily injury, is quite illogical on several counts:

1. If there is a possibility that something truly is or may be dangerous or fearsome, there are only two intelligent approaches you may take: (a) determine whether this thing actually *is* dangerous to your well-being; and (b) if it is, then either do something practical to alleviate the existing danger or (if absolutely nothing can be done) resign yourself to the fact of its existence. Bellyaching about it or continually reiterating to yourself the holy horror of a potentially or actually fearsome situation will not in any way change it or better prepare you to cope with it. On the contrary, the more you upset yourself about the existence of this dangerous situation, the less able you will be, in almost all instances, to assess it accurately and to cope with it.

2. Although it is perfectly true that certain accidents and illnesses (such as airplane accidents or the onset of cancer) *may* befall you one day, and that it will be quite unfortunate if one of these misfortunes *does* occur; once you have taken reasonable precautions to ward off such a possible mishap there is simply nothing else that you can usually do about it. Worry, believe it or not, has no magical quality of staving off bad luck. On the contrary, it frequently increases the probability of disease or accident by unnerving the vulnerable individual. Thus, the more you worry about getting into an automobile crackup the more likely you are, if you are driving the car (from either the front or the back seat!), to get yourself into just such a crackup.

Vietnam

3. The assumed catastrophic quality of most potentially unpleasant events is almost invariably highly exaggerated. The worst thing that can happen to you in life is usually death—and sooner or later you will have to die anyway. If you are truly in dire physical pain for a long period of time (as when you have an incurable cancerous condition and cannot find relief in drugs), you can always commit suicide. Virtually all misfortunes other than these which people continually worry about—such as loss of a loved one, missing a boat, or having a tooth pulled—turn out to be, when they actually occur, far less dreadful than one may have worriedly dreamed them up to be for a long time before their occurrence. The worst thing about almost any "disaster" is usually your exaggerated *belief* in its horror rather than anything intrinsically terrible about it. Life holds innumerable pains in the neck for all of us; but terrors, horrors, and catastrophes are almost entirely figments of our worried imaginations.

4. Worry itself is probably the most dreadful condition with which a

human being can exist; and most of us would probably be literally better off dead than "living" in its continual throes. If you are ever faced with the real danger of blackmail, injury, or death, and there is no possible way to avoid the issues involved, then you would better frankly and fearlessly face up to your problems, and accept whatever penalties (such as possible legal consequences) may accrue from facing them, rather than continue to live in fear. A life in jail or even no life whatever may well be preferable to spending the rest of your days running, hiding, and panting with fear.

5. Aside from the possibility of physical harm, what is there *really* ever to be afraid of? So people may disapprove of or dislike you. So some of them may boycott you or say nasty things about you. So your reputation may be besmirched, your name be considered mud. Tough; disadvantageous; rough. As long as you do not *literally* starve, or go to jail, or be harmed bodily by their censure, why give yourself a super-hard time about the wheels that turn in their heads? If you stop worrying and *do* something about their possible disapproval, the chances are that you will sooner or later counteract it. If there is nothing that can be done: tough again. That's the way the cards fall. Why make the game of life so much more difficult by fretting and stewing about its existing inequities?

6. Although many things seem terribly fearful to a young child, who has little or no control over his destiny, an adult is usually *not* in this precarious position and can either change the truly fearful circumstances of his life; or, if these are not changeable, can philosophically learn to live under such conditions without making himself panicky about them. Human adults do not *have* to keep reactivating fears that may have been fairly realistic in some earlier period of their lives but that are no longer valid.

Mrs. J. T. Borengrad provides us with an illustration of the foolish perpetuation of fears that were once realistic but that, at the time she came for psychotherapy, had no objective validity. As a child, she had learned to take whatever was said or done with hardly a word of protest because she had a sadistic father who would severely punish her for the slightest questioning of his authority. Then (quite likely because she believed she deserved no better) she married an equally sadistic man and remained with him for ten years until he became openly psychotic and had to be committed to a mental hospital, leaving her the full responsibility of rearing their two young daughters.

During both her childhood and her first marriage, then, Mrs. Borengrad lived under truly fearful circumstances. But not so during her second marriage. For a meeker man than Mr. Borengrad could scarcely be found; and he hardly ever lifted his eyebrow at her. Nonetheless, she became exceptionally disturbed and came to therapy in a veritable state of panic. Having majored in psychology in college, she stated her symptoms in somewhat sophisticated terms:

"It looks like I'm behaving exactly like Pavlov's dogs. I apparently got conditioned to react to anyone close to me with fear and trembling, with submission and underlying resentment, and I am going through the old conditioned response business over and over. Even though my husband is the kindest man in the world, and my teenage daughters are almost like lovely little dolls, I live in constant generalized fear. Ring the bell just before presenting the steak, and pretty soon the dog slobbers for the food he knows he's going to get. Well, ring the bell with me, and I immediately cringe with terror—even though the sadistic treatment I used to receive from my father and my first husband no longer follows its ringing. Just being present with any member of my family, bell or no bell, I quickly start cringing."

"Maybe it looks like conditioning to you," the therapist said, "but my own feeling is that the very word conditioning is so vague and general that it actually masks the detailed processes that are going on. Now let's look much more closely at these so-called conditioning processes. First, let's see what used to go on with your father and your first husband."

"They would get angry at some little thing that I did or didn't do, I noticed their anger, then I also saw how they followed it up—by punishing me severely in some manner. Then, naturally, whenever I began to see that they were growing angry, I immediately became very fearful of the punishment that would follow. And I either ran away or went into a panic state or asked them to beat me quickly and get the horrible thing over with."

"All right; that's a good description. But you left out a very important part of the process."

"What's that?"

"Well, you said that they got angry; and you knew you would be punished; and then you went into a panic state. But the second part of the process—the part where you knew that you would be punished—is being glossed over too easily. What you really mean, don't you, is that you perceived their anger and then, in a split-second, you told yourself something like: 'Oh, my heavens! There he goes again, getting angry at me for practically nothing. And now he's going to punish me for doing practically nothing. Oh, how terrible! Oh, how unfair! What a poor miserable, helpless creature I am to have an unfair father (or husband, as the case might be) who takes advantage of me like this and against whom I am too weak to protect myself!' Isn't this, or something much like this, what you said to yourself once you perceived your father's or your first husband's anger?"

"Yes, I'm sure you're right about that. Particularly with my father, I would tell myself how awful it was that I had a father like that, while Minerva Scanlan, my best girl friend, had such a nice, easy-going father who never even yelled at her and certainly never hit her or punished her in any other way. I was so *ashamed* to have a father like mine. And I thought I came from such a terrible family—so bad, in fact, that I wouldn't even want Minerva or anyone else to know just *how* bad they were and how badly they treated me."

"And with your first husband?"

"There, too. Only this time I wasn't so ashamed of him but of my *marrying* him. I kept saying, whenever he got angry and I knew he was about to pounce on me, 'Oh, how could I ever have been so stupid as to marry anyone like him. After I saw so much of this kind of thing at home, too! And then I went right out and repeated this horrible mistake, voluntarily. And now I'm staying with him, when I should have the guts to leave, even if I have to work my hands to the bone to take care of the children myself. How could I have been so stupid!' "

"All right, then. Note how we not only have the stimulus, the anger of your father and your first husband, and the conditioned response, your great fear of punishment, but we also and more importantly have your self-blaming *interpretations* of the horror of the stimulus. Thus, whereas you theoretically could have told yourself, 'There goes crazy old dad getting angry again, and he's probably going to punish me unjustly. Well, too bad; but I can survive his punishment and eventually, as I grow up, get away from him and live in a non-punishing environment.' You actually largely said to yourself, '*I'm* to blame for coming from such a crazy family and for being so weak as to let the old buzzard take advantage of me.' And, with your first husband, whereas you could have said to yourself, 'Too bad: I made a mistake in marrying this sadistic individual; but I'm strong enough to get away from him and leave him to his own sick ways.' You again said: '*I'm* to blame for making this terrible mistake of marrying this bastard; and now I'm too weak and idiotic to get away from him.' "

"What you seem to be saying, then, is that it wasn't necessarily the actions of my father and my husband—their anger followed by their punishment—that conditioned me to be so upset when I was with either of them, but really my own unjustified interpretations of their actions."

"Yes, your own *partly* unjustified interpretations. For you were, of course, especially when you lived with your father, a little girl who appropriately *should* have been scared of your father's physical assaults; and no matter what you might have philosophically told yourself at the time, you were in some *real* danger, and it would have been inappropriate for you *not* to be frightened at all."

"But that was not exactly the case when I was married to my first husband."

"You're quite right: it wasn't. Again, with him, you might have had a little reason for fear, since he was psychotic and he could have literally killed you when he got angry. But as you yourself pointed out before, you also could have easily, or with some but not too much difficulty, left him—which was not true when you were a girl living in your father's home. So much of the so-called 'conditioned' fear with your husband was distinctly your own doing: the result of your falsely telling yourself that you couldn't cope with the situation, were a dunce for having married him in the first place, and were a slob for staying with him. If you had told yourself other and more sensible things than this, you would soon have left him—or might even have stayed and been very unafraid of him."

" 'Conditioning,' then, is something of a cover-up word for what we largely do to ourselves?"

"Yes, very often. In Pavlov's case, don't forget that *he*, Pavlov, conditioned the dogs from the outside: he completely controlled the event of whether they would or would not get their piece of steak when the bell rang. And in the case of your father, since he was much bigger and stronger than you, he also largely controlled the event of whether or not you would be severely beaten once he got angry. But not entirely! For had you had a better and different philosophy of living when you were with your father—which not very many but some few young girls of your age do somehow manage to acquire—you could have (unlike Pavlov's dogs) changed the situation considerably. Thus, you could have somehow influenced your father and induced him to punish one of your brothers or sisters, rather than you; or you could have managed literally to run out of the house most of the times you knew he was about to punish you; or you could have accepted your punishment more stoically and not been too bothered by it; or you could have tried many other gambits to change or ameliorate the effects of your father's behavior. But because of your poor philosophy of life at the time—which, to be sure, your father among others helped you acquire—you passively submitted to his blows—and also blamed yourself for having such a father and for having to submit. So although your situation was indeed fearful, you helped make it positively *terrifying*."

"I can see what you mean. And with my first husband, I guess, I did even worse. There, I didn't have to submit at all; but I just about forced myself—with what you again would call my poor philosophy of life—to do so, and again to be absolutely terrified."

"Exactly. Although only some of your so-called 'conditioning' was self-effected in your relations with your father, probably the far greater part of it was self-wrought in your relations with your first husband. Where you could have nicely *un*conditioned yourself with him—by telling yourself how ridiculous it was for you to stay with and suffer the punishments of such a palpably disturbed man—you did the reverse and worked very hard to condition yourself still more."

"And what about my present state, with my second husband?"

"Your present state is an even better proof of the thesis we have been discussing than anything else. For you will remember, again, that in the case of Pavlov's dogs, when he kept presenting the bell without the steak, the dogs soon became unconditioned and stopped salivating, since they soon realized, or somehow signaled themselves, that the steak and the bell did not go together any longer. Accordingly, therefore, if you had been classically conditioned by the experiences with your father and first husband, both of whom were tyrants, you should have gradually got quite unconditioned by your several years of experience with your second husband, who is practically an angel when compared with the first two."

"He actually is. Unbelievably nice and unpunishing."

"But your merely being in his or your daughters' presence, you say, causes you to go into a state of panic?"

"Yes, I can't understand it. But that's just what happens."

"I am sure that you really *can* understand it, if you look a little more closely, and stop convincing yourself that you are 'automatically' conditioned by your past experiences. For if your husband's behavior is obviously not reinforcing your previously learned fear, and this fear still actively persists, then *you* must be doing something to reinforce it, to keep it alive, yourself."

"You really think I am?"

"You must be—unless we believe in some kind of magic. If you, as we just noted, were at least partly instrumental in setting up the original terrible fear of your father and your husband, even though they certainly also contributed mightily to the situational context of the fear, and if your present husband is not contributing to that context to any serious degree, who else but you *is* keeping the fear alive?"

"Hmm. I see what you mean. And what do you think that I'm telling myself to keep my fear alive?"

"What do *you* think? I am sure that if you start asking yourself you will soon start to see."

"What occurs to me, first of all, is that I am probably telling myself, or still telling myself, what you pointed out before: that I always was too weak and inadequate to do anything about myself and that I still am. And that therefore I *do* have something to be afraid of—my own weakness."

"That's a good point. These things usually become circular, just as you indicated. First, your father abuses you, then you tell yourself you can't do anything to stop his abuse, then you get terribly fearful. But, once you get fearful, and you only half-heartedly try to overcome your fear, you start telling yourself that you can't do anything about *that*. So you get fearful of becoming, and of not being able to do anything about becoming, fearful. Quite a pickle!"

"You know, I think that's exactly it. I used to be fearful of my father and my first husband—though really, as you're pointing out, of myself, of my weakness. And now I'm fearful of *remaining* fearful—of remaining weak. And even though my present husband and daughters are *not* abusing me, I'm afraid that I couldn't handle the situation if they *did* abuse me. I'm so afraid of being inadequate—and so afraid of being afraid—that I make myself panicky most of the time."

"Precisely. Then, probably, to take it one step further, you actually do get so frightened, and act so badly because you're frightened, that you then become convinced of your original hypothesis—that because you're so weak and inadequate, no one could ever possibly love you, including, especially, your own present husband and daughters."

"So I really start with a great need to be loved and a fear that, because I'm so worthless, I won't get this need fulfilled. Then because of my fear I behave badly. Then I note that I behave badly and say to myself: 'That proves how worthless I am!' Then, because I have doubly proved my 'worthlessness,' I get even more afraid that I won't be loved the next time. And so on, and on."

"Right. And then, going one step further, you hate yourself for being so weak and for having such a dire need for love; and you resent your present husband and daughters for not fulfilling your dire need to the exact extent you demand that they fill it—and for not making up for all the anger and punishment that your father and your first husband foisted on you. So that, mixed in with your terror, is a goodly degree of resentment—which only tends to make you still more upset."

"As you said before: Quite a pickle! But what do I do now to get out of it?"

"What do you think you do? If you're telling yourself sentences 1, 2, 3, and 4 to get result Number 5, and result Number 5 is highly undesirable, how do you manage not to get it again?"

"By *un*telling myself sentences 1, 2, 3, and 4!"

"Yes—or by challenging and questioning their validity."

"I have to ask myself, then, *why* I am so weak and worthless and *why* I can't stand anyone's anger."

"Yes. And also 'Why *don't* I deserve, now, to have a mild and cooperative husband and daughters?' And: 'Why, if I do happen to get frightened because I remind myself of some past threat that really doesn't exist any more, can't I then *see* what I am doing, and calm myself down pretty quickly?'"

"And if I try this kind of questioning and challenging and persist at it, then there's no reason why I have to continue to live in this kind of panic state I've been forcing myself into for such a long time?"

"No, no reason at all. Try it and see. And if it works, as I'm sure it will, that will be great. And if it doesn't then we'll quickly discover what *other* nonsense you are telling yourself to stop it from working."

"The main thing, if I understand you correctly, is that no matter what upsets me or what I am frightened at, it is now my *own* doing. It may not have been in the past. But it now is."

"In the main, yes. Occasionally, you may have a truly fearful circumstance in your life—as when you are on a sinking boat or in a car that is about to have a head-on collision with another car. But these kinds of realistic fears are rather rare in modern life; and the great majority of the things we now get panicked about are self-created 'dangers' that exist almost entirely in our own imaginations. *These* are your own doing; and these may invariably be undone by looking at your crooked thinking and straightening it out."

"O.K. What you say sounds reasonable. Let me do a little trying."

Mrs. Borengrad did try. Within the next several weeks she not only ceased being terrified when in the presence of her daughters and her present husband, but was able to do several other things, including making a public speech at her community center, a thing which she had never been able to do before in her life. She learned, and as the years go by she still continues to learn, that unlike Pavlov's dogs she can recondition or uncondition her feelings and her responses *from the inside* and that she does not *have* to respond to someone else's actual or possible anger with woeful feelings of fright.

In general, the most effective kinds of counterattacks against any needless and inappropriate fears that you may have may be taken along the following lines:

1. Track your worries and anxieties back to the specific sentences of which they consist. Invariably, you will find that you are telling yourself: "Isn't it terrible that—" or "Wouldn't it be awful if—". Forcefully ask yourself: "*Why* would it be so terrible that—?" and "*Would* it really be so awful if—?" Certainly, if this or that happened it might well be inconvenient, annoying, or unfortunate. But would it *really* be catastrophic?

2. When a situation actually is fearful—as when you are about to take a trip in a rickety old airplane—then the only sensible things to do are (a) change the situation (for example, don't take the trip) or (b) accept the danger as one of the unfortunate facts of life (thus, accept the fact that you may be killed in the rickety plane; that this is too bad if you are; but that life, to be reasonably lived, must be replete with considerable risk-taking). If a danger can be minimized, act to reduce it. If it cannot be minimized, or it would be more disadvantageous for you to avoid it than to risk it, then

you have little or no choice and you'd *just better* accept it. No matter how you slice it, the inevitable is still inevitable; and no amount of worrying will make it less so.

3. If a dire event may occur, and you can do no more than you have already done to ward it off, then *realistically* weigh the chances of its occurring and *realistically* assess the calamity that will befall you if it actually does occur. Although another world war *may* occur tomorrow, what are the chances that it *will?* If it does occur, what is the likelihood that you *will* be maimed or killed? If you are killed, will it *really* be much more catastrophic than your peacefully dying in bed ten or twenty years later?

4. To overcome a specific anxiety, verbal *and* active depropagandization are usually essential. You must first realize that *you* created the anxiety by *your* internalized sentences, and you must vigorously and persistently ferret out these sentences and challenge and contradict them. Then you must *also* push yourself to *do* the thing you are senselessly afraid of and *act* against your fear.

Thus, if you are afraid to ride on busses, you must realize that your over-concern is rooted in your own negative propaganda: in your telling yourself that busses are dangerous, that horrible things can happen to you in a bus, that if anything dreadful did happen on a bus you would not be able to stand it, and so on. And you must contradict this nonsense by showing yourself that busses are not very dangerous; that very few people are injured while riding on them; that if an unpleasant event occurs on a bus, you can handle it; and so forth. Finally, however, you must force yourself, over and over again, to keep riding on busses and to keep telling yourself, while riding, rational counterpropaganda to eradicate your irrationl self-sentences. The more you do the things you are afraid of *while* logically parsing and contradicting your self-imposed fearfulness, the quicker and more thoroughly your needless anxieties will vanish.

5. Most modern anxieties are intimately related to the underlying or overt dread of making public mistakes, of antagonizing others, of losing love. You should always suspect that some dire fear of disapproval lies behind your seemingly more objective fears and should continually and powerfully challenge and fight this basic anxiety of our time.

6. It is best to convince yourself—since this is invariably true—that worrying about many situations will definitely aggravate rather than improve them. If, instead of telling yourself how awful it would be if something happened, you tell yourself how silly, senseless, and self-defeating it will be if you *keep worrying* about this "awful" thing, you will have a much better chance of short-circuiting your irrational anxieties.

7. Try not to exaggerate the importance or significance of things. Your favorite cup, as Epictetus noted many centuries ago, is merely a cup of

which you are fond and your wife and children, however delightful, are mortal human beings. You need not take a negativistic, defensive so-what attitude and falsely tell yourself: "So what if I break my cup or my wife and children die? Who cares?" For you *should* care for your cup and your wife and children and will lead a more zestful and absorbing life if you do. But if you exaggeratedly convince yourself that this is the *only* cup in the world or that your life would be completely useless and worthless without your wife and children, you will only be falsely overestimating the value of undeniably good things and making yourself needlessly vulnerable to their possible loss.

It is good to remember, in this connection, that to enjoy a positive event wholeheartedly does *not* mean that you must catastrophize its absence. You may enjoy your cup, your wife, and your children wholeheartedly and truly care for them. But their sudden removal, although certainly a distinct loss and something that you should considerably *regret*, need not be *calamitous*. This loss, however difficult, merely removes *something* that you ardently desire and love—it does not remove *you*. Unless, of course, you *insist* on identifying your*self* with the people and things you love; and that kind of identification is emotional sickness.

8. Distraction, as we noted in the last chapter, may be a good temporary dissipator of groundless fear. If you are worrying about your plane's falling, forcing yourself to concentrate on a magazine or a book may give you some respite. If you are afraid that you are not making a good public speech, vigorous focusing on the content of your talk rather than on the reactions of your audience will often calm your fears. For deeper and more lasting removal of anxieties, however, a thoroughgoing philosophic approach, along the lines previously noted in this chapter, will be much more effective.

9. Tracking your present fears to their earlier origins, and seeing how though they were *once* fairly appropriate they *no longer* hold water, is often a useful anxiety-reducing technique. When you were a child, you normally feared many things, such as being in the dark or arguing with an adult. But you are now no longer a child. Keep showing yourself this and demonstrating that you can easily take certain chances now that it might have been foolhardy for you to take some years ago.

10. Don't be ashamed of still existing anxieties, no matter how senseless they may seem. Certainly it is wrong, meaning *mistaken*, for a grown person like you to retain childish fears. But *wrong* or *mistaken* does not mean *criminal* or *blameworthy*. And if people dislike you because you are anxious, that is largely their problem and is again nothing to worry about. Admit, by all means, that you are needlessly fearful; forthrightly tackle your silly worries; but don't waste a minute beating yourself over the head for being,

for the nonce, afraid. You have much better things to do with your time and energies!

11. No matter how effectively at times you combat your anxieties, and temporarily eradicate them, do not be surprised if they return from time to time. It is the nature of almost all human beings to fear again, at least from time to time, what they have once feared in the past, even though in general they are no longer afraid of this thing (Solomon and Wynne). If you once had a fear of high places and you conquered it by deliberately frequenting such places, you may still, on occasion, become afraid when looking down from heights. This is perfectly usual and expectable. In these circumstances, merely accept the returned fear, thinkingly and actively go to work on it again as you have done in the past, and you will quickly see, in most instances, that it returns to limbo.

Always remember, in this connection, that you are a mortal being; that humans have innate limitations; that they never *completely* overcome groundless fears and anxieties; and that life is a ceaseless battle against irrational worries. If you fight this battle intelligently and unremittingly, however, you can *almost* always be free from *almost* all your needless concerns. What more can you ask of a good life?

Acquiring
Self-Discipline
16

THE EASY WAY out is usually just that—the easy way out of the most rewarding satisfactions of *life*. Yet many—perhaps most—people swear by what we call Irrational Idea No. 7: *The idea that it is easier to avoid facing many life difficulties and self-responsibilities than to undertake more rewarding forms of self-discipline*. This idea is fallacious in several significant respects.

First of all, the notion that the easiest way out of life difficulties is the best way only considers at the very most, the case of action or avoidance at the exact moment of decision—and not in all the subsequent moments, hours, and days that are bound to follow this decision. Augie Mallick, for example, kept convincing himself that it would be terrible if the girl he had known for several years rejected his physical overtures. Every time he thought of putting his arm around her or holding her hand, he would be overwhelmed by his fear of rejection and would take the "easy" way out by drawing away from her. At the exact moment of his withdrawal, he sighed with relief. But for the rest of the night with her, and often for many nights following, he loathed himself and suffered the torments of the damned for his one moment of "ease." Short-run avoidance of fearful and difficult circumstances usually, in the long run, brings on far greater conflicts and self-annoyances.

By avoiding certain difficulties of life, moreover, you almost always tend to exaggerate their pain and discomfort. If Augie Mallick does take a chance, puts his arm around his girl friend, and actually gets rejected by her will this rejection actually hurt him as much as, in imagination, he thinks

144

it will? If he keeps getting rejected, will he *still* feel just as hurt? If he does get hurt, will his whole world fall apart? Almost certainly, if he keeps trying, the hard way, to win the favor of his girl, he will find that the answer to those questions is a pretty solid No.

Let us assume, again, that Augie does try, is rejected, and does get hurt (or, more accurately stated, does hurt himself by over-emphasizing the necessity of his getting accepted). Even so: will his self-hurt, as a result of his being rejected, be worse than his self-hurt as a result of his not *trying*? Probably not.

Still again: if Augie tries and fails, he will almost certainly *learn* something by his failure, while if he never tries, he will doubtless learn nothing. If he does things the hard way, his girl will probably ultimately accept him. And if she doesn't, the knowledge he acquires from being rejected by her, may well enable him to succeed with some other girl. Only if every single girl that he could ever possibly try to make an overture toward rejects him, will he have little or no gain from his experience; and this likelihood is infinitely small.

In the normal course of events, if Augie keeps trying, even against odds, he will ultimately succeed with *some* girl; while if he gives up quickly and foredooms himself to celibacy, his life will be a classic example of nothing ventured, nothing gained. But if he does venture, some kind of satisfaction will almost certainly be his; and quite possibly his gains will be enormous. Few of life's outstanding gratifications are achieved without taking considerable risks and facing distinct difficulties. Augie, in terms of time and energies expended, has his choice of: put up or shut up. And the less he puts up, the less he generally will fulfill his aliveness.

Similarly with the more negative side of the coin of self-discipline. If Janice, who wants to lose weight refuses to go through the continued difficulties of dieting, she will seemingly be taking the "easy" way out. But while she still enjoys her eating, will she also enjoy lugging around twenty extra pounds (particularly in summer), losing some of her best beaus to slimmer and trimmer girls, feeling tired and "blah" much of the time, and being a victim of several possible illnesses and ailments that often go with an overweight condition?

The story, then, is almost always the same when an individual takes the "easier" or unselfdisciplined way out of his life difficulties and responsibilities. Either his "easier" way is, in the long run, actually harder; or it continues to be easier—that is, less consuming of time and energy—but is also considerably less rewarding.

Take, by way of example, the case of Elmer Pinkham, a bright and potentially capable law school student who came to see me (R.A.H.) some years ago. He was an addict of the easy-way approach to life and knew all the angles of work-avoidance. Instead of buckling down to his studies, he spent considerable time learning the peculiarities of his professors—what they liked and did not like—so that he could induce them to give him good grades in spite of his continual goofing.

At the time Elmer came to see me he was having an affair with a fellow student but was finding the going rough. "Sally," he said, "is a great kid, but she is a very dependent character. I just can't have an ordinary affair with her—she's moved in. I mean completely moved in. I just am unable to get anything done any more. Not that I do much studying anyway; but with her around, I do absolutely none. We just make love, period. What I mean is period. And she's a pain in the hindquarters as well, since she wants me at her beck and call every single moment of the day and night and I can hardly go to the john without her tagging along. Other girls, whom I would like to see too from time to time, are absolutely out with Sally camping on my tail."

"If you find your relationship with Sally is interfering with your long-term plans to finish school and pass your bar exam and with your desire to have more time to yourself, why don't you get to work either to change the relationship with her or drop it?" I asked.

"I can't change it," Elmer replied. "Sally is just the way she is. She clings like a baby. There is no other way to relate to her. And I couldn't drop her— I just couldn't face her tears and her hysteria. Why, she'd be wailing around for weeks. And with some of the things she knows about me, how I cheated on some of my law exams and that sort of things, she might cause trouble too. I just couldn't go through the trouble of facing her and getting her to leave me."

"But with things the way they are, you say she's much more of a bother than she's worth. And, granted that it might be difficult to get rid of her, don't you think that it would be worth it in the long run."

"Yeah, I suppose so. But I wouldn't want to do it that way. I'd rather half keep her, you know. She is damned good in bed. And if I could only have less of her and not have her around all the time, that might be great. But how can I have it that way?"

"You mean: how can you have your cake and eat it? Isn't that what you really want?"

"Well, that's one way to put it. But maybe I can. Maybe there's an angle that I could work so that I could still have Sally, sort of on a part-time basis, and not be bothered by her so much or kept from seeing other girls sometimes."

"I can see you've already figured something out. Something real cute, no doubt! Now what's your plan?"

"Well, Doc, like this. I was thinking that if you would call Sally in and tell her you have diagnosed my problems and all that jazz and that you think it's necessary that she stop living with me, but just come around a couple of times a week, and stop being so sticky with me, you know—. Well, I thought you could fix it up with her so that I could still not have to give her up, not go through getting her all upset like, and keep the best part of our relationship going."

"You want me to help you do things the easy way with Sally. So that you won't have to face any responsibilities or difficulties and yet get exactly what you want. And you want me to sell Sally a bill of goods, so that she will be willing to accept half a loaf while you have your usual loaf and a half."

"Well, it would be easier on Sally that way, too, wouldn't it? She wouldn't get hurt or anything and would understand my position. You could easily arrange it, from your side. Such things must be all in your day's routine."

"It may surprise you to know," I said, "that my routine tends to run along other lines than being a kind of psychotherapeutic con man, easy-going fix-it expert, and emotional blackmailer. On the contrary, I help people to face and do things the hard way—because in the long run that way generally brings inner security and happiness. If I did what you want me to do not only would I be depriving you of the glorious opportunity to buckle down, for perhaps the first time in your life, to solving this difficult situation you are in and gaining some confidence that you actually *can* face and resolve tough situations that you encounter; but I would also be conniving to help Sally avoid making her own difficult decisions about whether to accept you on your terms or go on being the big baby she is. So my answer is a flat No. I intend to do you the service of forcing you, if possible, to face life's music this time, so that you may learn how to cope with it and yourself for a change and modify some of your obviously self-defeating, short-range hedonism."

"I am surprised at your attitude," Elmer said. "You have a reputation for being a liberal among psychologists. I've heard this from several people at the university. And yet you are giving me that old character-building song and dance. That old crap about 'chin up, sweet, clean, puritanical bird in the hand of God; work hard, be a good Christian, and you'll get a crumb from Jesus in the hereafter!' "

"You have the privilege of distorting what I say, if you wish. What I *am* saying, however, is this: The line of least resistance that you keep continually taking, in your school work, in your relations with Sally, and in some other aspects of your life that you've told me about is, almost certainly, not going to bring you what you really seem to want (and what you beautifully hide from yourself) out of life: namely, self-confidence and truly rewarding relationships with others. Whether you like it or not (and I am sure that you don't), you will not get maximum enjoyment in your work or your sex-love affairs until you learn to face the realities and difficulties of this world, figure out the best way of meeting instead of avoiding them, and act courageously and decisively in regard to them. This may sound to you like a philosophy of puritanical punishment, work for work's sake, and character-building for your heavenly salvation. But it's not. It's just one of the hard and cold facts of this highly unheavenly world."

"Maybe so, but I think I can do better than that. And I think I'll find another therapist with less austere ideals. There must be an easier road to happiness than the one you insist upon."

That's the last I heard of Elmer. For all I know, he is still shopping for the easy way of life and a less austere therapist to help him climb its roads. I would be willing to wager, however, that life will some day catch him up on his short selling of it and himself. At that time, if he has not softened himself up too much for eventual tackling of his basic problems, he may return for some serious psychotherapy. I'll probably still be at the old stand, with my "character-building" approach to life; and I shall, if he wants me to, be glad to welcome him back.

If avoidance of life difficulties and self-responsibilities leads, in most instances, to less rewarding activities and decreased self-confidence, full acceptance of the "harder" way of life is the only sensible and rational procedure. More specifically, this involves the following kinds of activities:

1. Although the taking on of needless tasks and responsibilities is not to be highly recommended, and is often a manifestation of masochism, you should determine what are the truly necessary activities of life—and then unrebellingly and promptly perform them. Necessary life tasks usually include: (a) tasks which are strictly necessary, such as eating, defecating, building a shelter from the cold, and so forth; and (b) tasks which are not strictly necessary for survival but that must be performed if one wishes to obtain desired goals. For example, brushing one's teeth to ensure their not decaying, or commuting in order to live in the country and work in the city.

2. Once you decide that a goal is necessary for your survival or highly desirable for your happiness (and not because *others* think you should attain it), self-discipline in regard to this goal can be attained by vigorous self-propagandization and forced action. In particular, you must first ferret out and forcefully attack your main *un*disciplining internal verbalizations: the nonsense that you keep telling yourself along the lines of "It is easier for me to remain the way I am," "I don't believe that I *can* discipline myself," and "Why should I *have* to do these unpleasant things in order to get the pleasant results I desire?" Instead, you must acquire a philosophy of life represented by these kinds of sentences: "It is definitely harder and less rewarding, especially in the long run, for me to do things the 'easy way' "; "I *do* have the ability, as a human being, to discipline myself, even though

it is quite difficult to do so"; and "Whether I like it or not, there *is* no other way to get the pleasant results I desire than by doing the unpleasant and time-consuming requisites to these results."

3. You must face the fact that, because you are a fallible human being, you often will have great difficulty getting started along a certain constructive line, and that normal principles of inertia will tend to hold you back and make the starting process quite a chore. You must therefore *expect* these problems to occur and prophylactically *accept* the fact that you will often have to use *extra* push and *extra* energy to get yourself on the road to self-discipline. Once you get going at brushing your teeth or getting up in the morning to travel to work, your task will tend to get easier and sometimes, even, enjoyable. But at the start it is *not* usually easy; and you must not expect it to be. Easy or not, you must keep convincing yourself that, if you want to obtain certain present or future results, there simply *is* no other way and it is to your own advantage (or sometimes your lesser disadvantage) to discipline yourself in a given manner.

4. Once you start on any self-disciplining task, you can sometimes make things easier for yourself: put yourself on some kind of a regular schedule or program; give yourself some sub-goals on any major project that you undertake; work on a piece rate basis (for example, force yourself to write so many pages or do a certain minimum number of exercises a day); or give yourself some intermediate rewards for your disciplining (permit yourself to go to a movie *after* you have completed this much studying or that much house cleaning for the day).

5. Guard against leaning over backward to be *too* self-disciplined or to do things the *too* hard way in order to achieve some magical rewards for your self-punishment. Most kinds of rigid adherence to rules, on the one hand, or inflexible rebelliousness against them, on the other hand, tend to be a throwing out of the baby with the bathwater and stem from emotional disturbance. Over-disciplining yourself can be just as self-defeating as avoidance of necessary discipline.

In sum: it *is* very difficult for the average or even the above-average individual to keep fighting against his or her normal tendencies to give up easily on hard tasks, to put off till tomorrow what really should be done today, and to slacken self-discipline long before it automatically develops its own momentum and begins to maintain itself with relatively little effort. All right, so it's hard. But it still continually has to be done if innumerable life responsibilities are to be adequately faced and solved and if long-range hedonism is to be appreciably achieved. And there *is* no other way. Avoid or cavil as you may, the piper still must be paid. If *your* goals and desires are to be attained, *you* must accept—and we really mean *accept*—

continual self-discipline. **Tough.** But that's what being human essentially means.

The only alternative is self-defeat; and this is the alternative that Oscar Jimson was taking when he first came to see me (A.E.) several years ago. Oscar, a young graduate student of psychology, was one of the brightest patients I ever had. But his Ph.D. thesis was just not getting done and all the important things he eagerly looked forward to doing in his chosen field of work were being everlastingly stymied because of what he called "my goddamned natural laziness." "Could it be," he asked, "that I'm just biologically this way and *can't* discipline myself the way that others much more easily can?"

I was not so easily sold on his biological hypothesis. "I doubt it," I said. "Especially since there are other aspects of your life in which you seem to do remarkably well in regard to self-discipline."

"You mean in my teaching?"

"Yes. You told me that in the classes you teach, you work very hard at preparing your lessons and really put considerable time and effort into them. And you take great pride in working so hard at it and being such a good teacher."

"That's right. I do work very hard in that area."

"Then what's this nonsense about 'natural biological laziness'? Obviously, if you can work hard at preparing your teaching activity you can work just as hard at writing your thesis and at the various other things you avoid doing."

"But that's different. In my class, I get an immediate amount of feedback or reward. My students love me and respond very favorably to the work I do in their behalf."

"No doubt. And I am sure that you well merit their approval. You give them something few other teachers do and they appreciate it."

"They really do."

"Great. But you're still proving *my* point—that when you *want* to do hard work, and when your reward for doing it is immediate enough, you have no trouble disciplining yourself to do it. When, however, the reward is somewhat remote—when the finishing of your Ph.D. thesis is a year or two away, and your professors are not going to give you much of a pat on the head until that year or two is up and the work is quite completed—then you idiotically tell yourself: 'Oh, I'm just naturally lazy. I can't discipline myself.' What you actually mean is, 'I'm so desperately in need of immediate approval that I *won't* discipline myself until I have a guaranty that I'm going to get it.' Quite a different picture, isn't it!"

"What you say sounds true. But is that the only reason why I'm refusing to work on my thesis and on various other things like that—because I demand immediate love satisfaction before I'll do anything?"

"No, probably not. There are usually other reasons why a human being, even when he's as bright as you are, will senselessly refuse to discipline himself in certain areas."

"And which of them seem to apply in my case?"

"Well, first of all there's the general principle of inertia. It *is* hard for people, even unusually sane people, to force themselves to get going and keep going on a long-term project like a Ph.D. thesis when they know perfectly well that it will be quite a time before they finish it and before they reap the rewards of their labor. Little children, you will note, are very difficult to motivate for any long-range project, no matter how much good it would do them to persist at it and finish it; and most adults all their lives retain much of this childish trait."

"So I'm still childish—eh?"

"Yes; but not necessarily in any unusual or abnormal sense. You just have a lot of *normal* childishness in you; and you are *normally* reluctant to give it up. Perhaps *that* is what you refer to as your 'natural laziness.' "

"Could be. But don't we all have some degree of this kind of thing? And why is mine more than somebody else's?"

"Well, for one thing, like so many highly intelligent individuals, you've had it a little *too* good most of your life as far as doing academic work is concerned. Being bright, you've found that you could get along very well, especially during grade school and high school, with much *less* work than the average child has to do to keep up with his subjects and still get good marks."

"You're right about that. I practically did no work at all during grade school and high school and still was always right near the top of my class. And in college, things were still easy."

"Exactly. So you didn't *need* to acquire good work habits until, quite recently, you got into graduate school. And now, since the competition is keener, and theses just don't write themselves, you do have to develop better work habits in the school area. But, having gotten along so well with a minimum of scholastic effort, you probably think that it's highly *unfair* that you shouldn't still be able to do so. So we come to the next point: you're *rebelling* against doing the thesis and some of your other work; you don't think you should *have* to exert yourself so much."

"Well, it *is* tough, isn't it? I never *did* have to do this kind of thing before."

"Yes, it is tough. So it's tough! But it still must be done—if you are to get the rewards that you now want. And no amount of childish rebelling is going to make it any easier. Quite the contrary: as you recently have been seeing."

"True. The more I goof, the more I fall behind, and then the harder it gets for me to catch up. Besides, my profs at school are becoming more than a little disgusted with me—and that isn't helping at all."

"It never will. Not only will your kind of dilly-dallying get others, such as your professors, disgusted with you; but it will tend to have a similar effect on yourself."

"I'll get disgusted with me, *too?*"

"Well?"

"Mmm. I see what you mean. Again, you've got me. I have to admit that as I've kept putting off my dissertation I've been thinking more and more, "Maybe I can't do it. Maybe it's just not my kind of task. Teaching—yes. And passing courses. But maybe this kind of thing is just beyond me.""

"Par for the course, those kinds of thoughts. First you refuse to buckle down to the job—because of the normal inertia and the abnormally childish habit patterns we've been discussing. Then, instead of getting the immediate approval you greatly crave and which you work your head off to get in your teaching, you get professorial disgruntledness and disgust. Then you say to yourself, 'You know, maybe I *can't* discipline myself,' or 'Maybe I *can't* do this kind of a project.' Then, because of your inordinate fear of failure, and your unwillingness to put your own negative hypothesis to the test, you run further away from working on the thesis rather than facing it. Then you engender still more professional displeasure and self-disgust. Finally, you're really caught up in the worst kind of a vicious circle and where you originally were childishly rebelling against doing the work now you're terribly *afraid* to try it. End of the line—and practically the end of you—if you don't stop this nonsense and cut this vicious circle."

"You make it sound real sick, my behavior."

"*Isn't* it?"

"Well—. What can I say?"

"Whatever you say isn't going to change things very much and make your behavior less sick. The real point is, what are you now going to *do?*"

"About my natural inertia, my childish rebellion, my inordinate demands for immediate approval, and my sick thinking that I *can't* do the thesis, merely because I've not at all tried to buckle down to do it?"

"Yes, you summarize the case very nicely. Now what are you going to *do* about it?"

"I suppose if I told you that I was going to stop this sick behavior and get right down to work on the thesis, you wouldn't believe me?"

"No—not till you actually started to work. But I wouldn't disbelieve you, either. For one thing I know perfectly well—that any person who works as well as you do in regard to your teaching—*can* work just as well on a project like a Ph.D. thesis. So the question is not at all whether you *can*, but whether you *will*. And maybe, now that you've been seeing just *how* inconsistent and self-defeating you are by not working on your dissertation, maybe you will."

"Goddamn it, I *hope* I will!"

"Hope is a very nice sentiment; but it's still not enough. You've got to be *determined* to overcome your childish rebelliousness and fear of failure. You've got to be *actively* determined. Which means actively ferreting out and vigorously challenging the anti-disciplinary nonsense that you've been feeding yourself for all these many years."

"You're right again. *Action* is the real key-word. We'll see!"

And we did see. Oscar Jimson got his thesis topic approved within the next few weeks, quickly buckled down to do his research on it, and a year later was a newly fledged Ph.D. in experimental psychology. He still is a fine teacher; and, in addition, one of the most all-around self-disciplined men I know in his field. Whenever I meet him at psychological conventions these days he facetiously stands at attention, gives me a Prussian Army salute, and exclaims: "ACTION! WORK! SELF-DISCIPLINE!" Only he's not really so facetious.

Rewriting
Your Personal
17 History

PERVERSELY ENOUGH, ONE of the most important psychological discoveries of the past century, emphasized by both the psychoanalytic and the conditioned response (or behaviorist) schools of thinking, has been most harmful to many individuals. And that is the idea that human beings are most importantly influenced, in their present patterns of living, by their past experiences. This perfectly sane and potentially helpful observation has been time and again used to create and bolster what we call <u>Irrational Idea No. 8</u>: *The idea that the past is all-important and that because something once strongly affected one's life, it should indefinitely do so.*

Yesterday, in the course of one of my typical working days, I (A.E.) saw twelve patients; and every single one of them, to one degree or another, believed that he or she *had* to be behaving in a certain disturbed way because of previous conditioning or early influences. A forty-year-old, highly attractive divorcee, for example, told me: "I couldn't possibly be more active in meeting men, as you are trying to induce me to be, when I've never done anything of the sort before in my life." A young wife said that she would rather have her husband lose fifty thousand dollars in a business venture than to be out of work again—because she was sure that he would not be able to find satisfactory employment in view of the fact that he had had so many poor jobs before. A remarkably good-looking, well-educated, and bright young man of twenty-two confessed that he couldn't imagine himself getting a satisfactory girl friend again if his present one left him, because "I have been conditioned from childhood to feel that I'm not good enough to go out and get anyone I want, so how can I ever expect to do this?"

So it goes, through most of my working days, with one patient after another directly or indirectly indicating that the unkind, heavily sunk-in ravages of his or her past life cannot possibly be overcome in the present or future—unless I somehow magically help him or her to undo this pernicious influence. To which I normally respond:

"Rubbish! Whatever your early conditioning or the pernicious influences of your childhood were, their effects never linger on, today, just *because* of these original conditions—but because you still *carry* them on, because you still *believe* the nonsense with which you were originally indoctrinated. Now when are *you* going to challenge and tackle your own often-repeated beliefs and thereby *uncondition* yourself?" And the battle of therapeutic de-indoctrination continues merrily apace, until (usually) I win or (sometimes, alas) the patient flees from me and the necessary work he will have to undertake to rid himself of his pernicious past influences.

Like these patients, most people in our society appear to believe that because something once significantly affected their lives, or was at one time appropriate or necessary to their existences, this thing must remain important forever. Thus, they believe that because they once had to obey their parents they still, as adults, should do so. Or because they were once victims of their environment, they still have to be. Or because they once were superstitious, they must continue to believe in their early-acquired nonsense.

A strong belief in the continuing importance or enormous significance of the past is illogical for several reasons:

1. If you still let yourself be unduly influenced by your past experiences, you commit the logical error of over-generalization. Because a thing is true under *some* circumstances hardly proves that it is equally true under *all* conditions. Because your father may have been unkind when you were a child and you had to fight against his exploiting you does not mean that *all* men are equally unkind and that you have to keep being on guard against them. Because you were once too weak to stand up against the domination of your mother hardly means that you must *always* remain that weak.

2. By allowing yourself to be too strongly influenced by past events, you cease to look for alternative solutions to a problem. There is rarely only one possible solution to a difficulty, and if you remain flexible in your thinking you will keep casting around till you find a better one than is immediately apparent. But if you believe that you must be unduly influenced by your past experiences, you will tend to think mainly in terms of prior, and usually quite inadequate, "solutions."

3. Many aspects of behavior that are appropriate at one time are decid-

edly inappropriate at another. Children, in particular, often devise various methods of solving their problems with their parents—such as by wailing, balking, or having a temper tantrum when they want their own way. These devices may be effective for youngsters; but when carried into adulthood may be thoroughly ineffective since other adults will not respond to the same devices unless employed by children. If you stick, therefore, to problem-solving devices that were effective in the past, you will often find them highly illogical in the present.

4. If you remain notably influenced by your past you will maintain what the psychoanalysts call "transference" effects—meaning that you will inappropriately transfer your feelings about people in your past life to those who are around you today. Thus, you may self-defeatingly rebel against your boss's orders today because they remind you of your parents' highhanded orders of twenty years ago. Such transference relationships are often most unrealistic and unrewarding.

5. If you unchallengingly continue to perform in a certain way because you have done so in the past, you will fail to gain many new experiences that might well prove to be exceptionally enjoyable. Thus, if you continue to have homosexual relations mainly because you enjoyed having them in your early teens, you may never try heterosexual relations and may never discover that they can be considerably more satisfying than homosexual acts. Or if you refuse to try for a job as an accountant because you were once fired from a similar job, you may never become competent enough to retain and enjoy another accounting position.

6. Unquestioningly accepting the influences of the past amounts to your being thoroughly unrealistic in many instances since the present is *not* the past but usually significantly differs from it. Riding in a Model T Ford on today's superhighways can be dangerous because the road and traffic conditions for which the Model T were designed no longer exist. Treating your wife the same way that you treat your mother may, because she definitely is *not* your mother, easily bring trouble.

In sum: although the past, as the psychoanalysts and the behaviorists have clearly seen, indubitably exists and definitely influences people to repeat old patterns of behavior, it is not *necessary* that it wield the enormous influence that it often does. You *can* change human nature, no matter how long a past condition of behaving has existed—otherwise we, like our ancestors, would still be living in caves.

Your basic personality, moreover, is *not* so inalterably set, in the light of your past experiences, that it need require a "deep" analysis of many years to restructure. If, with the help of any effective psychotherapeutic procedure, with participation in an intensive program of psychological reading, lectures, and group discussion, and with (above all!) continual self-questioning and challenging of your own basic assumptions and philosophies of living, you will keep working hard at changing your "basic nature," remarkable results can very often be achieved within a few months to a few years' time.

True, most people are more or less resistant to making drastic changes in themselves. This is largely, as we have been trying to show throughout this book, because they keep *reinforcing* their old beliefs—telling themselves, over and over, that Negroes *are* no good, or that failing at a job *is* terrible, or that they *should not be* forced to bake their cake before they can eat it. But this fact, rather than proving that "human nature" cannot be changed, really signifies just the opposite. Precisely *because* we keep re-living our past mistakes as a result of *our* self-sentences, we can normally change these mistakes by changing our own sentences. Just as our present behavior largely stems from our past experiences, our future activities will follow our present performances. And we, by determined thinking and practice, can enormously regulate and control our activities of today.

Harold Stover came to therapy with a quick and vicious temper which, he said right at the start, he just had to get rid of if he wanted to marry the girl of his dreams. "You've got to help me, Doctor Harper," he pleaded. "Because Grace says that if I fly off the handle once more in her presence that's it, and I'm all washed up with her. She said that you helped her immensely, a couple of years ago, when she kept getting angry at her boss all the time. And unless I let you help me, too, she's had it."

"Well, I can only do my best," I said. "Or, rather, help you do your best. But, first of all, tell me a little about how your big, bad temper originated."

Harold then told a fairly typical tale of how, since early childhood, he had raised the roof when even the slightest thing went wrong. And with some encouragement, too, since he remembered his mother proudly telling some guests that from his early nursing days he would howl with rage if she tried to get him to do anything he didn't want. "Harold had his own mind at birth," she was fond of saying. And it appeared that somehow this only child of hers, who insisted on having his own way at all times, appealed to the mother.

Under the circumstances, it was hardly surprising that his mother's evaluation of his temper tantrums as being natural, inevitable, and vaguely cute and desirable came to be adopted by Harold himself. He looked upon his temper as a normal and effective means of getting what he wanted from his mother and various other people, especially women, who were sufficiently intimidable. When Grace refused to be intimidated, and frankly told him that he could peddle his fish elsewhere unless he stopped acting like a big, churlish child, he realized that he had reached the end of the temper tantrum line and that he would do better casting about for more suitable means of continuing life's journey.

It was not hard to show Harold what the origins of his tantrums were; and he soon quite agreed with me that there was no use in blaming himself for having developed the way he did, since his mother had so obviously trained him to be that way, and there was no point, anyway, in self-recrimination.

"But where do I go from here?" Harold asked. "How do I get over this stuff, now that I know how it arose? Isn't it true that anything that goes back practically to birth, and is so deeply a part of my behavior patterns over so long a period of time, is going to be practically impossible to get rid of?"

"No, I replied, "it isn't so at all. It's perfectly true that, considering how long you have been having your childish temper tantrums—or how long, really, you have thought it perfectly *good and proper* to have them—you're going to have a decidedly *difficult* time in fighting them out of your life. So it'll be difficult. But not half so difficult as it will be if you *don't* fight to get rid of these self-defeating reactions."

"But how? *How* do I fight them out of my system?"

"The same way basically, as you put them *into* your system."

"But didn't we just get finished saying, a while ago, that my mother put them into my system, by her rewarding me for having the tantrums, and thereby conditioning me to keep having them?"

"No, not exactly—although it may, at first blush, seem like that. Actually what happened was that your mother rewarded you, all right, for having your fits of temper; but also, and more importantly, that you accepted and kept looking for further rewards. That is to say, you didn't only say to yourself: 'Ah, there goes Mother again, indicating that I can jolly well have my temper tantrums; so I might as well continue having them.' What you also said was: 'Ah, Mother allows herself to be intimidated by my tantrums. And Father goes along for the ride as well. And Florence, the maid, lets me get away with the same kind of thing. Now let me see: whenever I want anything that they at first won't give me, I'll look for people like Mother and Father and Florence and yell my bloody head off until they give it to me. I know that this will make me something of a bother to these people, but why should I care about that when I keep getting what I want? For it's really terrible, it's horrible not to get what I want. And I would much rather get it, even if I have to keep bothering people, than not get it. And if some people won't give me what I want when I scream and yell, then to hell with them. I'll just find other people to be with who *will* give me what I want.' Wasn't it something along these lines that you kept saying to yourself?"

"Come to think of it, I guess you're remarkably close. For I do remember, now that you've mentioned it, that I once had quite a lot of friends, when I was a small child, and was one of the most popular boys in my neighborhood. But when I found out that some of them wouldn't stand for my temper tantrums, and wouldn't let me have my way when I went into a fit, I somehow cut them out of my acquaintanceship and wound up, after a while, having a sort of bunch of toadies who would keep giving in to me. And I must admit, now that I think of it again, that these toadies didn't include some of the brightest and most able kids on the block. But I stayed with them anyway, in order to keep getting my way."

"You were willing to sacrifice, then, some of your brightest and most able friends in order to keep getting your immediate wants fulfilled. And isn't that the pattern that you've followed since that time, giving up long-range goals or more able friends in order to surround yourself with toadies who would quickly gratify you, just as your parents and maid originally gratified you at a moment's squawk?"

"Yes, I guess it is. But I still don't see how I'm going to get out of this pattern of behavior."

"As I said before—the same way you got into it. For if your dedication to tantrums stems largely, as I am contending, not just from your having been trained to have them, by some outside force, but from *your* having trained yourself to have them, to take the easier and shorter-range hedonistic way out of your problem of getting your wants immediately gratified, then you can equally well train yourself *not* to have these temper fits, and instead to favor long-range hedonistic aims."

"Just as *I* said to myself, "Well, go ahead, Harold, have your fits in order to blackmail others to do your bidding,' *I* can now say to myself, 'Stop the nonsense, Harold, and get what you really want out of life—longer-range and more deeply satisfying goals like winning Grace, for example—by behaving like an adult and *not* having any more fits.' Is that how I can do it?"

"Yes. And just as you, partly as a rationalization for keeping your present mode of going for immediate gratification instead of longer-range goals, are now telling yourself: 'How can I ever expect to change, to lose my tantrum habit, when it goes back to birth and is an inextricable part of my personality?' so you can tell yourself, instead: 'No matter how long I've had this childish habit, nor how many people I've cajoled into going along with it, I am *now* defeating my own best ends with it, so I'd better work my backside off, *against* my habit and *for* myself, to behave differently."

"What you seem to be saying is that I must now accept the fact that it is not so terrible to lose out on some immediate pleasure, but that I am a big boy and can stand such a loss; and that, for my *greater* good I'll just *have* to change my ways."

"Yes, I am asking you to make more of a *philosophic* than a *motor* change in your habits. And I am sure that if you accept an adult philosophy of life, for the first time, you will not have much difficulty in acting in an adult way from here on in."

"But suppose I try what you say, and all goes well for awhile, and then I fail, and have another real fit of temper again?"

"Suppose you do. As long as you do not use your slip to 'prove' to yourself that you really *were* born to have temper tantrums, and you definitely *can't* change, it will remain just that: a minor slip. And you will soon go back to changing for the better again, until your relapses become fewer and fewer, and eventually perhaps disappear completely."

"As long as I stick to the present and keep working for a different future, I can practically forget about the long negative conditioning of the past?"

"Right. As long as, every time you feel urged to have a fit of temper, or actually slip for a short while into having one, you say to yourself: "Well, there I go again. I must have told myself some nonsense all over again to make myself slip. Now let's see what it was. And how can I use this relapse to help myself avoid another temper outburst *next* time?' If you calmly, interestedly look at your slips, and your internalized sentences that are causing them, in *this* manner then it will only be a matter of time when your negative conditioning of the past turns into the positive conditioning of the present and your problem is solved."

So it proved. Six weeks later Harold Stover reported: "Would you believe it? Grace and I actually got engaged. You'll be getting a formal announcement just as soon as they are printed up. And *she* was the one to do the pushing. 'Look, darling,' I said, when she suggested it the other night, 'I know that I haven't had any temper outbursts for the last six weeks now, and I'm certainly glad for your sake and mine that I haven't. But how do you know that I'm really cured, and that I won't have one again tomorrow?' 'That's not the point, Harold,' she replied. 'I don't know that you won't have one tomorrow again—though I doubt that you will. But it wasn't really your outbursts that I was against but the little-boy, you've-got-to-give-me-ex-actly-what-I-want *attitude* that went with them and caused them. And *that*, your attitude, has changed remarkably since you've been talking to Dr. Harper. And I feel sure that *that* won't change back to the old attitude very quickly. If it does,' and she smiled in her inimitable manner at this point, you know how she smiles, Doctor, 'well, I can always divorce you.'"

Grace and Harold did marry; his new grown-up attitudes did not change back to the old little-boy ones; and they are still managing to stay out of the divorce court. There is every reason to believe that they always will.

Almost any other intelligent and hard-working person, too, can overcome the influence of his past, or stop acting in accordance with what the psychoanalysts call his classic transference, if some of these techniques are tried:

1. Accept the fact that your past is important and that you are bound to be significantly influenced by it in many ways. But accept, equally, the fact that *your present is your past of tomorrow.* You cannot today make a single right-about-turn and be an entirely different person from the one you were yesterday. But you can *start* changing yourself significantly today so that *eventually* you will be a quite different individual. By doing new kinds of thinking and undergoing new experiences in the present, and by accepting your past as a *handicap* rather than a *total block,* your tomorrow's (or the day after tomorrow's) behavior may well be radically different from today's.

2. <u>Objectively *acknowledging* your past errors, instead of moralistically *blaming* yourself for them, you can learn to *use* your disadvantageous past for your own present and future benefit</u>. Instead of automatically repeating your past mistakes because you *once* made them, you can calmly *observe* and *question* these misdeeds. All traditions and customs that you generally follow, in fact, can be periodically reviewed and rethought: so that you can separate the wheat from the chaff and (if desirable) change your life accordingly.

3. <u>When you find that you are strongly held by some past influence that is defeating your current goals you must persistently and forcefully fight it on both verbal and action levels</u>. Thus, if you find that you keep acting like a little child toward your mother and consequently failing to do what you really want to do in life, you must keep convincing yourself: "I do *not* have to continue to act this way. I am *no longer* a child. I can speak up to my mother and tell her what I really think is right and what I actually want to do. She has no power over me any more and cannot hurt me or prevent me from doing what I want unless *I* let her. I do not want to hurt her needlessly; but neither do I want to hurt myself. I know that I once thought disaster would ensue if I stood up to her; but this is nonsense—it won't. There is nothing to be afraid of but my *own* silly beliefs about disaster. Now let's have no more of this bosh. Enough is enough!" On the counter-propaganda front, you must seek out and forthrightly tackle any irrational influences from the past. You must show yourself how ridiculous they are; how they are only harming rather than helping you; how you would be much better off if you removed them.

4. As ever, to effect a solid change in yourself, you must accompany your counter-propaganda with action. You must deliberately *work* against the influences of the past: *force* yourself, for example, to act toward your mother in a more adult fashion, to risk her disapproval, to say and do things that you previously would have been petrified to do lest you shock her. If

you never in all your life talked to a stranger in a bus, went to a party alone, kissed a girl on your first date, or did similar things that you very much would like to do, *force* yourself, give yourself absolutely no peace, until you try and try again these terribly "fearful" but actually harmless acts. No nonsense! Don't just think: *act!* Years or decades of past fright and inertia may almost always be overcome by days or weeks of present forced practice.

5. Remember, above all: the past *is* the past. It has no magical, automatic effect on the present or future. At most, your past habits make it harder for you to change than to remain stationary. Harder, but not impossible. Work and time; practice and more practice; thinking and doing; these are the unmagical keys that will unlock almost any chest of past defeats and turn them into possible present and future victories.

Accepting Reality

18

LET'S FACE IT: reality often stinks. People are not the way we would like them to be; this is not the best of all possible worlds; even half-perfect solutions to many of life's serious problems and difficulties just do not exist.

But this is *still* no reason for an individual's being desperately unhappy. It is not imperfect or unkind reality which makes millions of humans miserable, but their unthinking addiction to Irrational Idea No. 9: *The idea that people and things should be different from the way they are and that it is catastrophic if perfect solutions to the grim realities of life are not immediately found*. This idea is idiotic for several reasons:

1. There is no reason whatever why people *should be* any different from the way they are, even when they are palpably acting very badly or immorally. It would certainly be nice if they *were* different and if they did not act badly. But the fact is that they *are* the way they are and *do* act badly. And it is grandiose if you tell yourself, "Because I don't *like* people the way they are, they *shouldn't be* that way." Similarly, although it would be lovely if things and events often were *not* the way they are, they frequently *are* that way. And again, there is no reason why they shouldn't be, just because you would *like* them to be different.

2. When people and events are the way you would like them not to be, there is actually relatively little pernicious effect they can have on you unless you *think* they can. If your wife acts nastily or your friends are unfriendly, their behavior may well be annoying or not ideal; but it is rarely truly as bothersome as you, by your intolerance, may *make* it. Similarly,

163

•

when things or events go wrong, that is unfortunate, and may affect you adversely. But the adversity thereby caused you is rarely half so bad as you think it is or as you make it by telling yourself "Things *shouldn't* be this way. I can't stand it!"

3. Assuming that people are actually harming you and events are really going poorly, your becoming upset about what is happening will still do you no good. On the contrary, the more upset you become, the less you will be able to change people or things for the better. Thus, if you become incensed because your mate is acting irresponsibly, the chances are that he or she, feeling angry at your criticism, will act even more irresponsibly.

4. As Epictetus pointed out two thousand years ago, although we do have the power to change and control ourselves to a considerable degree (if we work hard and long enough at modifying our own beliefs and actions), we do not have a similar power to control the behavior of others. No matter how wisely we may counsel others, they are still independent entities and may—and indeed, have the right as individuals—to choose to ignore us completely. If, therefore, we become unduly aroused over the way others act, instead of paying more attention to how *we* respond to their actions, we are upsetting ourselves over an outside event that is largely beyond our control. This is akin to tearing our hair because a jockey, a prizefighter, or an actor is not performing the way *we* think he should perform. Very silly business indeed!

5. Upsetting yourself about other people and events will usually sidetrack you from what should logically be your main concern: the way *you* behave, the things *you* do. If you control your own destiny, by the proper cultivation of your own garden, the most harrowing things that happen will not perturb you too much and you will often be able to help change other people and things for the better. But if you unduly upset yourself over outside happenings, you will inevitably consume so much time and energy that you will have little left for the proper cultivation of your own garden.

6. The notion that there is an absolutely right or perfect solution to any of life's problems is highly improbable, since few things are all black or all white and there are normally many alternative solutions, each with various advantages and disadvantages, to almost any problem. If you compulsively keep seeking for the absolutely best or perfect solution, you will tend to be so rigid and anxious that you will be fairly certain to miss some highly satisfactory compromises. Thus, the individual who *has* to see the best TV program that is on the air at a given time will probably keep anxiously turning from one channel to another and will end up by having seen *none* of the programs.

7. The disasters that you imagine will occur if you do not quickly get a

perfect and absolutely "right" solution to one of life's realities rarely actually occur—except by arbitrary definition. If you *think* it is catastrophic to make a wrong decision—to marry the wrong person, for example, and wind up with a divorce—you will most likely *bring* disaster on your head when you discover your mistake. If you think that it is regrettable and unfortunate, but *not* catastrophic, to make exactly the same wrong decision, you will most likely bear your mistake very well—and perhaps even learn a great deal by it.

8. <u>Perfectionism is, almost by definition, a self-defeating philosophy.</u> No matter how close you may come to running the perfect race, living with someone who displays flawless behavior, or arranging things in your life so that you are absolutely certain of their outcome, you will never really achieve your perfectionist goals. For humans are *not* angels; events are *never* certain; decisions *cannot* be absolutely correct at all times. Even if you temporarily achieve perfection in some goal, your chances of remaining at this ultimate peak are nil. Nothing is perfectly static; life *is* change. Whether you like it or not, you must accept reality the way it is: as being highly imperfect and filled with most fallible humans. The only alternative is continual anxiety and desperate disappointment.

Take the case of Laura Gerand. Laura came from a close-knit family. She had been her father's favorite child but had felt that her mother preferred her two sisters and two brothers to herself. Then her father died when Laura was twenty, and left a large amount of insurance to his wife. One of Laura's main problems, and one which she brought up continually during the early sessions of psychotherapy, was her great concern about her mother's ability to manage the money she had been left. According to Laura, her mother kept extravagantly throwing this money away on all the other family members except herself.

Said the therapist, after hearing a number of Laura's complaints and seeing that she probably intended to keep making them ad infinitum:

"Why are you so concerned about what your mother is doing with this money, anyway? After all, it *is* her money; it *was* left to her by your father; and she *has* a perfect right to do with it what she likes—to throw it down the sewer, if that pleases her."

"Yes, I realize that, of course," Laura replied. "But you see my mother always had my father to look after money matters before. Now she doesn't and she doesn't know how to say 'No' to my greedy brothers, sisters, and in-laws."

"Do you want some of the money yourself, for some special purpose? Is that what's bothering you?"

"No, I'm doing quite all right. I have a good job and opportunities for advancement. And the boy I'm engaged to is doing very well too and comes from a well-to-do family. So I don't want a cent of her money for myself. Not a cent."

"Then what's the problem? Why don't you just forget about what your mother is doing with her money and go about your own business? Apparently she hasn't asked any advice from you about it; and if she wants to give all the money to your brothers and sisters and their families, that's her privilege."

"But how can she behave that way—throwing away the money like that, when she may need it later? And giving all of them everything they want! Why, in no time at all the money will be entirely gone!"

"Perhaps so; but that's *still* her problem. Besides, you have already called to her attention the fact that you think she is spending too much too fast, haven't you?"

"Oh, yes. I spoke to her as soon as I saw, a few weeks after my father's death, what she was doing."

"And she said?"

"To mind my own goddamn business!"

"Well?"

"But how *can* she do this? It's terribly wrong of her to act this way. Can't something be done to stop her?"

"Let's assume, for the moment, that it is wrong or stupid for your mother to be spending the money the way she is—"

"Oh it is; it is!"

"Well, I'm not sure that everyone—especially your brothers and sisters— would agree that it is. But let's assume that it is wrong—that almost any sane and objective person would agree that it is. So what? So it's wrong. But hasn't your mother the democratic right to be wrong? Are you going to take away that right from her?"

"But—! But is it *right* to be wrong?"

"No, obviously it isn't. If she's wrong, she's wrong; and she can't, at one and the same time, be right. O.K.: so she's wrong. But you still haven't answered my question: Doesn't every human being, including your mother, have the right to be wrong? Or do you want to *force* them, if you can, to be perfectly dead right?"

"I'm not sure what you mean."

"Well, let's put it this way: It is certainly desirable, you and I will grant, that human beings be right instead of wrong, that they make fewer rather than more mistakes. And if your mother is wrong about her spending this money—as we are assuming for the sake of discussion that she is—then it would be highly desirable if she stopped being wrong and stopped spending the money the way she is spending it. But let's suppose that she's wrong, dead wrong, about the spending, and that she's just *not* going to stop being wrong—she's going to continue to spend the money badly, to squander it on your brothers and sisters and their families."

"But *should* she?"

"That's just the point—why *shouldn't she?* Why *shouldn't* she be wrong if she is, and continue to be wrong if she wants to continue to be? Why shouldn't she be a fallible human being, like all of us, and make one mistake after another? Would you want her, really expect her, to be an angel?"

"No, I wouldn't."

"You *say* you wouldn't; but do you really *mean* what you say? For here she is, your mother, dead wrong according to our hypothesis; and you're insisting that she not be wrong, that she be right. But she *is* wrong and is determined to continue being so. Now it seems to me that she'd have to be something of an angel, under these circumstances, not to be wrong—or to stop being wrong when she wants to go on continuing to be. And what you really mean, of course, is that you want her to do things *your* way with the money rather than *her* way. And even more than that, you want her to *want* to do things your way rather than hers. And you're giving her no democratic right whatever to want to do things *her* way—however wrong, according to you, me, and even the world at large, that way may be."

"But I still say: *Should* a person be wrong, when she can just as well be right?"

"But that's a rhetorical question. Because, obviously, if people *could* just as well be right, they probably would be. And when they are wrong, it means either that they want to be right, but somehow can't be as yet; or that they don't even want to be right—and therefore certainly can't be."

"I—I really don't know what to say."

"Well, think about it a little more, and I'm sure that you'll see that some of the things I'm pointing out are true, and that you just haven't been considering them. Suppose, for example, that you were in your mother's place instead of your mother being there and that you were doing something wrong—say, spending a lot of money rather recklessly and foolishly."

"I'd be wrong if I did—just as wrong as she is."

"All right, let's suppose you'd be wrong. But the point is: Wouldn't you have a *right* to be wrong—to make your own mistakes? Suppose your mother came to you, in those circumstances, and advised you to stop spending the money the way you were doing; and suppose you thought over her advice, but still decided to go on spending your money foolishly. Again: wouldn't you have the *right* to do things your way instead of hers, and make your own mistakes?"

"I see what you mean now. Even though I was wrong, I'd have a perfect right, as a human being, to do what I wanted, and perhaps by doing it to prove to myself that I was wrong."

"Exactly. For don't forget that people like your mother—or like you would be in this illustration, we are supposing—practically never *think* they are wrong when they are making their mistakes. Later, perhaps, they realize how wrong they were. But not at the time they are making the mistakes. Now how else can they learn, in these circumstances, *except* by making their mistakes, and finally proving themselves to have been wrong?"

"I guess you're right there. There *is* no other way, actually, that they can learn how wrong they are, is there?"

"No, not for all practical purposes. They *could* see how wrong they are merely from your or someone else's pointing it out to them. But if they don't, then what else can they do but make their mistakes and *then*, in retrospect, see that they were wrong?"

"But isn't it a shame that people have to act that way first and *then* see that they are wrong?"

"It probably is a shame—but that's the way human beings are. Most of the time they *first* make their mistakes and *then* they recognize them. If they were angels, they doubtless would behave differently. But they aren't angels—they are fallible humans. Besides, look at the advantages of their being so fallible and of our permitting them to be so."

"What advantages?"

"Well, for one thing their fallibility leads them to have experiences, and often quite valuable experiences, that otherwise, if they were more cautious and less fallible, they might never have. Memoirs would be quite dull reading if people were as infallible as you would like them to be!"

"Oh, I'm sure we could make *that* sacrifice to create a better world!"

"Maybe so. But there's an even more important point. If people made fewer mistakes the way *you* want to force them to do—by not only bringing their errors to their attention but punishing them severely for such errors —would the fascist-type world that we then would have be worth living in? If you, for example, really could and did force your mother to stop her rash spending, and let's even suppose that you were technically correct in doing so (though actually, of course, you *could* be wrong and she *could* be right), how do you think she and millions of other people like her would enjoy being supervised by people like you? How would you, for example, enjoy being told, by people like your mother, what kind of a job you could work at, whom you could marry, and just how much money you could spend each week?"

"I don't suppose I'd enjoy it at all."

"I don't suppose you would. And yet isn't that what you're really propos-ing: that a small group of 'correct' and largely infallible people have the power to tell a much larger group of 'incorrect' and fallible people exactly how to run their lives? And if this kind of society existed, wouldn't it be most dictatorial and fascistic—and would you want to live in it?"

"You seem to be saying that allowing people to be seriously mistaken about their behavior, and even to defeat their own ends by their mistakes, is the price we have to pay for democracy."

"Well, isn't it?"

"Hmm. You may be right."

"As I said before: think it over. Besides, there's another aspect of your problem with your mother that we have to face and that perhaps you're not facing."

"What is that?"

"Simply that although you set up the situation as if she is hurting herself, and you are on the outside merely watching her self-defeating game, we have to suspect that really, underneath, you may feel that she is hurting *you* and that she is not playing *your* perfection-seeking game."

"You think that I really want her to love me as much as or more than my brothers and sisters and that I am using her spending as an excuse to force her to do so?"

"That's certainly a possibility. Surely, from your standpoint, a less than perfect family circle has existed, especially since your father's death, as he was the one who mainly cared for you. Now under the guise of helping your mother spend her money better, you may be trying to get your *own* way, break up some of her closeness with the other family members, and achieve the 'ideal' situation that *you* think should exist. Then, when you cannot attain this 'ideal' and cannot achieve the certainty of your mother's love that you probably always wanted and never got, you grandiosely refuse to accept reality and start wailing about *her* wrongdoings."

"But if what you say is true, isn't it natural for me to want to get closer to my mother and to get back some of the love that she's kept from me all these years?"

"Yes, it's natural for you to *want* to do so; but your means of achieving your desires are quite distorted and ineffective. If you truly accepted the reality of her favoring your brothers and sisters, and worked hard to change this reality—say, by being exceptionally nice to her yourself—that would be a sane enough program for you to follow. But instead you deny the reality that you consider so unfair and imperfect—pretend that you are *not* troubled by your mother's favoritism of the other family members—and then keep flaying your mother on a supposedly different issue entirely. And your sharp criticism of her, of course, will only help *preserve* the poor reality that you actually seem to want to change."

"By keeping after her about the spending of the money, the way I do, I just keep antagonizing her further and give her good reason for favoring the others—is that what you mean?"

"That's exactly it. By refusing to face and temporarily put up with the grim reality of your family life, and by unconsciously telling yourself much of the time that 'It's unfair! It shouldn't *be* this way!' you deviously induce yourself to act in the very manner that will almost certainly help perpetuate and aggravate this unpleasant reality. While, on the other hand, if you ungrandiosely accepted, for the present, the ungracious position you're in, you might well be able, as an intelligent and hard-working person, to do something to correct the situation."

"My, you've certainly given me a lot of food for thought in this session! I'm going to have to think over very carefully what we've talked about and see whether I really have been doing what you say and whether I have been covering up my own perfectionism and refusal to accept reality by keeping after mother about her spending."

"By all means think about this carefully and see whether you do not find that same of the hypotheses I have suggested accurately fit your situation."

Laura did think things over; came to the conclusion that even though she still felt that her mother was mistaken, that was not the main issue involved in her own being upset; and for the first time began to accept, quite democratically, her mother's and others' right to make their own mistakes and errors. Within the next several months, her relations with her mother were enormously improved and some of the mother's reckless spending, possibly because of these improved relations, did stop. More importantly, Laura went back to cultivating her own garden more effectively and began to get along better with her fiancé, whose imperfections she had previously been covertly simmering about, but whom she could now accept in a much more uncritical manner.

Some general rules for combating your own perfectionism and grandiosity and learning to accept reality even when it shows some of its most unpleasant aspects are these:

1. When people act badly in relation to you or to themselves—as they often do in this world—ask yourself whether their behavior is *really* worth getting excited about. Do you actually *care* what these people do? Do their actions truly *affect* your life? *Will* these people change, no matter how much time and effect you spend helping them? Do you *want* to spend sufficient time and energy to help them? Do you actually *have* it available to spend? Unless you can answer questions like these with a resounding 'Yes!' wouldn't it perhaps be better if you stayed somewhat aloof from other peoples' errors and shortcomings and merely offered them, especially when asked, moderate advice and help?

2. Assuming that you do consider it highly worthwhile to become in-

timately involved with helping others change their ineffective or poor behavior, try to do so in a relatively calm and unfrantic way. If you really want people to change for their own (or even your own) good, you will almost always be most helpful by being permissive, uncritical, and accepting. Do your best to see things from *their* frames of reference, rather than your own. Firmly reject, if you will, their self-defeating *behavior* but do not reject *them*.

3. Even when people are specifically nasty to you, or actually harm you, it is still most important that you keep calm yourself and not condemn them severely or viciously retaliate. Whether you like it or not, they *are* the way they are; and it is childish for you to think that they *shouldn't be*. The more objective you are about their nastiness, the better an example you will be able to set them; the more constructive a plan you will be able to devise to induce them to stop their nastiness; and the less you will annoy yourself because of their behavior. If, when faced with difficult people (or things or events), you keep telling yourself how terrible and awful they are, you will only make your situation more difficult. If you tell yourself, instead, that: "this situation stinks—tough! so it stinks" you will at least prevent yourself from being annoyed at being annoyed and you will be much more likely to be effective in making the situation less stinking.

4. Ceaselessly fight your own perfectionism. If, as an artist or a producer, you would like to work on a near-perfect *work* or *product,* fine. But *you* will never be perfect; nor will anyone else with whom you are in contact. Humans are thoroughly fallible; life is essentially uncertain. The quest for certainty and perfection is largely motivated (a) by the childish fear of living in a highly uncertain and imperfect world; and (b) by the conscious or unconscious drive to excel all others, to be King or Queen of the May, and thus 'prove' one's absolute superiority over everyone else. Living without anxiety and hostility can never be attained unless you fully accept, as Reichenbach shows, that you live in a world of probability and chance, and unless you accept yourself because you *are* and not because you are "better" than anyone else.

5. Since there are no perfect solutions to life problems and difficulties, you simply must accept many compromises and *reasonable* solutions. The more you keep your eyes open for many alternative answers to a given problem, the more likely you are to find the best *feasible* answer to it. Impulsive and impatient choices are more likely to be ineffective ones. Think about, consider, and compare the different alternatives open to you. Try *objectively* to see various sides of an issue, with a minimum of prejudices and preconceptions. In the final analysis, however, you will have to make some kind of a plunge; and it is usually best to make this plunge *experimentally,* with the full acceptance of the fact that it *may* work out well—and it may *not.*

If you fail, that is unfortunate; but it is rarely catastrophic. And failure never—no, *never!*—has anything to do with your intrinsic value *as a person.* Humans only learn by doing and by failing—that is probably the main aspect of (highly uncertain and imperfect) reality that you must accept.

6. Assuming that you are able to choose wisely and non-perfectionistically among several present alternatives, you must still leave the door open to taking *other* choices in the future. For the best alternative that you may take today in solving a problem may not be the best one you might take tomorrow, any more than the kind of car you would buy today need be the same you would purchase ten years from now. Your own desires, outside conditions, and other people with whom you may be involved all may significantly change; and these changes should be taken into account in your choice among alternatives. Your attitude should therefore be one of what Kelly calls an outlook conducive to "a program of continuous construct revision." Or, as Korzybski and Magee would put it, life plan$_1$ may not be the same as life plan$_2$; and you must be realistically able to differentiate between your own preferences and goals, and the most feasible methods of achieving them, at one point in time and another.

Overcoming Inertia and Becoming
19   *Creatively Absorbed*

THERE IS NO rest for the weary; and, as we noted before, there is no easy way out of life's difficulties and responsibilities. Yet millions of civilized people seem to believe heartily in <u>Irrational Idea No. 10</u>: *The idea that maximum human happiness can be achieved by inertia and inaction or by passively and uncommittedly "enjoying oneself."* This notion is illogical for several reasons:

1. Human beings appear to be a species of animal who are not particularly happy or alive when they are inert, except for short periods of time between their exertions. Although they become tired and tense when they are ceaselessly active, they just as easily become bored and listless when they are constantly at rest. Passive "enjoyments," such as reading, play-going, or watching sporting events are quite entertaining and relaxing when engaged in fairly regularly; but a steady and exclusive diet of this kind of "activity" soon tends to pall and to lead to feelings of ennui and self-alienation.

2. The more intelligent and perceptive a human being is, the more he seems to require vitally absorbing activity to keep himself maximally alive and happy. Perhaps less intelligent people can sit in the sun day after day and need no other occupation for their full enjoyment. But highly intelligent adults can rarely be enthused and gratified for any length of time unless they have some rather complex, absorbing, and challenging occupations or avocations.

3. To some degree, human well-being would seem to *be* absorption in

173

outside people and events, or what Nina Bull calls goal-orientation. Highly negative emotions (such as depression, grief, and anxiety) on the one hand, as well as ecstatically positive emotions (such as elation, triumph, and manic joy) on the other hand, may *both*, when experienced for long periods of time, be pathological; while quiet, undramatic, persistent absorption in achieving some goal, and especially some long-range creative goal (such as writing a novel or working on a large scientific project) may well be the most satisfying kind of activity.

It is notable, however, that even highly negative feelings (such as continual anxiety) or positive emotions (such as great elation) are unusually absorbing and unpassive occupations for those who keep experiencing them. Above all, they are *active* participations in life; and that is perhaps why so many seemingly unhappy people resist giving up their severe feelings of depression or mania. Intense *absorption* seems to be the common denominator of practically all forms of aliveness—including even the emotionally disturbed forms.

4. What we usually call *loving* or being *in love*, as opposed to desiring to *be loved*, is one of the main forms of vital absorption. In fact, the three main forms of being vitally absorbed in anything are (a) loving—or being absorbed in other people; (b) creating—or being absorbed in things; and (c) philosophizing—or being absorbed in ideas. Being inert, passive, or over-inhibited normally keeps you from being absorbed in any of these three major ways—and hence from truly living. Living essentially means doing, acting, loving, creating, thinking. It is negated by any prolonged amount of goofing, loafing, or lazing.

5. Although, as we pointed out previously in our chapter on self-discipline, it is *initially* harder for many or most people to get themselves into vitally absorbing activities, and it is *at first* easier for them to sit on their backsides and do little or nothing, in the great majority of instances the individual who fights against this initial difficulty and propels himself into activity comes to enjoy his actions (and sometimes, also, their results) far more than he would continue to enjoy his prolonged inactivity. The game normally *is* worth the candle—if you keep playing it long enough.

6. People who lead a lazy, passive existence and who keep saying that "nothing really interests me very much" are almost always (consciously or unconsciously) defending themselves against some irrational fear, especially the great fear of failure. Viewing failure with horror, they avoid certain activities that they would really like to engage in; and after sufficient avoidance, they conclude, in all sincerity, that they are not interested in these activities. They thus cut off one potential piece of their life space after another, and may well end up in the sad position of not being interested in anything. In some respects, these apathetic, listless, and bored individuals

are even more unhappy than are the actively anxious and hostile people of the world: who at least, as we indicated a few paragraphs back, are *absorbed* in their fears and hatreds.

7. To some extent, self-confidence seems to be intrinsically related to activity. The reason, in the last analysis, you know that you *can* do something you would like to do is because you have already proven, by your past behavior, that you *have* done it or something akin to it before. A child who never tried to walk would hardly acquire confidence in his being able to walk—or to swim, or ride, or do almost any other kind of muscular activity. This is not to deny that the dire need to succeed at difficult tasks and projects is one which, in our society, is largely drilled into us by cultural competition propaganda. It is. And much of our "pride" or "self-confidence," therefore, is actually *false* pride and *false* confidence: born of this dire need to succeed.

There is some reason to believe, however, that even with a minimum of social upbringing, a human being is a kind of animal that has to accept certain challenges and at least *try* various tasks if he is to have confidence in himself. And the philosophy of inertia and inaction, especially when it is motivated by fear of failure, blocks the development of self-confidence and self-respect.

8. Action, as we have been stressing throughout this book, is often required to break the pattern of your own self-defeating behavior. If you have almost any habit pattern that is sabotaging your health, your happiness, or your relations with others, and you want to change it for a more effective pattern of living, you will just have to work forcefully against this habit, with both verbal-propagandistic and activity-deconditioning approaches. Time and effort are the essence of human growth and development. The more inert and inactive you are, the more you are certain to block your own strongest desires, to sabotage your own healthy ends.

9. Inertia has a tendency to become perniciously cumulative. The more you refrain from doing some activity—especially, again, out of fear—the more you normally become used to *not* doing it, and it then becomes harder and harder to get yourself to do it. The more, for example, you keep from doing the writing or the painting that you keep telling yourself you really want to do, the more difficult you find it, eventually, to get down to doing it; and, as noted above, you frequently lose interest entirely in doing it. Human beings easily become habituated or acclimated to what they do, even though what they do is entirely senseless and self-defeating. A little inertia, when excused and coddled, therefore tends to lead to more inertia —and so on, almost ad infinitum.

An excellent case in point is the condition of fixed homosexuality, which literally tens of thousands of American males become addicted to every year, largely because it originally seems to be an "easy" way out for them —considering, as has been pointed out, how difficult we often make it in this country for the young male to fulfill himself sexually with the young female. Jack Monroe, one such homosexual, came to therapy when he was twenty-five, after he had had, since the age of fifteen, an exclusively homoerotic background. He had been attracted to girls at a very early age, but had not had the courage to date any of them, for fear that they would look askance at his pimply face and his long, gangly body; and he had found easy solace in older homosexual males, who accepted him the way he was and even made most of the overtures themselves.

After ten years of highly promiscuous homosexual behavior, including one arrest and a recent attempt to blackmail him at his place of business (where they did not suspect his homosexual proclivities and would have been shocked to learn about them), Jack decided that it was about high time he attempted to "go straight." And he came to see the therapist with the knowledge that he, unlike a good many psychoanalytic practitioners, strongly felt that homosexuality was a learned rather than an inborn anomaly and that it definitely could be cured.

At first, Jack was quite cooperative. He seemed to accept the fact that he would have to make some drastic changes in his thinking; and he did not resist the therapist's homework assignments (a common part of rational-emotive psychotherapy) which involved his forcing himself to make dates with girls. When, however, it came to carrying out the second part of this assignment—which was to start making some sexual overtures to the girls he was dating—Jack started to balk and to bring forth various excuses. He was going with one particular girl, Tammie, who seemed favorably inclined toward him and would probably respond if he tried to kiss or pet her; but he never started.

"It seems to me," he said to the therapist in the course of the seventh session, "that it would be futile for me to kiss and pet her until I feel a strong urge to do so. Otherwise, it will just be artificial and mechanical."

"With that kind of attitude," said the therapist, "you'll probably wait forever. For how can you possibly, with your longstanding homosexual background, strongly *want* to kiss Tammie (or any other girl)? How, for that matter, could you strongly want to eat oysters until you had first tried them, several times perhaps, and finally *knew* that you enjoyed them?"

"But I could strongly want to *try* oysters for the first time, to *see* if I might like them."

"Exactly! If you had no silly fear of oysters, you probably *would* want to try them for the first time, to see if you would cultivate a taste for them. But that's just the point: you *do* have a silly fear of girls. And while you have this fear, it is ridiculous to ask that you should *want* to kiss them or do any-thing else in the line of sexual advances."

"All right: but how do I get over my fear?"

"Just as you would get over your fear of oysters, if you had one. First, by convincing yourself that oysters are *not* terrible, awful, and death-deal-ing. And, second, by forcing yourself to try and to keep trying them until you *proved*, in action, that nothing horrible occurred when you ate them."

"So I should try telling myself that it is *not* too terrible to kiss girls, and then should keep kissing and kissing and kissing them?"

"Right. For no matter how much you try the first part of this de-indoctri-nation process—the part where you keep telling yourself that it is *not* ter-rible to kiss girls—nothing much is likely to happen until you also try the second part. For every time that you get a chance to kiss Tammie and don't do so, you are actually reindoctrinating yourself, all over again, with your fears: telling yourself, that is, that it *is* or *would* be frightening if you kissed her. Or, in other words, you are saying to yourself, by your inactivity, 'All this fear of kissing Tammie may be nonsense *in theory* but it sure as hell is real *in action*. Boy, it's difficult to do!' And by repeating to yourself how dif-ficult it is to do, you actually of course keep *making* it just that difficult."

"According to your way of looking at it, then, I have to keep subjecting myself to actions that counteract my fears of women before I can really ex-pect to expose to myself the absurdity of these fears. Is that right?"

"Right as can be."

"But I just *can't* go ahead and kiss Tammie, feeling the way I do. And if I forced myself to do so, against my own fundamental tastes, it would be bound to be such a disagreeable experience that it might well hinder rather than help me become heterosexually interested."

"Why should it? If you had a fear of swimming, and after showing your-self many times that there was no real danger and that in a shallow pool you couldn't possibly drown, you hesitatingly plunged, would it be likely that your swim would be so unpleasant that you would never go in the water again? Or would it be more likely that, once you were in the water, you would quickly *see*, what you had been theoretically but not too effectively trying to tell yourself, that the pool *is* shallow and that you *can't* possibly drown?"

"I guess I'd soon see that the swimming wasn't dangerous. But is this a fair analogy? In swimming, all I would have to do would be to plunge into the water. But in trying to behave heterosexually I have to go through a most complicated set of thoughts, feelings, and actions that aren't *me*."

"True. But in swimming, too, you might be surprised how complicated a set of thoughts, feelings, and actions you would have to go through before you could swim well. For plunging into the water is but the *first* step. After that, you have to get used to the feel of the water, learn not to swallow too much of it, practice moving your arms in certain coordinated ways, see that you breathe properly while you are swimming, and so on, and so forth. There are perhaps a hundred different thoughts, feelings, and acts that you would have to undergo while swimming that you probably have never before undergone while, say, walking, riding, or dancing. And these movements and these feelings *become* you as you practice them. You *grow* to like them after a time; and many of them, in fact, you grow to like only after you have become thoroughly proficient at them—which may be weeks or months later.Thus, although you first may dislike using a breast stroke in swimming, because you have started with a crawl stroke, once you keep trying and become proficient at the breast stroke you may come to like it far more than the crawl position. Your liking to be and being a fine breast stroke swimmer then *becomes* part of your swimming personality. Whereas at first it was entirely foreign to you, it later may become most natural."

"It all sounds very easy, the way you put it. But *how* am I to force myself to kiss Tammie when I really don't want to do so?"

"Very simply: by forcing yourself. Just as you would force yourself to plunge into the swimming. And by, as I said before, fighting against your present nonsense: your telling yourself that it would be horrible if she rejected your kiss, or indicated that she didn't like it, or let you have some sex satisfaction and *then* rejected you. Plunging means plunging—there's no other way."

"Even against my own *feelings?*"

"*Especially* against your own feelings. For your feelings, I must keep insisting, are nothing but arbitrary fears. You don't even *know* it would be unpleasant to kiss Tammie: never having tried! And what you are really against, and have no so-called *feeling* for, is not the kissing (for I repeat: you can't even see how unpleasant that might be, until you've tried it; besides you know perfectly well that it can't be *that* much different from kissing a male, which you've done frequently and somehow survived); what you really feel negative or blah about is the idea of your *having* to take the bull by the horns, *having* to work at conquering your fear and your inertia. Isn't that *really* what you have feelings against?"

"Well, yes: now that you mention it. I *don't* like the idea of having to go to all this goddamn trouble to enjoy myself, if I ever actually will succeed in enjoying myself, with a woman when, as you well know, I already get a heck of a lot of enjoyment out of being with men."

"Ah, so that *is* it! As it so often is, in cases like yours. You would like to change, to become heterosexual—*if* there were little or no work involved in doing so. But since it *is* a pain in the neck and *does* require all kinds of effort and practice, and since you already can enjoy yourself sexually with males without this kind of effort and practice, you don't see why you should *have* to change. That's exactly why so few homosexuals do overcome their fear of heterosexuality—and why so few other kinds of neurotics thoroughly overcome their particular kinds of fears and hostilities: because they want to do so magically, without work, without practice."

"But they can't, can they?"

"No, they damn well can't. There is no magic. There is no easy way. And the principles of human inertia are tough ones to conquer; they really are. But there is, of course, no other way. In your case, either you must force yourself to kiss Tammie, and to keep on kissing her till you *learn* to enjoy it; or else you must go on being exclusively homosexual, with all the enormous disadvantages thereof in this society, for the rest of your life."

"So, no matter how I feel about kissing her, I'd darned well better try it."

"Yes. The real point is not how you feel about kissing Tammie, but how you feel about *yourself*. If you really like yourself and want to get over this homosexual neurosis, and all the trouble which it has led you into and will doubtlessly continue to cause as long as you live in this society, you will try kissing Tammie, just as you would try swimming, or try adjusting to the armed forces if you were drafted into them against your will. Only, kissing females should be a little more enjoyable, once you have tried it, than swimming or adjusting to a period of service in the armed forces!"

Jack, for once, did try. The very next date he had with Tammie, he avoided going out with her (which previously he was only too eager to do) and instead stayed home with her and forced himself, literally forced himself, to try some petting. Much to his surprise, he discovered that her body was much softer and nicer to touch than that of most of the males with whom he had previously had sex relations; and it was she, this time, who had to put *him* off, saying that she didn't feel she knew him well enough yet to go as far as he obviously wanted to go. He could hardly wait to date her again. In his therapy session that followed this first attempt at heterosexual petting, he said:

"Let me be the first one to admit it: I was dead wrong. And you were one hundred per cent right. My negative feelings about kissing Tammie were entirely the result of my fear and resentment. I could see that when I first put my arm around her. I almost died a thousand deaths, fearing that she would push me away or, worse yet, make a laughing remark, like I used to hear my sisters make when they were telling each other how stupid and silly most of their boyfriends were and how they just couldn't stand their kisses or caresses. But I pushed ahead anyway. I could almost hear you saying to me: 'See! it *is* fear. What do you mean you have no *feeling* for kissing the girl?' And I said to myself: 'Damn right it's fear! But it's not going to be this way forever. Screw it all, it's not!' And I kept my arm around her, and drew her to me, though my heart was beating like a goddamn drum or something. And before I knew it, much to my surprise, she had turned her face up and obviously wanted to be kissed. Imagine!—*wanted* to be kissed by an old faggot like me! 'Well,' I said to myself, 'Here I'm scared as hell that she'll reject me and dump me out of the window or something and she really wants it, *she really honest-to-blazes wants it!*' I didn't hesitate after that. I just grabbed her and got the sweetest, juiciest kiss I never knew even existed before. 'Hell,' I said to myself again, 'so *this* is what I've been fighting against all these years, and keeping myself from working to get. Hell, hell, hell!' That was it. No more of that crummy fear and fighting for me. I know the game's not over, and I've got a long, long way to go yet. And I know I'll still have to force myself at times. But once that initial old inertia starts to go—just as you said was the case—things can get awfully jumping enjoyable!"

Jack Monroe was on his way. Within the next year he had several affairs, with Tammie and two other girls; enjoyed all of them immensely; and is now engaged to Tammie and is looking forward to marrying her soon. His sexual interest in males has vanished to the near-zero point and he is quite sure that whatever little interest in them he has can easily be kept under control for the rest of his life. His work (as a draftsman) has also improved considerably; he is saving money for the first time in his life; and he finds himself much less resentful toward both males and females.

"How can I take the time," he said at one of his last psychotherapy sessions, "to hate others and make up excuses for their holding me down when I'm so busy, these days, caring for Tammie, devoting myself to my work (which becomes more pleasurable almost every day), and doing everything possible to plan for my marital and vocational future? Inertia and passivity are for the birds! Too bad I haven't got more time to find some other interesting projects to sink my teeth into!"

In many important respects, then, it would appear that action, particularly when it takes the form of creative, intensely absorbing activity, is one of the mainstays of happy human living and that anyone who (consciously or unconsciously) believes otherwise and who lives by a philosophy of inertia and inaction will sabotage his own potential satisfaction. More specifically, the kinds of actions which can be taken to help bring about fuller living can include the following:

1. You should make a definite attempt to become vitally absorbed in some persons or things outside yourself. Loving persons rather than things or ideas has some distinct advantages: since other people can, in their turn, love you back and can beautifully interact with you. But loving some long-range activity or idea—such as being vitally attached to an art or a profession—also has its great rewards, and in some respects may be more dur-

able, varied, and all-involving than loving a member of the other sex or a close relative. Ideally, you should be able to love both persons *and* things; but if you are, especially at a certain period of time, thoroughly absorbed in one *or* the other, you may still be a happy and reasonably complete person.

2. Try to find some persons or things in which you can honestly be absorbed for *their own* sake and not for other "ego-raising" reasons. It may be fine and noble if you love your own children; or your orphaned younger brother; or if you are devoted to one of the helping professions, such as teaching, psychology, or medicine. But you have a perfect right, as a human being, "selfishly" to devote yourself to the prettiest girl in town or to an avocation, such as coin collecting, which has relatively little application to human welfare. It is unlikely that you will genuinely love anyone or anything very deeply unless you follow the courage of your *own* convictions and do not try to win the accolades of others by forcing yourself to be interested in what you think *they* would like you to be.

3. In devoting yourself to any field of endeavor it is wise to choose a challenging, long-range project or area rather than something simple or short-ranged. Most highly intelligent individuals will not for very long remain highly absorbed in simply making a sexual conquest, stamp collecting, playing checkers, or weight lifting: for these are pursuits that can be mastered in a short length of time and that then often become boring and unchallenging. Rather, try to select a goal such as writing a fine novel, being an outstanding physicist, or winning and retaining a high-level marital relationship, since this kind of pursuit is likely to remain intriguing for some time to come.

4. Don't expect vital absorptions to be self-evident or to develop quickly. Because of inertia, fear of failure, or ignorance of the true depths of a given subject, you may at first have to push yourself, experimentally and forcibly, into a certain field of endeavor, and make yourself stick at it for a reasonable length of time, before you really begin to become absorbed in and fascinated by it. Before you conclude that you definitely do not enjoy your relationship with a given person or your preoccupation with a given project, give it an honest, fairly prolonged try. Then, if you still are not enamored, you can look around for a different kind of absorption.

5. It is sometimes a good idea to vary your interests and have some minor side projects going, even if you are absorbed in some major endeavor. This is particularly true where the main person or thing with which you are involved may not be around forever, and where you may therefore be wise to have some alternate involvements available. But even aside from this, man is a creature of variety as well as of sustained goals; and you can easily go stale if you only concentrate on one pursuit. If, therefore, you vary your

reading, your hobbies, the organizations to which you belong, and your circle of friends, you may remain more vitally alive than if you routinely keep doing the same thing over and over again.

6. Inertia and inaction may be combatted by tracking down your own irrational anxieties and hostilities that almost invariably lie at their source. If you are self-defeatingly inert, you almost certainly are telling yourself some nonsense—such as "It is easier and better for me to let others do things for me than to do them myself" or "Wouldn't it be terrible if I risked writing that novel and miserably failed?" You must force yourself to *see* that you are saying these self-sabotaging sentences and must challenge, question, contradict them, most vigorously and consistently, until you change them for saner, motion-impelling self-verbalizations.

7. Self-talk is not enough. In the final analysis, you must literally force yourself, propel yourself, push yourself into action. Often, you must make yourself—yes, *make* yourself—undertake specific *acts of courage:* beard an employer in his office, ask a very beautiful girl to dance, take your idea for a book to a publisher. And you must keep forcing yourself into action long enough and often enough until the action itself becomes easier and easier, and often even enjoyable.

8. It is sometimes valuable, deliberately to adopt a role that is quite different from your usual one and for a period of time to force yourself to live up to this assumed role. If you are actually shy and retiring, and for a day or a week can act as if you are one of the most outgoing and assertive individuals you know, you may find it relatively easy, after acting out that role, to *be* less inhibited. The more you force yourself to do a thing that you are "sure" you cannot do, the more you may prove how mythical your "certainty" is and may show yourself that you *can* do this thing.

20 Living Rationally in an Irrational World

A MORE IRRATIONAL world than the one in which we presently live could hardly be conceived. In spite of the enormous advances in technical knowledge made during the last century, and the theoretical possibility all of us living in peace and prosperity, we actually exist perilously close to the brink of local strife, world war, economic insecurity, political skullduggery, organized crime, business fraud, sexual violence, racial bigotry, labor and management inefficiency, religious fanaticism, and scores of similar manifestations of idiocy and inhumanity.

On a more personal scale, conditions are equally bad or worse. None of us—no, not a single, solitary one of us—can fail to have intimate encounters, almost every day of our lives, with several individuals (be they bosses or employees, husbands or wives, children or parents, friends or enemies) who are stupid, ignorant, ineffective, provocative, frustrating, vicious, or seriously disturbed. Modern life, instead of being just a bowl of cherries, more closely resembles a barrel of prune pits.

Nevertheless: a human being in today's world does not *have* to be unhappy. Wonderfully enough, along with his being endowed with more than his share of inanity and insanity, man *also* has a remarkable capacity for straight thinking. And, as we noted in the opening pages of this book, if he intelligently organizes and disciplines his thinking and his actions, he can live a decidedly self-fulfilling, creative, and emotionally satisfying life *even* in the highly unsatisfactory world of today.

The main practical points that we have made in this volume may be summarized as follows:

Your desires and emotions are not mysterious, uncontrollable forces that drive you to do their bidding. Although they are deeply rooted in your physical and historical being and are therefore partly beyond your *immediate* control, they are also closely allied to your thinking and are consequently largely within your *eventual* control. Where the wishes and feelings of lower animals and of young children are almost entirely dependent upon their inborn urges and the influences of their surrounding environment, the human adult is the one being who, with thinking and action, can radically alter his own emotional responses and considerably control his own destiny.

Thinking, like emotion, is a complex bisocial process that is intimately related to your perceiving, moving, and desiring and does not have a completely pure and independent existence. Although you cannot maintain perfect control over your thinking, you can—by observing, analyzing, questioning, and changing the sentences of which it largely consists—significantly change and regulate it. At the same time, by controlling a considerable amount of your thinking in this manner, you can also learn to change and regulate much of your emoting.

Emotional disturbance or neurosis essentially consists of letting your emotions run away with you: of being hysterically over-concerned about certain people and things on the one hand, or being defensively under-concerned on the other hand. While some individuals may be physically predisposed to become seriously disturbed, most neurotics appear to learn to think in an ignorance-based or irrational manner and thereby disturb themselves. Although potentially capable of thinking straight and effectively controlling their behavior, they become habituated to thinking illogically and forcing themselves to engage in self-defeating behavior.

If you would control your emotions effectively and keep yourself from leading a self-defeating, neurotic existence, you must discard the major irrational ideas that you (and millions of your fellow members of this society) acquired early in life. These ideas, which once may have been appropriate (in view of your helpless state as an infant and child) or which always may have been irrational and inappropriate resulted from (a) your early inability to think straight (particularly your childish insistence on immediate gratification rather than on future gains and your being unable to accurately distinguish real from imagined dangers); (b) your dependence as a child on the planning and thinking of others; (c) the superstitions and prejudices inculcated in you by your parents; and (d) the indoctrinations of the mass media of the society in which you were reared.

Although, as you grew older, you probably challenged and questioned your early-acquired irrational premises to some extent, you also held on tenaciously and defensively to many of them, and have kept reindoctrinating yourself with them until the present. It is this reindoctrination—which unconsciously but very forcefully and persistently goes on day after day—which mainly serves to keep your original irrationalities alive, in spite of the devastating results which they continue to have on your adult behavior. And it is largely by closely observing your self-sentences and making yourself fully aware of your continuous reindoctrinating processes, that you can learn to contradict and counter-attack the irrational ideas with which you originally were reared and which you are now perpetuating.

At the same time, because your irrational thinking has (over the years) led to pernicious forms of action or inaction (to tendencies, for example, to lash out at others impulsively or anxiously to refrain from doing what you really want to do in life), you must *actively* as well as *thinkingly* challenge your hostile or inhibited ways of behaving. Thus, you must literally *force yourself* to give up childish impulse gratification (such as lying, stealing, attention-getting, or addiction to drugs or alcohol) or to do the things you are illogically afraid of doing (such as socializing, courting members of the other sex, or going for job interviews).

Only this kind of double-barreled, simultaneous attack on your deeply-ingrained irrational ideas and self-defeating behavior is likely to be truly effective. For vigorous thinking about your emotional upsets or inhibitions will serve to pave the way to appropriate action or restraint; and forceful counteraction against your anxieties and hostilities will serve as the very best form of de-propagandization of the silly ideas that lie behind them. Thinking *and* doing are *equally* indispensable in attacking your oldest and deepest self-defeating tendencies.

Some of the major irrational ideas which you must strongly and persistently challenge, as well as forcefully propel yourself to act against, include these all-pervading beliefs of our society:

1. You should challenge the belief that it is a dire necessity for you to be loved or approved by almost everyone for almost everything you do. Instead, you should try to stand on your own two feet; keep the approval of others as a *desirable* but not *necessary* goal; seriously and self-correctively consider other people's criticisms of you without dreadfully hurting yourself with their negative evaluations; and continually and mainly strive to do what *you* really enjoy doing rather than what *other people* think you ought to do in life.

2. Give up the notion of trying to be thoroughly competent, adequate, and achieving in all possible respects. Try to *do* rather than to do *perfectly*. Try to better your own performances rather than those of others. Strive, if you will, to be a better artist, ballplayer, or business man than you now are; but do not delude yourself that you will be a better *person* if you

achieve your goal. Strongly desire and work for success in your chosen fields; but be ready to accept failures as undesirable but not dreadful—as having nothing whatever to do with your intrinsic value as a human being.

3. Get rid of the idea that certain people are bad, wicked, or villainous and that they should be severely blamed or punished for their sins. Accept your own and others' wrongdoings objectively and unmoralistically: as misdeeds to learn from and to correct in the future. Fully acknowledge the fallibility of yourself and others and make due allowances for the possibility—indeed, the practical certainty—of your and their continuing to make numerous errors and mistakes. Learn to distinguish between an individual's being *responsible* for his actions (which he frequently is and should be) and being *to blame* for these actions (which he never should be). See that when you blame yourself or others you are being perfectionistic and grandiose, and that you are thereby invariably helping to perpetuate rather than correct your or their misdeeds. Never confuse an individual with his acts, a person who acts badly with a bad *person*.

4. Combat the idea that it is terrible, horrible, and catastrophic when things are not going the way you would like them to go. When conditions are not the way you would prefer them to be, calmly and determinedly try to change them for the better; and when, for the moment, they cannot be changed, the only sane thing to do is quietly to accept them (and wait and plan for the time when they finally can be changed). The greater your loss or frustration is, the more philosophic you must be in regard to it: the more you must accept the fact that it is bad and undesirable—but *not* catastrophic or unbearable.

5. You should reject the hypothesis that human unhappiness is externally caused and that you have little or no ability to control your sorrows or rid yourselves of your negative feelings. Instead, you should realize that most of your own misery is created by your own irrational thinking, your own self-propagandization; and that you can eliminate most of your despair or anger by changing your thinking or your self-talk. If you ferret out your own illogical *shoulds, oughts,* and *musts* and replace your childish demands with realistic preferences, you need rarely make yourself anxious or upset.

6. You should rid yourself of the idea that if something is or may be dangerous or fearsome, you should be terribly occupied with and upset about it. You should seriously question the real dangers about the things you fear and see what the actual probabilities are of their occurring or leading to terribly dreadful consequences if they do occur. If you are to live fully and creatively, you simply have to accept certain inevitable dangers and risks that go with contemporary life. Most of your over-concern is doubtless definitional—follows from your own catastrophizing internalized sentences—and can be eliminated by your observing and questioning your

definitional assumptions: especially your assumptions that you must always please others and achieve remarkably well.

7. You should stop trying to run away from many life difficulties and self-responsibilities. Short-range hedonism, or the insistence on immediate gratifications, is a senseless philosophy in most instances and must be surrendered for a harder-headed, longer-range approach to pleasure and enjoyment. You should determine what are the truly necessary activities of life—and then, no matter how unpleasant they may be, unrebelliously and promptly perform them. Although acquiring a considerable degree of self-discipline may seem unduly difficult, in the long run the "easy" and undisciplined way is the harder and less rewarding way and is clearly self-sabotaging.

8. You should surrender the idea that the past is all-important and that because something once strongly affected your life it should do so indefinitely. While considering your past history seriously and trying to do your best to learn valuable lessons from it, you should realize that your present is your past of tomorrow and that working to change the present may enable you to make yourself a radically better future. Continual re-thinking of your old assumptions and re-working of your past habits can help eradicate most of the pernicious influences from your childhood and adolescence.

9. You should give up the notion that people and things should be different from the way they are and that it is catastrophic if perfect solutions to the grim realities of life are not immediately found. Whether you like it or not, reality *is* reality and simply must be accepted as it is before you can set about changing it. At times, you have to accept many compromise and reasonable solutions rather than perfect and certain solutions to life problems.

10. You should combat the idea that maximum human happiness can be achieved by inertia and inaction or by passively and uncommittedly "enjoying yourself." Make a definite attempt to become vitally absorbed in some persons or things outside yourself; and find persons or things in which you can honestly be absorbed for their *own* sake rather than for the sake of being socially approved. In devoting yourself to any field of endeavor, try to choose a challenging, long-range project or area of work. Force yourself, by specific acts of courage, to take risks, to act against your own inertia, to be committedly *alive*.

Summing up. While taking good care to avoid needlessly and gratuitously hurting others, you should consistently try to be *you*: on the one hand, to be self-interestedly devoted to those pursuits which are likely to bring *you* the greatest satisfaction in your relatively brief span of life; and, on the other hand, to be lovingly, absorbedly devoted to people and things outside yourself because *you* truly enjoy this kind of involvement. Your paramount absorption should unashamedly be the fulfillment of your own desires, your morality that of enlightened self-interest and unabashed individualism.

The sane and truly enlightened individualist, however, will not define his *desires* as *demands,* nor his *preferences* as *needs.* He will be carefully considerate of others because he realizes that only by such consideration can he hope to build and sustain the kind of world *he* wants to live in. And he will be lovingly devoted, in most instances, to selected other people because through such intimate relationships he can more fully know and enjoy *himself.*

These, then, would appear to be some of the most essential rules for following the sound and intelligent life: a life, that is to say, based on knowledge and reason, and dedicated to the proposition that through your reasoning powers you may best achieve a highly satisfying emotional existence. Will the following of these rules absolutely ensure your living a maximally creative and happy life? Not necessarily: because, as we have several times noted in this book, there are some important intra- and interpersonal factors that are not entirely within your control.

Accidents and physical ailments do occur. Environmental circumstances sometimes are impossibly constricting. War and famine, pestilence and destruction still, even in this relatively enlightened age, show their ugly fangs. But the human spirit, when freed of ignorance and cant, has remarkable resiliency. However bowed and bent it may temporarily be, it still may throw off its unthinking and conventionalist chains, and rise above some of the meanest physical and ideological handicaps.

You, as a human, potentially have that spirit. If you resolutely strive to think, fight to act, you can probably use it to good effect. If, after making a concerted effort to question your own basic premises and to propel yourself to act against your self-defeating habit patterns, you still find yourself beset by intense, frequent, or prolonged feelings of anxiety or hostility, then you probably need psychotherapeutic help. By all means, in these circumstances, go for intensive psychotherapy—even a little of which may be enormously helpful in setting you on the right track.

If you are not too emotionally blocked or upset to benefit from the rational approach to human living that we have outlined in this book, then try to see what you can do by working, working, and (yes, everlastingly) working at it. Good luck—and good reasoning!

References

(Items which are starred in this list of references may be of particular help to readers who are interested in additional reading.)

*Adler, Alfred. *Understanding Human Nature.* New York: Greenberg, 1927.

*Adler, Alfred. *The Practice and Theory of Individual Psychology.* New York: Harcourt, Brace, 1939.

*Alexander, Franz, and French, Thomas M. *Psychoanalytic Therapy.* New York: Ronald, 1946.

*Anderson, Camilla M. *Saints, Sinners and Psychiatry.* Philadelphia: Lippincott, 1950.

*Ansbacher, Heinz, and Ansbacher, Rowena. *The Individual Psychology of Alfred Adler.* New York: Basic Books, 1956.

*Bach, G. R. *Intensive Group Psychotherapy.* New York: Ronald, 1954.

*Brenner, Charles. *An Elementary Textbook of Psychoanalysis.* New York: Doubleday, 1957.

*Brown, M. Bevan. *The Sources of Love and Fear.* New York: Vanguard, 1950.

*Cameron, Norman and Magaret, Ann. *Behavior Pathology.* Boston: Houghton Mifflin, 1951.

Cobb, Stanley. *Emotions and Clinical Medicine.* New York: Norton, 1950.

*Dollard, John, and Miller, Neal E. *Personality and Psychotherapy.* New York: McGraw Hill, 1950.

Ellis, Albert. *An Introduction to the Principles of Scientific Psychoanalysis.* Provincetown, Mass.: Journal Press, 1950.

Ellis, Albert. *The Folklore of Sex.* New York: Charles Boni, 1951. Rev. ed., New York: Grove Press, 1961.

*Ellis, Albert. *The American Sexual Tragedy.* New York: Twayne, 1954. New York: Lyle Stuart, 1959.

Ellis, Albert. *New Approaches to Psychotherapy Techniques.* Brandon, Vermont: Journal of Clinical Psychology, 1955.

Ellis, Albert. "An Operational Reformulation of Some of the Basic Principles of Psychoanalysis." *Psychoanalytic Review,* 1956, 43, 163–180. Also published in Feigl, Herbert and Scriven, Michael (Eds.), *Minnesota Studies in the Philosophy of Science, Vol. I.* Minneapolis: University of Minnesota Press, 1956.

*Ellis, Albert. *How to Live with a Neurotic.* New York: Crown Publishers, 1957a.

Ellis, Albert. "Outcome of Employing Three Techniques of Psychotherapy." *J. Clinical Psychol.,* 1957b, 13, 344–350.

Ellis, Albert. "Rational Psychotherapy." *J. General Psychol.,* 1958a, 59, 35–49.

Ellis, Albert. "Rational Psychotherapy and Individual Psychology." *J. Individual Psychol.,* 1958b, 13, 38–44.

Ellis, Albert. "Neurotic Interaction Between Marital Partners." *J. Counseling Psychol.,* 1958c., 5, 24–28.

*Ellis, Albert. *Sex Without Guilt.* New York: Lyle Stuart, 1958d.

Ellis, Albert. "Rationalism and Its Therapeutic Applications." *Annals of Psychotherapy,* Monograph No. 2., 1959a, 1, 55–64.

Ellis, Albert. "The Treatment of a Psychopath With Rational Psychotherapy." *Quaderni di Criminologia Clinica,* 1959b, 2, 173–184; *J. Psychology,* 1961, 51, 141–150.

Ellis, Albert. "Requisite Conditions for Basic Personality Change." *J. Consulting Psychol.,* 1959c, 23, 538–540.

Ellis, Albert. "Treatment of a Homosexual With Rational Psychotherapy." *J. Clinical Psychol.,* 1959d, 15, 338–343.

Ellis, Albert. "Guilt, Shame, and Frigidity." *Quart. Rev. Surg. Obstet. & Gynecol.,* 1959e, 16, 259–261.

Ellis, Albert. "Does Morality Require Religious Sanctions." *Controversy,* June, 1959f.

*Ellis, Albert. *The Art and Science of Love.* New York: Lyle Stuart, 1960a.

Ellis, Albert. "There is No Place for the Concept of Sin in Psychotherapy." *J. Counseling Psychol.,* 1960b, 7, 188–192.

*Ellis, Albert, and Abarbanel, Albert (Eds.). *Encyclopedia of Sexual Behavior.* 2 vols. New York: Hawthorn Books, 1961.

*Ellis, Albert, and Harper, Robert A. *Creative Marriage.* New York: Lyle Stuart, 1961.

Ellis, Albert, Krassner, Paul, and Wilson, Robert A. "An Impolite Interview With Albert Ellis." *The Realist,* March and May, 1960.

Epictetus. *The Works of Epictetus.* Translated by Thomas W. Higginson. Boston: Little, Brown, 1899.

*Erikson, Erik. *Childhood and Society.* New York: Norton, 1950.

Fenichel, Otto. *Psychoanalytic Theory of Neurosis.* New York: Norton, 1945.

*Freeman, Lucy. *Fight Against Fears.* New York: Crown, 1951.

Freud, Sigmund. *Collected Papers.* New York: Hogarth Press, 1924–1950.

Freud, Sigmund. *Basic Writings.* New York: Modern Library, 1938.

*Freud, Sigmund. *An Outline of Psychoanalysis.* New York: Norton, 1949.

*Fromm, Erich. *Escape from Freedom.* New York: Farrar & Rinehart, 1939.

*Fromm, Erich. *Man for Himself.* New York: Rinehart, 1947.

*Fromm, Erich. *The Sane Society.* New York: Rinehart, 1955.

*Fromm, Erich. *The Art of Loving.* New York: Harper, 1956.

Gardner, Wallace J., Licklider, J. C. R., and Weisz, A. Z. "Suppression of Pain by Sound." *Science,* 1960, 132, 32–33.

*Hall, Calvin S. *A Primer of Freudian Psychology.* Cleveland: World Pub. Co., 1954.

Harper, Robert A. *Marriage.* New York: Appleton, 1949.

Harper, Robert A. "Marriage Counseling: Art or Science." *Marr. Fam. Living,* 1951, 13, 164–166.

Harper, Robert A. "A Marital Case: With Two Years' Marital Follow Up." *Marr. Fam. Living,* 1952, 14, 133–149.

Harper, Robert A. "Should Marriage Counseling Become a Fullfledged Specialty?" *Marr. Fam. Living,* 1955, 17, 359–362.

Harper, Robert A. "Communication Problems in Marriage and Marriage Counseling." *Marr. Fam. Living,* 1958, 20, 107–112.

*Harper, Robert A. *Psychoanalysis and Psychotherapy: 36 Systems.* Englewood Cliffs, N.J.: Prentice Hall, 1959a.

Harper, Robert A. "Marriage Counseling and the Mores: A Critique." *Marr. Fam. Living,* 1959b, 21, 13–19.

Harper, Robert A. "A Rational Process-Centered Approach to Marriage Counseling." *J. Individual. Psychol.,* 1960, 16, 197–207.

Harper, Robert A., and Harper, Frances R. "Are Educators Afraid of Sex?" *Marr. Fam. Living,* 1957, 19, 240–244.

Harper, Robert A., and Harper, Frances R. "Sex Education." In Ellis, Albert and Abarbanel, Albert, *Encyclopedia of Sexual Behavior.* New York: Hawthorn Books, 1961.

*Horney, Karen. *The Neurotic Personality of Our Time.* New York: Norton, 1937.

*Horney, Karen. *New Ways in Psychoanalysis.* New York: Norton, 1939.

*Jacobsen, Edmund. *You Must Relax*. New York: McGraw-Hill, 1942.

*Jones, Ernest. *The Life and Works of Sigmund Freud*. 3 vols. New York: Basic Books, 1955–1957.

*Jung, C. G. *Two Essays on Analytical Psychology*. New York: Pantheon, 1953.

*Knight, John. *The Story of My Psychoanalysis*. New York: Pocket Books, 1952.

*Korzybski, Alfred. *Science and Sanity: An Introduction to Non-Aristotelian Systems and General Semantics*. Lancaster, Pa.: Science Press, 1933.

*Low, Abraham A. *Mental Health Through Will-Training*. Boston: Christopher Publishing Co., 1952.

*Maslow, A. H. *Motivation and Personality*. New York: Harper, 1955.

*May, Rollo. *Man's Search for Himself*. New York: Norton, 1953.

*Mowrer, O. Hobart. *Psychotherapy: Theory and Research*. New York: Ronald, 1953.

*Mullahy, Patrick. *Oedipus; Myth and Complex*. New York: Hermitage, 1948.

*Munroe, Ruth L. *Schools of Psychoanalytic Thought*. New York: Dryden, 1955.

Orlansky, Harold. "Infant Care and Personality." *Psychol. Bull.*, 1949, 46, 1–50.

Ortega y Gasset, Jose. *The Revolt of the Masses*. New York: Norton, 1932.

Peller, Lili E. "The Child's Approach to Reality." *Amer. J. Orthopsychiat.*, 1939, 9, 503–513.

*Rank, Otto. *Will Therapy and Truth and Reality*. New York: Knopf, 1950.

*Reichenbach, Hans. *The Rise of Scientific Philosophy*. Berkeley: University of California Press, 1953.

*Russell, Bertrand. *The Conquest of Happiness*. New York: Pocket Books, 1950.

Santayana, George. *The Life of Reason*. New York: Scribners, 1905.

*Silverberg, William V. *Childhood Experience and Personal Destiny*. New York: Springer, 1952.

Sewell, William H., Mussen, Paul H., and Harris, Chester W. "Relationships Among Child Training Practices." *Amer. Sociol. Rev.* 1955, 20, 137–148.

*Stokes, Walter R. *Modern Pattern for Marriage*. New York: Rinehart, 1948.

*Sullivan, Harry Stack. *The Interpersonal Theory of Psychiatry*. New York: Norton, 1953.

*Thompson, Clara. *Psychoanalysis: Evolution and Development*. New York: Hermitage, 1950.

*Tillich, Paul. *The Courage to Be*. New York: Oxford University Press, 1953.

*Vincent, Clark E. *Readings in Marriage Counseling*. New York: Crowell, 1957.

*Wolberg, Lewis R. *The Techniques of Psychotherapy*. New York: Grune & Stratton, 1954.

About the Authors

ALBERT ELLIS WAS born in Pittsburgh and grew up in New York City. He holds a bachelor's degree from the College of the City of New York; and M.A. and Ph.D. degrees in Clinical Psychology from Columbia University. He has taught at Rutgers University and New York University; has been Chief Psychologist of the New Jersey State Diagnostic Center and then Chief Psychologist of the New Jersey Department of Institutions and Agencies; and for the last several years has been in the private practice of psychotherapy and marriage and family counseling in New York City.

Dr. Ellis is a fellow of the American Psychological Association (and President of its Division of Consulting Psychology) and of the American Sociological Association and the American Association for the Advancement of Science. He is the President of the Society for the Scientific Study of Sex; and has been a member of the Executive Committee of the American Academy of Psychotherapists, the American Association of Marriage Counselors, Psychologists in Private Practice, and the New York Society of Clinical Psychologists. He has been Chairman of the Marriage Counseling Section of the National Council on Family Relations and an Associate Editor of *Marriage and Family Living*, the *International Journal of Sexology*, and the *Journal of Sexual Research*.

Dr. Ellis has published well over a hundred and fifty papers in psychological, psychiatric, and sociological journals and has authored or edited the following books and monographs: *An Introduction to the Principles of Scientific Psychoanalysis, The Folklore of Sex, Sex, Society and the Individual* (with A. P. Pillay), *Sex Life of the American Woman and the Kinsey Report, The American Sexual Tragedy, New Approaches to Psychotherapy Techniques, The Psychology of Sex Offenders* (with Ralph Brancale), *How to Live with a Neurotic, Sex Without Guilt, The Art and Science of Love, What is Psychotherapy?, The Place of Values in the Practice of Psychotherapy, The Encyclopedia of Sexual Behavior* (with Albert Abarbanel), *Creative Marriage* (with Robert A. Harper), and *A Guide to Rational Living* (with Robert A. Harper).

ROBERT A. HARPER was trained in psychology, anthropology, and sociology at Ohio State University, where he received his Ph.D. degree in 1942; and then took post-doctoral training in psychotherapy in Detroit, New York, and Washington. He has taught at several leading universities and directed counseling clinics and counselor training programs at both Ohio State University and the Merill-Palmer Institute in Detroit. During World War II, Dr. Harper served as a psychiatric social worker in the United States Army. Since 1953, he has been in the private practice of psychotherapy and marriage and family counseling in Washington, D.C.

Dr. Harper is President of the American Academy of Psychotherapists and of the American Association of Marriage Counselors. He is a Fellow of the American Psychological Association, a member of the American Group Psychotherapy Association, a charter member of the Society for the Scientific Study of Sex, and a member of the Executive Committee of Psychologists in Private Practice. He has been Chairman of the Marriage Counseling Section of the National Council on Family Relations, an Associate Editor of *Marriage and Family Living* and of the *Journal of Sexual Research,* and the Book Review Editor of the *International Journal of Sexology* and the *Journal of Family Welfare.*

Dr. Harper has written more than fifty papers for professional publications and numerous articles in popular magazines. He is also author of *Marriage, Psychoanalysis and Psychotherapy: 36 Systems,* and co-author of *Problems of American Society* (with John F. Cuber and William F. Kenkel) and *Creative Marriage* (with Albert Ellis). *A Guide to Rational Living* is the second of a series of collaborations by Dr. Harper and Dr. Ellis and will be followed in the near future by a major volume on *Rational Psychotherapy* and a multi-volumed *Handbook of Psychotherapeutic Techniques.*